LO,
I AM WITH YOU ALWAYS

Christian Autobiography of: Douglas D Thornberry Jr,
Brother in the Lord; Dreams, Visions, Visitations,
Intervention and Inspirations from the Lord,
The Words of the Lord, within Matt. 28:20.

DOUGLAS D. THORNBERRY JR.

Lo, I Am With You Always
Copyright © 2020 by Douglas D. Thornberry Jr.

All rights reserved. No part of this publication may be reproduced, distributed, or transmitted in any form or by any means, including photocopying, recording, or other electronic or mechanical methods, without the prior written permission of the publisher or author, except in the case of brief quotations embodied in critical reviews and certain other noncommercial uses permitted by copyright law.

Although every precaution has been taken to verify the accuracy of the information contained herein, the author and publisher assume no responsibility for any errors or omissions. No liability is assumed for damages that may result from the use of information contained within.

Library of Congress Control Number: 2020906757
ISBN-13:   Paperback: 978-1-64749-104-8

Printed in the United States of America

GoTo Publish

GoToPublish LLC
1-888-337-1724
www.gotopublish.com
info@gotopublish.com

CONTENTS

PREFACE vii
INTRODUCTION viii
Chapter 1 1
   Innocence of Life 1
   Awareness of Being 4
   Unexpected Dinner Guest 5
   New Home and New Brother 6
   Problem Child 7
   Coming to know Jesus 7
   Little Red Fire Truck 9
   Burned to Learn 10
   Brothers in Bondage 11
   Vision from the Lord 12
Chapter 2 15
   Divorce 15
   God Hates Divorce 20
   Love Triangle 21
   Memories of My Dad 24
   Family Divided 29
   Rejection & Rage 32
   Out of Control 36
   Poor Ole Dad 39

Chapter 3 43
- Cave In 43
- Playing Tag 43
- Frozen Nightmare 45
- Sole Saved 47
- No Where to Turn 48
- Sheltered With a Friend 50
- Leap of Faith 52
- Trying to Survive 54
- What is Family? 57
- Blessings-N-Prayer 59

Chapter 4 61
- Rejected by My Step-Father 61
- Arrival in St. Louis 63
- Rejected by My Step-Mother 65
- Abandoned for a Reason 68
- Learning Forgiveness 71
- Last Chance 71

Chapter 5 74
- Home Away from Home 74
- Camp Atterbury 75
- Tomato Soup 76
- Remember the Homeless 80
- Camp Gary 82
- Worst Thing... I Ever Did 84

Chapter 6 89
- Graduating from Job Corps 89
- Lonely and Searching for Life 91
- Lost and Rejected 92
- Destined for Hell 94
- Dream #1 – Place of Rest 97
- Dreams #2 – Though the Eyes of Jesus 101
- Dream #3 – Life is so Short... 104
- Eternal Gift of God 106

- God is Love 108

Chapter 7 110
- New Beginning 110
- Meeting and Courting of My Wife 115
- Families Beginning 124
- Last Spin 126
- In Search of a Better Home 127
- Florida Bound 130

Chapter 8 135
- Hello Florida 135
- Beware of "Ouija Boards 136
- In-Laws Visit 144
- Stress of Marriage 146
- SEPARATION 149
- Change in Direction 156

Chapter 9 160
- Beginning of a New Horizon 160
- 1ST Night with Friends 161
- 2ND Night with Joyce's Friend 162
- 3RD Night with Friends of the Lord 162
- The Story of Gideon - Explained 163
- Put me to the Test 166
- Honoring Commitment 168
- Remembering Our Commitments 170
- God Honors Commitment 173
- God Honors Prayer 177
- Broken Bottle 183

Chapter 10 185
- Journey Home 185
- Family Re-United 188
- Iranian Hostages 195
- Family Addition 197
- My Sons Blessings 197

Chapter 11 203

    Trust in the Lord 203
    Professional Experience's 206
    Failing the Lord 208
    Second Opportunity 211
    Smiling Fish Dream 212
    Too Many Dreams 213
    FISHER OF MEN 215
    TEN COMMANDMENTS..220
    Worked Myself... Out of a Job 221
    Reprieved from Reassigned 223

Charter 12...226
    Finally, Home Again 226
    Living the Dream 228
    Dreams... Do Come to an End 229
    Ministry of Helps 230
    Life Changing Event 233

Chapter 13...241
    Wake-Up America 241
    AMERICA IN NEED OF PRAYER 241
    Post 911 - DREAM..241
    Interpretation 242
    We must find Love, Peace & God. 243
    Prayer of Salvation 244
    Jesus is Coming... Soon 245

Chapter 14...247
    In God We Trust 247
    America... The Blessed..250

SCRIPTURE 254
    Closing Thoughts, Salvation & Prayer,
        with Scriptures. 256

PREFACE

First and foremost, I want to thank the Lord for life and the time to share what I've been, so richly blessed with. It's for this reason that I'm dedicating this book to all my brothers and sisters in the Lord, Jesus Christ. My primary reason for writing this book is to offer words of encouragement and to refresh those seeking a recharge in faith and hope; to lift those up in spirit that trust in Jesus and to help those who do not know the Lord to have a better understanding: Jesus is... our only Lord and Savior.

INTRODUCTION

This is why we are alive; to help and love one another as sisters and brother, helping each other. My oldest daughter says, "Alive-N-God." Life as we know it, would be insane without Him; Jesus. To be or not to be, is not the question. The real question is; "Do you know the Lord?" To know Truth (knowing God) or not to know truth (separation from God) is not a question, but rather a decision. To deny Truth (Jesus) is to be denied by God which means, separation from God... Forever!

The following stories are reflections of my own personal life, dreams, visions, visitations, and more importantly; inspirations from God. These stories and other misc. writings are short and complete as best, as my memory serves me. Some will seem unbelievable but never the less, factual and true. Some may seem gruesome, a bit bizarre, but all presented to you, as words of truth. I'll also be sharing some of my trials and tribulations that I've been so graciously blessed with. Some of which I even recognized, as they were taking place, but most... after the fact.

During my first recollections in life, I did not realize the presence of anyone or anything, except for what my five natural senses led me to believe. As time went on, I became fully aware of my surroundings, as all people do, which is; I'm not alone. None of us are! Some of us may wish or believe otherwise, or even think that we are alone, but in the end, when the reality check comes in focus; the obvious will become clear; that there is a God, and as for Jesus? Well, He truly is God's one and only begotten Son, who is actually, God in the flesh;

who stepped down from His thrown... to battle and defeat Satan on the Cross.

He's the only perfect one, as man, who could provide us hope and salvation through our acceptance of Jesus Christ, as our Lord and Savior; a gift from God, whom we celebrate each Christmas.

> *John 1:1-2In the beginning was the Word, and the Word was with God, and the Word was God. The same was in the beginning with God.*

(Therefore: The Word is Jesus and Jesus is, God in the Flesh)

This ensures us, as Sons and Daughters of God that by believing and trusting in Him... we have Eternal Life. We will live in a place, in the presence of the Lord, to live in true happiness, peace and harmony without any wars, hate, hunger or sorrow toward anyone or anything. We shall live as one with God through His son, Jesus Christ, forever. Praise God!

It's true! All things do become, as New! Your very being, becomes righteous with God and this is only possible through God's Love, Mercy and Grace. All you need to do is to accept God's Personal Gift; the Gift of His Ultimate Sacrifice made by God Himself, as Jesus. It is He who came to live and die in this world, and the first to rise from the dead on the third day, only to return to his Throne, where He is "Lord of Lords" and "King of Kings", and He will be coming again, soon... to receive His own.

The Lord God Almighty really does love us. It's out of this Love, He has made a provision for all of us, so that we may once again, become "Righteous" as it were in the beginning before the "Great Fall into SIN" by Adam and Eve who separated man from God. God also, separated us, from the "Tree of Life" so we wouldn't eat thereof, and live in our sins, forever. However, we were provided a second "Tree of Life" given unto all to partake-of, which provides us the means of becoming righteous, so we can once again, be with God. This "Tree of Life" of course, is "JESUS" and we are the branches, and we shall all be bearers of fruit, and everyone shall be known by their fruit; good or bad.

> **Matthew 12:33** *Either make the tree good, and his fruit good; or else make the tree corrupt, and his fruit corrupt: for the tree is known, by his fruit.*

It was after His dissension, from the Throne of God" to live and die in the flesh, unto the Resurrection from the Dead, to His Ascension back to the Throne of God that we were sent His Holy Spirit to dwell within us, as Jesus had promised. This Holy Spirit is the Spirit of God and the Spirit of God is God, and God is Jesus and Jesus is God, who guides and dwells within us, as the Holy Spirit of God... for the three are one, as stated within the Word of God.

> **1st John 5:7** *"The Three are ONE! For there are three that bear record in heaven, the Father, the Word, and the Holy Ghost: and these three are one."* **(Jesus is... the Word.)**

So, there is, but one God; God the Father, the Son and the Holy Spirit, and as such, God dwells with-in his Saints through His Spirit. We who confess Jesus as Lord and Savior are the Sons and Daughters of God who have accepted God's Gracious Gift of Salvation; freely given through the Blood of Jesus, who walks with us and guides us daily, throughout all the days of our lives, as His Holy Spirit lives within us. All you need... is to accept Jesus as Lord and if you haven't done so, as of yet? Just listen to that voice deep within, for it is His Holy Spirit calling out to you.

The following is an inspiration came to me one day, which is: "There is but one way to love the Lord, and that is with everything... He has given you!" Know too, if it weren't for Him; none of us would have anything, or even exist. We should give Him thanks daily, for we are His, and so richly Blessed with life, as we know it, here on earth... in His presence. Praise God!

I'm sure there are many people who can share their own personal testimonies and walks in life with Jesus and like most; my experiences, be just that, personal to them, as are mine to me, but I have had a deep desire and inspiration within to share them.

For God is an Awesome God. He is literally, everywhere and in everything; be it good or bad, existing or non-existing, or yet to come. He knows all! He doesn't necessarily approve of all, but life is full of trials and tribulations, and He loves us and is with us, always. It's absolutely wonderful, knowing we have such a wonderful GOD... the Great "I AM"; having His Holy Spirit dwelling within us, knowing he is with us, guiding us, never to forsake us.

If, you knew me personally, and knew where I came from; only then, would you understand and appreciate the fact, that I would even consider writing a book. I could count on my hands, the number of books I've read from cover to cover, as a child... not because I can't read, but because, as a youngster; I never developed good reading habits. It's truly essential and important for a child to grow and develop the ability to comprehend and have communication skills, especially with today's technologies.

As most children in my era though, I was far, too active to sit still long enough to read anything, except for super hero comic books and to this very day, I still have bad reading habits, except for certain books that were necessary. I'm referring to technical books; books that are required to maintain employment and further ones education. The only real book that I always take my time in reading is, the Word of God; the Real Book of Hero's!

Yes, the Bible is full of Hero's, Life, and Gods Word; the Living Word... the Hero of Heroes; Jesus Christ, God Almighty, the Bright and Morning Star, the Author and the Finisher, the Alpha and Omega, the one and only True Living God! There is no other God; No, not one, except for the Great, "I Am." He is God!

I've read this great book: "The Bible"; the "Word of God", from cover to cover. I've read the New Testament many times, as well as the Old Testament; Psalms, Proverbs and other books.

They're all good for the soul. I'm a slow reader, because I prefer to read each and every word; one word at a time, to digest and understand each morsel of knowledge and wisdom. This is especially true when being fed these words of understanding that grow each time we partake of the word. So, I'm sure you'll understand why, it's not taken me just months, but literally years to write this book. I've read over these pages more than I care to admit which is not bad for a 9th grade education, but I did obtain a GED, followed by an Associate's Degree in Theology, in 2009.

In fact, this book has literally taken me decades to complete, considering this task, which is quite an undertaking for me. Especially, knowing how little I have read and the lack of my communication skills. So please bear with me and pardon my grammar, spelling and English. I'll do my best. My only hopes are that you will enjoy and are drawn closer to the Lord, and become more aware of His presence; the very essence of your being. This is because, you are His creation, in His image, and one of a kind, and yet, so unique and special; a child... of God's.

Finally, I want to give thanks to the Lord too, for the love of my life; my wonderful wife; Joyce, and our three beautiful children. All of which are a product of the Love, God blessed us with, including our seven grandchildren. We're all on loan to one another because we all belong to Jesus, who has purchased us for a great price; His precious blood which means, we are His and as such we should serve Him and help others to know Him as Lord.

Acts 20:28 Take heed therefore unto yourselves, and to all the flock, over which the Holy Ghost hath made you overseers, to feed the church of God, which he hath purchased with his own blood.

So, as you can see; we are... the church; sanctioned to be overseers by God's Holy Spirit and are to go forth into the world and feed the Church, which has been purchased with the blood of Jesus and as such, I remind you of these words spoken by Jesus.

"Lo, I am With You Always."

Please Note: It is the writer's intent, excluding any publishing cost; to give the majority of the sales for this book; to those who are homeless, hungry and in need of assistance and prayer. It is your support that will enable me to help accomplish this and it is greatly appreciated. I just want to say, bless you and thank you for your generosity, and as such... you are partakers of this endeavor.

CHAPTER 1

"My Early Years"

Innocence of Life

I life began at the St. Louis Jewish Hospital in St. Louis, Mo. My mother told me I was also born with long black hair all over my face and body that made me appear to be more Jewish than all the other babies, which were actually born in the Jewish faith. No, I'm not of Jewish descendent. I am a Born Again Christian, Saved by the Grace of God and have the Holy Spirit dwelling within me; uniting me as one, with my Lord and Savior; Jesus.

> *John 17: 21 That they all may be one; as thou, Father, art in me, and I in thee, that they also may be **one** in us: that the world may believe that thou hast sent me.*

It's for this reason, that by my accepting Jesus as my Lord and Savior, that I too, am a descendant from Father Abraham, as well as David; allowing me the right to lay claim to being a descendant of Israel. This is true, only because of Jesus Christ; my Lord and Savior. It is through His personal sacrifice and the lying down of His life, that we might have life, and that we might have it... more abundantly.

> ***John 10:10*** *The thief cometh not, but for to steal, and to kill, and to destroy: I am come that they might have life, and that they might have it more abundantly.*

So, it is Jesus whom we should follow and serve; carrying our cross daily, throughout our lives, because it is the Blood of Jesus that has purchased all of us. Therefore, we are His and He is our Savior and soon coming King. The Lord of Lords and King of Kings, and He will rein forever and ever more, Amen. So, give God the Praise and the Glory, for He truly does love us... all of us, for we are made in His Image. Thanks and Glory unto God.

> ***John 3:16****"For God so loved the world, that he gave his only begotten Son, that whosoever believeth on him should not perish, but have eternal life."*

Life continues after birth, as it does... after death; but, it is between the two where childhood memories begin. These memories begin at some point in our early years, sometimes at an unbelievable early age and some sooner than others. All of this is just the beginning of our journey through life while in this earthly vessel, which we will come to know and explore with each passing day. Some of these memories may not always be something we can recall very clearly, if at all. Yet, other memories may be as clear as if, they took place, just yesterday. This could be because of some exciting or traumatic event. I believe all these memories and experiences serve a purpose. They are the very substance and essence of our being that accumulates into adulthood, and through-out our lives, as a guide from our experiences, as what to do and not to do; to sin or not to sin, or to know or not to know... especially, when it comes to our Lord. We've all been given the Freedom to choose, but know this; there is but one way only, to choose... so, choose wisely.

> ***John 14:6****Jesus saith unto him, I am the way, the truth, and the life: no man cometh unto the Father, but by me.*

I am a strong believer that the first two or three years of any child, are the most critical, growth and development years. It's for this reason, I feel it is essential and in the child's best interest to be raised in a home environment with the parents. This is to develop stability and strong personality traits from each parent to know the Lord, and about love, truth, knowledge and wisdom.

> **_Proverbs 16:3_** *Commit thy works unto the LORD, and thy thoughts shall be established.*

> **_Proverbs 22:6_** *Train up a child in the way he should go: and when he is old, he will not depart from it.*

However, there are those less fortunate who have no choice, or just prefer having their freedom. Instead of raising their child at home, they may have to choose a daycare facility, be it within the confines of a business or that of an individual's home. True, day care centers have their place and do serve a purpose; to fill a necessity when options are limited. However, remember these centers can, and do, reach maximum capacity. So, the quality of care may not always be what one desires for their loved ones and definitely, cannot equal that in which, only a parent can provide.

Than undeniable, real love and compassion that only a mother can give, can never be matched by another, not even a father, let alone some day care facility. No, I'm not down on day care centers. Some people have no other recourse and are forced into this type of an arrangement. Some may even think that their child may receive a modest education. Maybe they will, and then again, maybe they won't. However, if a child needs security, true love, and attention; then mom would be the natural preference. Obviously, anything less, may not meet the child needs, which can again, only come from the child's mother and in some cases, an affectionate and gifted father. Granted too, there are again those fine and reputable places available that provide an excellent quality childcare service with some education, but I'm certain everyone would agree, there is truly, no place like home... in the arms of a mother. As for the children, while in the innocence of life; they really do know the difference and can sense the genuine love of a loving mother, or that of a substitute; someone else, other than mom or dad.

Home is where the heart is and where true love should always be found; unconditional love. This type of love comes from the natural bonding that takes place from the very first moment a child is conceived to the day of delivery and then placed beside the very mother that will feed and nurture this child in a way that only, a mother can do. The father's role is more that of being a provider; the head of the house, but will also take on the role as his wife's helpmate, more commonly known, as dad; the hero and a role model, as is the mother, among other things.

Awareness of Being

Like all people, I too, have memories that allow me to recall events in my early years; from infancy throughout childhood that may be questionable by some, but true! I can remember some things, as far back as two years of age and even earlier, such as lying in a baby buggy. Only the Lord knows how old I was for sure. Joyce, my wife jokingly says my mom must have kept in a buggy until I was twelve. She's one of my many blessings from the Lord, but at times; Joyce can be somewhat of a real smart-aleck, but a real genuine blessing, from God. Thank you, Lord.

This is the earliest of what I believe to be my first memories that go back to an age that I'm not really certain of. I may have only been a six months old... give or take, where I was lying in this baby buggy, as I had said. I may have even been slightly younger; I don't really know, but the event is truly, amazing.

It was mid-morning while my mother was taking me for a stroll. There were two neighbor ladies that stopped her to visit and to see me. My mother was directly behind me, as she towered over me, where I was lying. One woman was directly in front of the carriage and the other was to my right; obviously, east of the buggy. As she stood there, she swayed back and forth, as they visited. The morning sun was directly behind her and as she swayed back and forth, the sun was beaming in and out of my eyes. It was extremely bright and blinding, causing me a great deal of pain and discomfort. I remember the lady in front of me noticing my fussing and she mentioned it to my mother who then peeked down to see, if I was alright. She reached down to reposition my bottle resting on a blanket, lying on my chest and pulled the buggy canopy up over my head as to protect me from the sun's rays; saying her good-byes and headed home.

I know this memory sounds unbelievable, but it's true and only exist because of the traumatic event, causing me pain. I believe most of our memories are embedded through special events, be they of a traumatic event or a pleasurable experience, and are... the very substance, of our being.

Unexpected Dinner Guest

I recall my sister and me receiving a couple cute, Easter baby chicks. We fed them regularly in the back-yard and they grew, and they grew, and they grew. They grew so big, that I can remember holding my hand out, waist high to feed them. They would take the feed right from the palm of my hand. They were enormous in size. Actually, I was a toddler, possibly 2 or maybe 2½ years of age, so these chickens appeared huge to me. As I was feeding them one warm summer day; I remember being barefoot and wearing only my under-wear as my dad stood over me. He made small talk with me, telling me my aunt and uncle was coming for dinner that afternoon. Now, I don't remember my chicken's name, but Peaty comes to mind and I do remember asking my dad, if Peaty could come too, and he said, "of course." I was so excited and I really loved my pet chicken. When we all sat down for dinner and began eating... I remembered and began looking for Petty. I looked at my dad and asked, "Hey dad, where's my chicken"? It was then that my dad responded to me saying, "He's here. He's the guest of honor." I looked again and said I don't see him, so I asked, "Where is he?" It was then he said, "You're eating him!" All I could say is... Ahhhh! Actually, I really don't recall for sure how I reacted, but I do recall the event with good reason... he was my pet. Afterwards, we all went outside to watch the 4th of July fireworks. So, this day of events compounded with the love and joy of a pet, to the shock of eating him, along with the excitement of the fireworks; has provided me a clear memory, of that particular day. Whenever, I would mention this day to my parents, they would only tell me that I must have over heard them speaking about it, but I was there and I do remember it well. In short, I believe childhood memories are the provisions given us, to help develop our individual personalities. Mine I believe, started out with a little bit of trauma, but God's been watching over me the whole time, as He does for all His children, whether we are aware of His presence or not. Especially, the little ones, and in all sincerity; we're all His children... who have childlike faith; believing and trusting in the Lord, as our Lord and Savior. Thank you, Jesus.

New Home and New Brother

First let me say, while we yet lived in our first home; I'm one year and two days younger than my older sister, Donna who was 2½ years old at that time, and holding a butter-knife. I don't really know why, but she walked over and inserted it into an electrical outlet. Sparks shot out, setting her clothing on fire and she screamed! My folk's ran in from the kitchen, into the living room and my dad picked her up in a blanket putting out the fire that left no burns. I often wondered where she got her red hair.

Looking back at that particular time frame though, I would say that my family appeared to be the typical, normal, All-American family. Well, as normal as what I knew normal to be at that age, with lots of love from a loving and caring, mom and dad. When I was 2½ years old, my mom became pregnant with my little brother Dennis who was due that November, only two months after my third birthday. With my mother expecting, and being as big as she was, she always managed to find the time and room in her lap, where I'd cuddle, as she'd read me a story book.

It was during this time I remember going out and looking at new homes and seeing all the beautiful colorful paints with colors that I'd never seen before. I looked in awe at their beauty and remember the fresh smell of the yellow paint. We needed a new home with more space and finally, we found just the right house. All this occurred that summer before my mother went to the hospital to give birth to my brother, Dennis. We all stayed with my aunt and grandmother until November. I remember stacking pennies as high as I could before they toppled, only to do it again and again on top of their kitchen table. It was covered with a red and white checkered table cloth. Finally, we moved into our new three bedroom home with a full basement. I was so excited about having a new home and little brother. We found a church that had just been built and we began attending Sunday school and Church services, but prior to this? I don't remember ever attending Church Services or Sunday school; but, we were a happy family with a whole lot of love, and a new baby brother.

Problem Child

One Sunday after moving in, Donna and I were eating dinner at the kitchen table, built for two. For some reason she flipped a beet at me from her fork. Not knowing better and thinking this to be a game, I flipped a couple back at her, missing her as she ducked, hitting the bright, freshly painted canary yellow wall. She and I burst into laughter and our parents heard us and asked what was going on in there and came in to investigate. They were just in time to see my red beets sliding down the wall and this was just the beginning of the many feuds Donna and I would have where I would always, be to blame as the "Problem Child."

Coming to know Jesus

It was after that with Dennis coming into our lives, that we began attending this new church, as a family. We even helped the new pastor and his wife move into their new home. I don't recall attending church prior to this, as I said earlier, but I come to love the beauty of the house of the Lord with its huge white, mighty roman style pillars, and the double-door entrance... wow!

I remember too, my first Sunday; attending a Sunday school in a room, full of kids. It was located right next to the nursery where

Dennis was staying and the sanctuary was located on the opposite side of the nursery. I remember slipping out to see Dennis as I would be heading for the bathroom and peeking into the sanctuary, and as most young children, I loved sitting with my mom and dad. So, I would sneak into church services. This ceased though, when I moved ahead with each passing year by advancing into different classrooms. I didn't like this primarily, because it prevented me from slipping out to see my brother, making it next to impossible to slip into the sanctuary where I really wanted to be, with my mom and dad, who loved me.

Whenever I was able to do so, my parents would let me sit in the Sanctuary. I just had to be very quiet and like all kids, I'd become so bored that I would climb into their laps and fall asleep. We not only attended church on Sunday, but Wednesday evenings too, but it was during Sunday school that I met Bobby Grammer who was my Sunday school teacher and a great man.

As a family, we went to special events too, and eventually my sister was baptized. I was the jealous brother who naturally had to be baptized too, thinking I was missing out on something. So, a few weeks later, possibly a month or two after Donna's baptism, I was baptized at the early age of eight or nine. I didn't really understand what being baptized meant and unaware of the true meaning of salvation, but eventually, I came to learn of the love of Jesus from Bobby. It was through the years that I would come to love Bobby and his family too, and eventually, they would come to play a very important role, throughout my life.

As time went on my parents stopped attending church as often; stopping all together, but I continued thanks to Bobby. He would go out of his way after dropping of his family at church and then came by to pick me up. Had he not done so, I may have not continued going to church either. Even after church services, Bobby would go out of his way to make certain, I'd get home safely. As I became older, I walked the 1/2 mile out of my own desire to attend church. My brother and my sister stopped going completely as well, but Bobby was always there for me. He was so energetic, and devoted to Jesus and a perfect gentleman.

One Sunday, he invited the whole Sunday school class to come and eat Sloppy Joes and I had the privilege of meeting Bobby's wife; Sue, for the first time. Actually, Bobby's wife's was absolutely lovely and treated me as her own, as she did all of us. Everyone ate 2 or 3 Sloppy Joes, but as for me; I put away 8 or 9, if not more. I don't know why, but I was always hungry, but though the years, I really come to love and know this family and claimed them to be my adopted family, and they have always been there for me, and I do mean... always, without fail.

Little Red Fire Truck

One thing for certain, is that my sister, brother and I always had a big Christmas and we received so many gifts making our Christmas's, so memorable. I don't recall celebrating the birth of Jesus until after Joyce and I were married. We too, celebrated Christmas with lots of gifts; but we would sing "Happy Birthday to Jesus" with a birthday cake, topped with a little manger scene.

There is one Christmas, as a child, I remember well. My little brother had just turned three and he received a little red fire truck that he would pedal round and round inside the house. He'd go in circles from room to room; living room, down the hall into the kitchen, around the stair well, into the dining room and then back into the living room, and so on and so on. He loved clanging his little shiny, chrome plated bell, as he peddled endlessly. Dennis would stop to detach the ladders mounted on the sides of the fire truck and would place them up against the sofa. He pretended, as he climbed up one side and down the other. Well, I don't know if it was his imagination or fascination with fire, or just because he had a little red fire truck, but early one morning, he apparently went a little, too far. It was about 3AM when Dennis had awakened and got out of bed and began peddling his little red fire truck, round and round in his endless loop of circles. As he did, he pulled on the string, clanging that silly little chrome plated bell. He was just clanging away as he yelled, "Fire... Fire!" Thank God he did! Because, it woke all of us up out of a sound sleep. My mom was the first to rush down the hallway saying, "What, are you doing out of bed so early?" as she turned into the kitchen, and just in time. She yelled fire to my dad, saying, "Dennis set the kitchen on fire." It was because of the stove's control knobs being located on the front of the stoves back then where Dennis could reach them. As such, he turned on a burner where a skillet that had been left the night before, which started a grease fire. It obviously, just started and my dad's quick actions were just in time. All I can say is, Thank God for that little chrome plated bell. I don't recall seeing that little red fire truck anymore after that. It just disappeared!

Burned to Learn
....

What I do remember though is afterwards; my dad went back to bed and my mom stayed up. She heated an empty pot on the stove to teach Dennis not to play with fire. Then she carried it into the living room and sat down calling Dennis to her. She then placed him between her legs and held him down, as she bent him over her leg; pulling down his PJ's. As she did, she placed that hot pot on his bare buttocks. Dennis screamed in agony as his flesh immediately blistered, sticking to the pot. I remember hearing my dad calling out to see if she needed him. She said, "No, everything's taken care-of, so go back to sleep, you need to go to work in the morning." So my dad never knew about Dennis or the abuse we witnessed, nor will we ever forget.

It wasn't too much longer after that though, possibly several weeks since his last incident. Dennis was obviously healed and had forgotten the warning not to play with fire. Well, one would think that Dennis would have learned from his lesson, but not so! He was caught trying to light matches in a closet this time and my dad wasn't home from work, yet. So again, my dad never knew what took place this time either. I didn't know what my mom was doing, was child abuse at the time. I just didn't know then, or earlier. As far as I knew, this sort of thing was normal and acceptable punishment for bad boys and bad girls. All I could do is watch in shock and horror as I saw what unfolded. My mom placed a towel over her lap, as she sat and held Dennis again, between her thighs at the knees while facing her. She had crossed her legs to prevent his escape and dowsed his hands with lighter fluid. She then asked, "Do you want to see what fire can do to you?" as she set his hands ablaze. She allowed the flames to burn for 8 to 10 seconds if not longer and as the fire licked at his hands and fingers, she asked, "Do you ever want to play with fire again?" Dennis screamed, "No", as he shook his hands frantically, trying to fan out the flames. She asked him, "Do you promise?" He screamed, "I promise mommy, I promise"! Afterwards, she wrapped the towel around his hands to put out the fire and only then did Dennis lose his obsession with fire.

Brothers in Bondage
············

It was during this same time frame that I experienced my first Vision, which I'll share shortly. Please understand this though. My mom had become so concerned about my brother possibly setting the house on fire, that she took drastic measures to the extreme which included me. This was done due to the loss of some neighbors up the street that had actually died in a fire just a few months earlier while they were fast asleep that gave off an unforgettable stench that filled the neighborhood.

My mom said, she wasn't going to have this happen to her. To make sure of it, she literally strapped my brother and me to our bedposts in our separate beds having a walkway between us. She used some of her many plastic belts with perforated rows upon continuous rows of holes covering the full-length of each belt. She strapped a couple of them together to securing my right leg to my lower right bedpost and then my left hand and wrist to the adjacent, upper left bedpost. Dennis was done similar, only opposite of me that allowed us to face one another.

My dad protested, but my mother's determination prevailed. She always seemed to have things her way, one way or another. So, there we lay… and there was absolutely, no way of setting ourselves free. Even if, we had to. One morning, I remember raising my head up and looking down the hallway and then over to my brother where he laid tied up and fast asleep. I said, "Hey Dennis, can you get loose?" He said, "No!" I looked back down the hall and yelled, "Mom! Hey, Mom!" She hollered back to me, "What?" I said, "Come and untie me!" Then she said, "Why? It's too, early to get up." Then I said, "Well, I got to go to the bathroom and you better hurry-up because I got to go, really bad." She came in laughing and set me free and I managed to make it to the bathroom, just in time! These episodes where just the beginning of the abuses we as a family would start to experience, for what I'm sure my mother did with good intentions, knowing too, that she really did love all of us, but she feared for our lives. Either way, I still love and still pray for her.

Vision from the Lord
············

As I learned to love and trust in the Lord, I came to find out that He's always been with me as far back, as I can remember. My first real confirmation of such was during this time frame of being strapped to the bed. It was then I encountered my first vision as I lie there… not understand the meaning of it, until years later.

I was awakened by a voice telling me to get up and go over to the dresser. I said, "I can't", but then I heard, "Yes you can." So, I sat up to my surprise, looking at the dresser; an old make-up desk that had a large round mirror in the center with two sets of drawers on each side and a recessed table top about 6" lower than top of the dresser. So I walked over to this dresser with my eyes fixed on something I hadn't seen earlier; 3-stacks of coins.

`Now, I didn't know where the coins came from, but there they were, sitting on my dresser. As I stood there looking at them, this voice asked me, "Do you see the coins?" Now I didn't count them but I would venture to say that there were 20 coins stacked on the right, 30 coins on the left with 40 coins in rear, all tightly stacked together in a group. I answered the question by saying, "Yes." They appeared to be large, possibly silver dollars and while I was looking at them I heard this same voice say to me, "Look into the mirror." So, I looked into the mirror and I could see what appeared to be a reflection of the coins. I was asked, "Do you see the coins in the mirror?" I said, "Yes."

Then I was told to reach into the mirror and to pull the coins over to first set of coins that were setting on my dresser. So, I reached into the mirror, as if it were an open window; interlacing my little fingers around the three stacks of coins. I pulled on them ever so gently, as not to topple them; pulling them back through the mirror onto my dresser. I placed them right beside the first set, now totaling six stacks of coins. After I had done this, I was then told to look back into the mirror and much to my surprise, as I did; I saw the reflection of six stacks of coins in the mirror, but didn't have the understanding, as to why.

As I said earlier, I didn't come to the realization of this vision until years later when I became aware of God's presence. What I do know though, is that God has blessed me all my life. Basically speaking, I've never had to really want for anything that I didn't already have or want within reason. I know this to be true, because I am so richly blessed in all that I have and do, for the Lord is, as He has always been... right here inside of me through His Holy Spirit.

Again, this was my first vision and it took place when my brother and I were tied to the bed post because of Dennis playing with fire. If, this were not a vision... then it was an illusion or a dream, but surreal, as if I were wide awake in my room, at that very moment. This is why I'll always refer to this as my first vision, because to me; it happened and is an embedded memory forever. I believe too, this vision was given to me, to let me know not to worry about anything; that the

Lord would always be here for me, and to take care of me as He has always done. He's available to all people that believe and receive Him; reaching out to Him, trusting Him, walking in faith.

As you continue, I will be sharing many other blessings that the Lord has given me and has done for me as a Christian; not to boast but hopefully, to share and strengthen your faith. I too, will do my best to share these blessings in a humble way. One may even think these blessings were intended for me personally, as to let me know of the love God has for me, but I do not cast these pearls before swine, but to brothers & Sisters of the Lord.

I believe too, however, that the Lord would have me share these experiences, as to allow others to see the awesome power of God. No matter how insignificant some of these stories may appear to some, know this; I know that I know, that I know that I know... Jesus Christ is Lord, and that He loves all of us, and He is here for each of us, if we would only reach out with open hearts and open minds, to the presence of God. Then watch the mighty presence of God work within, and around you. But, "Seek ye first the kingdom of God and all these things shall be added unto you." Also, one must come to know and trust in Jesus Christ, as the Son of God; the one and only True Living God; the Almighty and Powerful... the Great I Am. There is none other, but one God!

CHAPTER 2

"Casualties' of Divorce"

Divorce
....

I do not recall... my parents ever fighting, especially having any kind of knock down drag out over anything. If they did, it must have been done quietly, behind closed doors, except for one particular day. It was just one of those days that I'll never forget and I know this because, I caused it, so to speak... even though, I wasn't at fault. As I said, if my parents argued or fought, it must have been behind closed doors, but not that day... and was about money, bills, and dishonesty, all of which I knew nothing about.

It all began when my dad came home from work and asked my mother "Is there any mail?" I was naïve and innocent at the age of seven or eight and didn't know, or understand certain things. I'd like to believe that in my youth, as in all small children; I was an honest person. I attended church and was living life, as I was led to believe, with love and honesty. So, what my mother said to my dad was incorrect and in all honestly, I didn't know she did so... intentionally. So, when my mother said, "No, there wasn't any", I thought to myself that my mother had made a mistake; she must have forgotten. This is because, just moments before, I seen her put it with other mail.

So, in my innocence I said, "Yes, we did mom. Don't you remember, you just put it under my mattress?" My mom looked at me rather strangely. It was after this, there were no more walls and we heard it all. My dad stormed through the house and went straight into my bedroom and there it was; the mail! Apparently, it had been collecting for a while consisting of eight or more items, which I myself, had just learned about. My dad became so furious, he began yelling and then it was my mom that began hollering back at my dad. He was so up-set that he threw a glass ashtray into the coat closet door that exploded; shattering shards of glass everywhere. Then he stormed out of the front door to his car and my mom followed him out the door, going to her car.

As my dad was starting his car, my mother had reached into the back of her car to get a crow-bar. She raised it over her head as she quickly approached my dad's car where he began backing out of the driveway. She threatened to lay it across the driver's windshield, if he even tried to drive anywhere but back into the driveway. So, he eased the car back into the driveway and put it into park. Then they both went inside the house to talked behind closed doors, none of which we could hear, nor understood.

After my mom and dad had exchanged words with each other they emerged from the bedroom. Things appeared to have calmed down a bit behind those closed doors, but when my dad came out, he left. My mom said that he just needed to get away and have some quiet time; to be alone and think. It was then that divorce became an issue and my mother explained what divorce meant. I pleaded with her, begging for them not to get a divorce, saying; "No mom; I love you and Dad. Please, don't get a divorce. I'm sorry! I didn't know!" I felt like they were getting a divorce because of me, but she said no. She blamed his mother for interfering with their marriage and called my dad a momma's boy. Then she remembered... and blamed me for saying something about the mail under the mattress. I explained to her why I said what I did, but to no avail. My mom was raised by nuns in an orphanage and learned her ways through the abuse she received. She was a good mother and I really do love her so, even today. She was just a victim of abuse too, and misguided.

Now, my dad was an injured vet due to a mortar shell blast during WW-ll. He wore a leg brace on his right thigh and calf, which allowed him to walk. He kept a dozen or more 42" long spare leather-strap laces hanging on a hook behind my bedroom door. It was out of frustration and anger after my dad left that my mother just lost it. She called me into my bedroom and picked up my dad's laces. She asked me, if I knew what they were and I said, "Yes, they're dad's laces." She said, "Yes", as she folded them and knotted them together asking, "But do you know what they call this when you do this to them? I said, "No." She said, "It's called a cat of nine tails and do you know why?"

Again, I said, "No." and she said, "Here, let me show you!" As I sat on the side of my bed facing her, she drew her arm back over her head and then stepped forward with this homemade whip. I had never experienced a beating before so out of fear, my reflexes were to raise my arm to protect myself, as I heard this thing cutting through the air with a loud swish. I did this, just in case she swung this thing a little too close, thinking it might hit me, accidently of course. Wrong! It wrapped around my left forearm. In a fit of rage she tried to jerk it back to break it free several times, but it was all entangled around my arm and I didn't really feel any pain. It was probably blocked from me out of fear, but after she untangled it, she pulled her arm back over her head again. I put up both my hands up this time with my palms facing her, yelling; "Mom, hey Mom, wait; wait a minute. Times" as I crossed my fingers in front of her face, which meant... stop, hold everything; I needed to say something. "Mom! Wait a minute; I got something to show you!" She stopped long enough to say, "What"? I said, "Look! Look at my arm", as I gazed at my left arm. I had never seen anything like that before. I said, "You broke dad's straps. See, they broke off and wrapped around my arm. Do you see them" as I pointed at them; digging at them with my fingernails trying to peel them off. She laughed and proceeded to hit me again and again, on my arms and my back. It was then I come to learn these broken pieces of straps were actually welts that I had never experienced. It was afterwards that she began punching my outer thighs causing my legs to cramp up into a Charlie-Horse, as she laughed out loud. Then she asked me what seemed to be a really stupid question at the time, as she continued to punch me. She asked, "Does it hurt"? Out of protection, I laid back onto my bed screaming, "Of course it hurts... saying that's a stupid question!" I ask her to stop hitting me, but she continued. Why to this day, I'm not certain, but something told me to raise my feet in the air for protection, so I did. Then she stopped beating me and drew herself back up against the wall, clasping her right hand with her left hand, which had hit the heel of my foot. She began crying; yelling at me. Saying, "Look what you've done! You've broken my knuckles." as she hit me with her left hand, leaving in tears.

Throughout my childhood and adult years I was reminded of her suffering with arthritis. She'd say "Look at me! Look what you've done. You did this to me." Yes, I felt the guilt, for years.

I remember too, on those hot summer days how I would always have to wear a hot, winter flannel lined, leather hat with earflaps hanging loosely on each side of my head and had to wear long sleeve flannel shirts. Why you might ask? They were entirely too hot to be wearing and when I complained, my mom would tell me that I had to wear them if I wanted to play outside because I was allergic to the sun. I eventually through the years come to realize that they were to hide all my marks and bruises.

My older sister, Donna seemed to be the one that could do no wrong and she beat on me, too. Today though, I know Donna's beatings were out of frustration and it was her way of fighting back, but I didn't know it at the time. I told my mom about it, but she would never listen to me over Donna, because Donna was the eldest. She was considered to be the mature one, but one day my mom heard me screaming where we had been playing on the side of the house in the shade. I wasn't wearing my hat and my sister struck me on the head with the end of a stiletto type spiked high heel, which drew blood. Fortunately, my mother had been looking out the window and saw what had happened. Donna was scolded for it, but she denied it claiming innocence. So for lying, my mom punished her by strapping her to a support beam at the bottom of the stairs, in the basement. I watched and listened to Donna as she yelled and screamed while our mother was tying her up. Donna begged my mom not to do it or leave her in the basement. Afterwards, my mom came up the stairs and closed the door, leaving Donna sitting in the dark on the cold concrete floor with all those water bugs and roaches. I don't know how long Donna was down there but she kept banging the back of her head on the steel beam, creating a loud vibrating noise that could be heard throughout the whole house: BONG! My mom yelled down to her that she would not be untied until she quit misbehaving. Eventually, she quit screaming and banging her head and then, just wept. Finally, mom released her.

I still love Donna and until just recently, I haven't had a clue as to her whereabouts nor seen her but maybe 2 or 3 times in 40+ years. We haven't spoken to one another but once, in over 25 years. I've prayed to see or hear from her, to let her know she's my sister and that I love her and to share Jesus and now we have.

It wasn't much longer after all this took place that my folks finalized their divorce and my mother moved, leaving the three of us with my dad which was almost unheard-of in those days. It was then I began burdening myself with the blame for years to come. Also, I did not see or understand everything that went on and there are so many embedded horror stories. Some of which I did not share, and some that I have; not to dishonor or discredit my parents whom I love, but only to share... God's intervention.

These events though are the very substance that has made me into, who I am today and has shown me what to do, and not to do in life. All these embedded past memories I have had to work through, by myself? No! Thanks be... unto the Lord who was, and still is with me. He has walked with me through all these heart-aches where I blame myself, but I was just a kid struggling to survive; to grow up and be someone that my parents would be proud of. However, on occasion I still looked back and wonder, what if... and did I really cause my folks to get a divorce? The only thing that keeps my thoughts in check is the fact that, if my mother had been more honest, open, and had more patience when it came to materialistic things, I believe our family would have survived. What is really strange about all these events though are the bond; the bond between a mother and a child, no matter what. It's that love; referred to as unconditional love, and believe me; I still have a strong love for my mother. But, all you parents out there, in short; love your children and again, do not tear their hearts apart with guilt or blame, and do not blame yourself or your spouse for whatever path the two of you have chosen. Remember too, this really does hurt the children and only leads to confusion, guilt, anger and rage, and may even cause them to withdraw into their own little world of depression, which may take years to overcome, if ever. Trust me, I know!

God Hates Divorce

Remember your vows to one another and more importantly, your vows to God; to Love and Honor... for better or worse, until death, do us part. Well, God hates divorce, for to divorce is to divide and to divide is to separate, as in death; for we are joined together, as one. Therefore, the death of a marriage... is the severing of the unity within a marriage; the bonding of two, as one; brought together through God, who says:

> **_Matthew 19:6_** *wherefore they are no more twain, but one flesh. What therefore God hath joined together, let not man put asunder.*

Marriage reflects the ultimate and supreme way where two persons; a man and wife, are joined together, as one. In marriage, where two are united as one, follows the same principle, as the marriage that will take place between the Lamb of God; our Lord, Jesus Christ and His Bride... the Church; when united as one. Only then, it is for all eternity. Eternity, meaning forever and not... until death do us part, as it is between a man and woman, as it has been from the beginning with Adam and Eve. It was because of Adam and Eve's disobedience, which caused our death and separation from God. It is through Jesus Christ that by faith, we are brought back into righteousness with God, having life ever-lasting. God's promise is His Word and His Word is Truth and when we accept Jesus as our Lord and Savior, we are then brought into his fold; the Church; the Bride, and we are united as one with God, forever!

Satan originally, robbed us of our Righteousness and the Dominion God gave man in the beginning, through Satan's lies and deception. But, it's through God's Love, Mercy and Grace that He sent Jesus to die in our place to set us Free from death; to restore us, into Righteousness; Praise God! For we are created in God's image and His love for us is that of a father, who loves his own, which is why He sent Jesus; the only perfect one, pure enough to be sacrificed... to save man, from the grips of death.

So, it is through the sacrifice of Jesus that we now belong to Jesus Christ, our Lord and Savior and soon coming King. Other passages confirming this unity called marriage between a man and a woman, and are as follows:

> *a.) But from the beginning of the creation, Male and female made he them. b.) For this cause shall a man leave his father and mother, and shall cleave to his wife; c.) and the two shall become one flesh: so that they are no more two, but one flesh. d.) What therefore God hath joined together, let not man put asunder.*
>
> ***a.)****Mark 10:6* ***b.)****Mark 10:7* ***c.)****Mark 10:8* ***d.)****Mark 10:9*
>
> *(Taken from the American Standards Version Bible.)*

Love Triangle
....

I look at marriage liken that of a trinity or the perfect triangle; the "Love Triangle" which has three equal sides and corners! The bottom surface; is one side having two equal corners, as the base which is needed for a sound marriage. This base having two corners represents you and your spouse. Both lower corners are held together at the base which is the life-line of their marriage, be it long or short in length. They also have two separate sides, which represents their own separate life lines rising to a third point; another corner, which is perfectly centered between the two, above the center of the base; being united at the very top of this Love Triangle. This third point represents God, as being equally centered and above all things. By keeping God in this position; in the center of your marriage and above all things; in the middle of your marriage... you will have the perfect balanced triangle; the Love Triangle and a Blessed Marriage. But, if one of the two in marriage pulls away from the perfect triangle it will no longer be symmetrically balanced or in unison, as a perfect triangle and will become disfigured and lop-sided. As this distance grows between one another; this also puts a greater distance between them and God, and the perfect will of God.

However, the closer we draw together by keeping our eyes on the Lord, the closer our marriage is drawn together and if one has done wrong, forgiveness is a must... to be forgiven and our marriage will be blessed; remaining complete, and united as one.

This acknowledges God... as being above all things and your marriage will be blessed, in God's will. This unity will hold you together, as one, but only if you allow God to remain above yourself and never elsewhere, such as, at the bottom of this Love Triangle, or your marriage will be top heavy and collapse. This is not the will of God, but the closer you draw toward God, the closer knit the Love Triangle becomes. So, if you want a happy marriage, and life; "Seek ye first the kingdom of God, and his righteousness; and all these things shall be added unto you." This will provide you true happiness and a solid marriage, by living in God's will, united as one and keeping God in the center of your marriage and above all things... including each other.

To do otherwise, could create conditions that I've come to know personally, being from a broken home; that can only lead to confusion and irreparable heartache that will linger with us... until God knows when. In short, the children will suffer more than anyone can ever imagine. I know too, that the parents don't intend to hurt their children, but do so, when it comes to divorce.

Let's not forget either; God will hold us all accountable for any oath put forth before Him and it would be better if a mill stone be placed around your neck and you be cast into the sea than to hurt even one of these little ones. What more can I say, but God have mercy on my parents; for I do love them dearly and please consider yourselves, if not your children... should separation or divorce ever come to mind, for God loves you. Again, believe me on this... God hates divorce.

My wife, Joyce and I have been married 50 years in June and contribute our longevity to putting Jesus first and ourselves last. This includes recognizing ourselves, as equals... residing at each end of the Love Triangle's base, which has drawn us closer.

By doing this, we are actually committed to each other and even talk to one another to make sure we know just what each of us want; as long as we are trying to keep our Lord first. Only then can we live in peace and harmony with one another. We, as others, have our ups and downs but we always remember our place in the Love Triangle. We also pray over our food at home or when we're out. We even say prayers together when we retire for the night, for there truly is power... when praying together.

The Word says that when two or more are gathered in my name that He is with us and whatever we ask in Jesus name; it shall be done to glorify our Father who is in Heaven. Not may be done or might be done, but will be done! You needn't do anything else but ask, believe, have faith and expect... to receive.

God does love us and He is committed to us, and the least we can do is honor our commitments to God and each other for, it is intended to remain as such. Again, this is because the word says that we are joined, as one. Since there are no marriages in heaven, then by death, we do depart, but while here on earth, to divorce, is to divide and to divide is again, liken that of a death. It breaks many hearts.

Personally, I want to be among the living and no, I judge not, for there is, but one true and righteous judge and he alone, is God. It's because of His Love for us that we have everlasting life. Thanks, be unto the Lord, and praise God!

Memories of My Dad

Everyone should have memories of their dad and I am no different. Some are excellent, some good and some not so good. Though they are few; this is because of his responsibilities, as being the man of the house, so he was almost always, gone... working on the job. It's not that he was a bad father, but he was a working man and had little time for family. After raising my own family I can relate to the following statement; someday when you older, you will understand. I did hear this and it's true in some cases, but not necessarily in all situations and now, as a man, I understand the devastation of divorce... period!

My dad and I did go to a few parks together that I can recall, where we went swimming and fishing. One time we went to an old mining slimes pit that was filled years earlier, as part of a reclamation project. On the opposite side of this pit was a lake where we went fishing, so we walked around the pit, rather than taking the chance of sinking into it. We fished into the late afternoon and were tired, thirsty, and hungry. With my dad being exhausted, he was not... up to walking, around that pit.

It was because of this, that my dad said to me, "Douglas, this pits been here for years and looks to be dry. How about stepping out there 5 or 10 feet for me to see how firm it is." So, I did. Then he said to jump up and down, as to test the crust build-up. So again, I did just as he asked, being naïve and not knowing better. As I did so, I said, "It's okay dad... come on, let's go!"

Not knowing better at the time; as the years passed... I often wonder, what was my dad thinking, especially with my dad stepping out onto that pit. It appeared solid at first and as he continued to step out slowly onto the crusted slimes pit. First one step, then two; then three and four, or more... and then all of a sudden, the crustation gave away. He yelled for me to get off, as he fell back toward the edge in an effort to evenly distribute his weight; flipping over, to crawl-off this thing. It was just a matter of moments and he'd already sunk up to his knees, as he scrambled to crawl back to the edge. He leaned forward and reached for anything and everything he could grasp, even the grass. He was only feet away and I remember the fear in his voice as he fought to pull his legs free and to crawl onto solid ground. All I could do was stand there; frightened, as he yelled; "Get back! Keep away!" Had he gone out any further, it would have been over, for both of us. I say this, because I may have gone out to help him and may have very well met the same fate. Apparently though, someone was watching over us that day and he managed to crawl to the edge. I feared for his safety, but he made it. However, the thought... "What if?" does come to mind. You know: as I was jumping up and down; what if... Ker-plunk?

As I said, I too, could have sunk into that pit with a single Ker-plunk and I would have been no more. It was years later that I came to realize, it was the Lord who was watching over us.

After that little test of fate, my dad decided it best to walk around the pit. Good idea! We were empty handed and headed home but not until my dad introduced me to "White Castles"; the best little tasting hamburger ever. I really miss those, here in FL.

My dad also took me to an indoor roller rink to go skating regularly and to an ice skating rink on occasion. We even went to some of the many old-time drive-in theaters, as a family. There were times during the snowy winter months too, that he'd take us to sleigh down some really steep hills, where he grew up in downtown St. Louis. There was another time he built me a home-made triple stick kite. It was one of the greatest things he ever built me. I bragged about that kite to my friends including my own kids, and of course I had to build them one, just to show them what I was talking about. It had a tail, as did mine, that was 80 feet long or more. Wow, what a kite! What a tail! This kite would soar straight up, as high as your string, was long.

When it comes to hunting though, I don't recall ever going hunting with my dad, but we went to an old camp site he knew about. We fished and then he unloaded his rifle. He asked, if I would like to learn how to shoot it. I said, "Yes!" and it was fun even though we only shot at tin cans. Those were the days...

He also went to a Cub-Scout function with me once where I had to carve a home-made wooden racecar for a special derby race. Other than that my dad and I never really spent much time together except maybe when he came home during the evening hours. I would force myself on him by jumping up on his lap when I could and he'd grab my neck around my collar bone. I'd do my best to get away as he held on and tickled me, but he'd cross his legs and trap me in his lap, so I wouldn't escape. Eventually though, I would manage to get past his knees and hit the floor, squirming to get out of his reach, tossing and turning.

Doing this maneuver just to escape once was usually enough. This was because of the metal brace he wore functioned through the use of steel knuckles on either side of his left foot and knee to assist bending them which enabled him to stand and walk with his leg injury. Those knuckles really hurt when he used them, as he squeezed my head to prevent my escape, but he never knew because I never complained. This is what I suppose most people would call quality time that I had with my dad and as for the love. Well, it was worth going back for seconds, but Ouch!

I was so ticklish around the neck that all he had to do was to point his finger and say freeze, like he was going to get me, and I'd just collapse to the floor in laughter, without even being touched. Sometimes he'd rub his 5 o'clock shadow on my neck as he hugged me. It felt like sand paper and I tried to get away only to have him point that finger and again and I'd just melt. I really loved my dad and as I said, I usually ended up on the floor in laughter, scrambling to get away. As I look back on those days though, they became fewer and fewer after the divorce. He was just too busy working or running around; rarely if ever at home. He never had any time for special events at school or otherwise. That's how it was, unless I was in trouble where we had to see the principal after school hours, only to be grounded.

So, all you moms and dads, please listen. I don't care how bad you think you two have it. You don't have it nearly as bad as your children do, or will. Those children you brought into this world... are a gift to you. They're a product of the love you two had once shared with one another, and more than likely, you still have it. This is because, believe it or not, even after a divorce.... that love still remains. You might not see it or feel it, but it remains. It's that small spot, or hole in your heart that can only be filled, by one another. Seek help for your children's sake and yes; you can separate or divorce, if you choose, but as for your children; they consist of the two of you and they cannot divorce, separate or be divided from within, or from you. They will never understand, and it will literally tear their hearts apart, from the inside out, and they'll be unable to choose between the two you.

I remember asking my mom and my dad continuously, do you love me? Even though they would say yes, I would continue to ask daily, because that love they once had for each other, appeared to be, no more. Because of that... I was, so insecure. I even began wondering, if God loved me at times, but thank God... He's never given up on me. He's always been right here inside me. It's taken me years and years to realize this, but He is with all of us, including you, whether you wish to accept it or not. He's that small still inner voice, calling you from within and it is up to you to respond. You have nothing more to do than to recognize that He is with you. So go ahead, speak to Him, trust Him, and have faith. You'll be surprised, because He will answer you, and does answer prayer, according to your faith.

Some of those moments, no matter how few they were, were truly the best times I ever had, including when I was allowed to join the Boy Scouts. It was great and I learned a lot of things, including how to survive. It helped make up for some of those times that we didn't spend together. But, to look back at them now? Those days were valuable but were no substitute for a father. I only wish I had spent more time with him. I wanted to hear him say that he loved me and that he was proud of me. This is all I longed for since I was a child and then finally, one day... he opened up and told me. I was 40 years of age at the time, but better late than never. He said that he loved me and that he was proud of what I had become. In doing so, I was flabbergasted!

Kids of all ages love, and want to be loved and to be accepted for who and what they are, by their parents. You and your children are no different. So love your children with all your heart, for again, they are on loan to you from God; a product of the love, God has given a man and his wife; to love, hold and cherish. For in the end we're all here for one purpose only, and this is to love and please God. I'm sure this is what you want, as I do. There are those times though when we all feel like such a disappointment, but thank God for first loving us. None of us deserve His love, but He too, needs our love. For God is Love and I believe this is why we should love each other; to love Him.

When we love one another we are returning this love unto the Lord for He dwells within each of us and again, we are made in His Image and Likeness; Love. It's because of this love, God sent His only begotten son, Jesus Christ to save the sons of men and there is no greater love than this, the gift of Love, from God.

> **_Isaiah 1:18_** *"though your sins be as scarlet, they shall be as white as snow; though they be red like crimson, they shall be as wool"*

By the way, I promised myself a long time ago that I would never divorce, for my children's sake nor put them through the heartache I endured. As such, and being just a child, I became distraught and a renegade. I did unspeakable things that I'm not proud-of nor care to mention, but I've asked the Lord to forgive me, who forgives and loves me... always, including you.

God will forgive us, if we seek his forgiveness and repent, for His Word is Truth, and it breaks my heart to speak of these things, but

I felt led to. So, whatever you do, remember this... do not put your children through divorce. If you do, then God help you, especially the children for they're going to really need some help from someone. Jesus is a specialist in these areas of love and compassion. Without Him they will truly be lost and alone, having no one in whom to turn to, for love and support, except for that of a dysfunctional family that has abandoned one another. Parents, you are the hero's in whom they love and look up to for guidance and direction, as their loving and trustworthy parents. You and your spouse are joined together creating a oneness that is united together in Holy Matrimony, and that which God has joined together, let no man... or woman, separate.

Also, it isn't good for anyone to be alone, especially a child. As it states in the Word of God; the Bible, which is, as follows:

> ***Ecclesiastes 4:10*** *For if they fall, the one will lift up his fellow; but woe to him that is alone when he falleth, and hath not another to lift him up.*

Family Divided
....

As a child; I tried to save my parents' marriage, as I'm sure any child would do. I begged and I pleaded. I even lied to my mother about my dad still loving her and lied to my dad about my mother still loving him. All, to no avail. I was so young, too young to understand and was heartbroken. Life, as I knew it was shattered. I even tried sabotaging any efforts of my mother getting married to someone else that I had hopes of preventing.

She moved in with some guy named Gil Armour who has since passed away. He only tolerated my sister, my brother and me for my mother's sake. I guess you could say we were part of the package. She wasn't given custody of us children, which was unheard when I was a child. In most cases, the mother was always given custody of the children unless the mother is proven unfit, so I come to learn. I didn't understand this at the time; so my dad said, no... she just didn't want us. I believe now that he was just trying to spare us the heart-ache, but the heart-ache is still very real, even today. I was so up-set over this that I questioned her about loving me and she claimed that she did. She claimed too, she would always love me. I believe she did, but then again, we did have to live with my dad and of course, I believed my dad, too. So, as one can see, confusion set in and one's belief is in question. No wonder why God hates divorce; for God is Love, and if Love is in question; what's a child to do?

I was 12 when we first came to visit and meet a man called Gil who was an alcoholic. We all sat together for dinner as a family in a four-star hotel suite. Gil was from the old school era where it was said, "Out of sight, out of mind." So when we finished eating, much to my surprise; he gave us taxi-fare for a round trip; to and from the theater, plus enough money to buy movie tickets and all the popcorn, candy and drinks we wanted.

Wow, if he was trying to impress us with all his money, it worked! I was in total awe, because he always seemed to have more than enough money, which my dad never seem to have.

As time passed, I realized that it wasn't my dad's fault that he was financially ruined. He was just a victim of circumstances. I say this because I remember when my folks were still together before Gil, I was lucky to even get a nickel for an ice cream. My dad just didn't have it! Why, I didn't know. I was just a little kid, but I remember getting up early one day and sneaking into my mom and dad's bed where they were asleep. As I did, my mom woke up and slid out of bed, saying she'd be right back. She went to the rest room and the came back stopping in front of the chair were my dad's slacks were lying. She smiled at me ever so big and as she did; she put her index finger over her lips as if to say, Shhh as she sheepishly went through his pockets in search of money which I can only assume she needed to pay bills. I was a kid then and didn't know any better or understand.

However, I loved my mom and dad and wanted them back together so much so, that I made a real effort to up-set Gil. This was done in hopes that Gil would come after me and that my mother would step in and rescue me and then return to my dad. That was the plan, but it was a bad idea. I used sneezing powder and cigarette loads that exploded in Gil's face and it gave him a chuckle, but was I blinded, by ignorance. It was after a few stout drinks and a fine meal consisting of New York Strips that Gil went into the living room to enjoy a cigarette with his drink in hand and as always, he asked for a tooth pick. So I gave him a hot cinnamon tooth pick that I bought, just for the occasion. Needless to say, with Gil being half-drunk; he flew off the handle asking me... No, he demanded to know where I got those toothpicks. I laughed as I told him that I bought them as a joke and he demanded I give him all the toothpicks, so I did. Then he grabbed me by the nap of my neck and led me to the bathroom and threw them into the commode, and as he flushed them; he crammed my head into the toilet. As he did so, he asked me if I still thought it was funny. I cried out to my mom, but she did nothing and I learned a valuable lesson... don't mess with Gil, or play any more stupid tricks on him. I thought my mother would come to my rescue, but she didn't and only scolded me instead. Imagine the rejection I felt, leaving more doubts, and confusion.

I wanted to live with my mother even though she was abusive but why? I don't know except that I loved her then as I do now, and will continue loving her all the days of my life. This love also applies to my dad, even though he lied telling us that she didn't want us. It was confusing and hard for us to except the truth when in reality, he may have known of our abuse, but he never mentioned it or questioned us about it, not even once.

Then again, he may have been telling us the truth. God only knows for sure. All I knew was that I wanted my parents together again, but it just wasn't meant to be. My mother finally married Gil, which explains why today's generations have so many problems. It's due to the number of divorces! Let's face it; divorce literally tears a family apart; physically, emotionally and mentally. Especially, for a child who is so easily crushed and scarred for years to come? Trust me, this agony can last a lifetime as one wonders; did I or did I not cause this and what if?

Rejection & Rage

During my childhood years, divorce was taboo not to mention illegal, except in certain cases. I become shunned by my friends because I was not allowed to play with them any longer due to my parents being divorced. It was like I had a disease or something that might be passed on to them. Naturally, I started hanging around with a rougher crowd and stopped going to church and skipped so much school that I can't even remember the number of days I missed. I started smoking in the 5th grade, broke into houses, stealing and vandalized things; ripping people off right and left. I even went on a joy ride in a stolen car once, which we wrecked. I've also done worse... like hurt people; a lot of people. I've even sent some to the hospital from the things I'd done. I got mad at one guy and knocked out his permanent front teeth just for telling me, "There is no Santa... stupid." I was so young and dumb and it still haunts me, to remember these things. I even broke my own brother's collarbone; not once, but twice... back to back, and he hadn't even been out of the cast, but a week.

I also, learned when I was younger from my mother, how to have him stand at attention, like that of a soldier with his eye's closed. Instead swatting him with a stick, I would rear-back and punch him in the mouth. If he flinched or pulled away; we'd do the same thing over and over, until he quit flinching. This event would never have happened had there been a parent around to teach us right from wrong and not just one parent, but both!

For being his big brother I was such a mean and terrible bully. It's a wonder that he or I ever survived childhood or that he'd even claim me, as his brother. He not only liked being around me, but he looked up to me and he loved me, but was rejected as I was, only by me. I've always said God was... and is, watching over me and has always taken care of me and obviously, He did so for my brother, too! It wasn't until adulthood that I would come to realize the importance of having a brother and just how much I really loved him, but I'll tell you more, and why later.

After the divorce, we always came home to an empty home without any adult supervision. Donna was always left in charge because she was the eldest. I honestly think she was missing something up stairs. She constantly picked on me while our folks were married, but after the divorce? In all honestly, I think she not only wanted to hurt me, but actually, wanted to kill me!

One cold wintery day as a practical joke, Donna set a bucket full of water on the top of the back screen door that was partially held open, by a snow drift on the back porch. She knowingly, locked the front door so I would have to use the back door and she stood there and watched me through the back door window as I waded through the snow, struggling to get up the steps. As I did, I grabbed the screen door handle and tried to pull it open, but I couldn't get it open enough to squeeze through. So I got between the door and the door frame to push it open and spilled water all over me. I became so furious, especially to see Donna in the back door window, laughing as I stood there sopping wet and freezing. I began banging on the door, threatening to break the glass window, if she didn't open the door and let me in.

Well, she unlock the door, but not because she was afraid of me, but because she had set up another stunt for me. As I opened the back door, it released a string that was pinched between the top of the door and door jamb; tied to a butcher knife pointing downward, toward the doorknob. When released? Well, thank God the knife missed my artery, as it stabbed my wrist. As time went on; I was stabbed in both wrists and forearms on many occasions and with some leaving deep gashes and puncture wounds scarring me... for life. I'm easily reminded of them often when checking myself for any signs of skin cancer.

I have five or more scares on my wrist and forearms that are still visible. I even have one on my stomach and my throat. Let me explain. Out of frustration, I decided to show her what it feels like to stand outside in the snow... all sopping wet. So, I set the same trap for her the very next day, and she had forgot what she did to me, but not for long and it proved to be a big mistake.

I had hurried home from grade school that next day to beat Donna home and to set-up the same trap. She came to the front door which was locked, causing her to use the back door and it worked, perfectly. The bucket poured all over her and like her, I laughed through the window while standing indoors behind the locked door. She was drenched, and began banging on the back door. She was so mad that she forgot to look up and as she opened the door and the same butcher knife, now stabbed her in the wrist. However, that a big mistake on my part. She now had the knife and was beyond being mad and much bigger than me.

She barged through the back door and slammed it shut. She grabbed me and slung me up against the back door while holding the knife up under my chin. She had a wild, wide eyed, crazed look about her and said, "Don't move!" and I didn't, because I was afraid, very afraid and I said, "I won't!" She said, "Too late, you moved", as she pulled the knife upward to cut me just under my chin. So, that's where I contribute a scar beneath my chin or not, though I'm not certain, but I have worn a full-beard most of my life to conceal it and have never forgotten her rage, that day.

Also, after pulling the knife upward beneath my chin, she did stab me in the stomach, but I believe my heavy padded coat protected me. Meaning, I don't believe the knife penetrated my coat but then again, I do have a small scar on my stomach that appears to have been from a puncture wound, but it may have been from another event. I really don't recall exactly, but I do remember her laughter as she walked away, tossing the knife into sink. Her abuse did neither of us any favors.

I recall another time where she chased me down the basement stairs and picked up a hatchet she seen; raising it over her head as if she wanted to hit me. The furnace was the only thing that saved me. It was in the middle of the basement, separating us. She scared the heck out of me and I needed to get out of that basement, as soon as possible, but I was trapped. As I tried to go one-way or another, she would head me off with her raised arm. I tried to talk some sense into her and apologized for whatever up-set her and then I saw my opportunity, and I leaped up the stairs. As I did, I turned the corner at the top of the stairs and just in time; leading into the kitchen, and I heard.. "WHAM!"

I turned around to look at what had happened, as heard my sister storming up the stairs and there it was; the ax! It was embedded in the back door with a split running up the door. I ran out the front door in fear for my life, yelling back to her that I was going to tell dad what she did. She said "Go ahead! I'll tell dad you did it, because it's your ax." I was stupid enough to believe her and feared a beating, so I never said anything to him.

There's another time where she chased me out the front door too, only she was chasing me with a pair of barber scissors. She followed me right out the front door and hurled them at me, which entered into the back of my right elbow and plunged down into my forearm. They were embedded at least 2½"to 3" into my right arm; entering just above the elbow and passing beneath my upper forearm's flesh. I held my hand wide open... stiff armed, as the pain shot down into my hand. I stopped and turned around looking toward the front porch in total disbelief, as she laughed.

She had real problems and must have thought that I had intentions on throwing them back at her, because she turned around and stormed into the house. I looked down at the damage done to my arm and pulled out the scissors where I now have, yet another scar to remind me of the terror. I never told my parents about any of this either, because I was always told, "She's the oldest and in charge." Therefore, not knowing any better, I never questioned this authority and just accepted this behavior as normal, even though she was wrong! She was the boss! I also, know how bizarre this story must sound, but God knows I'm telling the truth to the best of my recollection and if it weren't for some kind of intervention, I really don't think I'd be here today. Thank you, Lord.

Out of Control
············

As I said earlier, my mom married Gil, and the three of us were shuffled back and forth between living with mom and dad. As for my dad, he was always out and about regularly, gallivanting around town after work before coming home scouting the bars for a new lady friend. Obviously, we had no one at home, except for our grandma at 70, who had moved in to help with us kids. She came to stay but shortly afterwards, she had a stroke and went into the hospital. I wonder why? She came back home a couple weeks later using a walker at first and then crutches and unable to get up and down stairs, so she never came into the basement, which gave me my privacy. I grew a strong dislike of my grandmother whom I had loved dearly. I only gave her a hard time because of my mother, belittling her. She tolerated me but eventually, she moved out and because of me, I'm sure. I was so disrespectful toward her and called her names and said so many mean and hurtful things... blaming her for my parents' divorce, only because of what my mother had said. Not once did she say anything to my dad about my abuse or disrespect. She probably knew if she did, my dad may have beaten me within an inch of my life, which he almost did once.

He beat me and hit me so much one time that I too, fought him off with my feet. Finally, in an attempt to get him to stop, I said, "Why don't you just kill me and get it over with." It was only then that he stopped and left the room. I was just a mixed-up kid full of anger, confused and as for my grandmother? She truly was a good woman, deserving so much more than I offered.

My brother, sister, and dad lived upstairs and had walls where-as, I had no walls living downstairs in that dungy old basement which was just one big cold dark, damp room beneath the house. I slept in a double bed and I took great pride in my little section of the basement after semi-cleaning it. It was just a small little area within this huge roach infested, slum of an area full of cat fesses that my mother left behind. The up-stairs wasn't much better, but not nearly as bad as the basement. It had a bad roach infestation with piles and piles of dirty, old worn-out heaps of clothing, over-lapping one another from years earlier when we could fit into them. I literally had to wade through them, just to get to my side of that scary basement.

We had overhead lighting in five separate areas in the basement, which had pull-strings enabling the lights to be turned on or off. I added additional lengths to each of these strings by using kite-string, and strung them through eye-lets screwed into the floor joist. I laced them across the basement to a common place. I brought them all together and entwined them into a single light cord; hanging from just above where I slept within arm's reach.

I did this because I was so afraid of being in the basement with all the creeks and cracks, popping and snapping that occurred through the night, as well as having all those bugs crawling all around; especially in the dark. I even put an old table beside my bed, so I would have a place to put a glass of water, just in case I become thirsty. I did this because I hated the thought of having to get up in the middle of the night and having to wade over all those disgusting piles of worthless, mildewed, roach infested piles of clothing.

I more or less, accepted the filth and things as they were until this one night when I reached over to get a drink of water. Upon doing so, I felt something moving around in my mouth and spit the water onto the floor as fast I could and jerked the pull cord. This lit up the whole basement with five 100-watt light-bulbs and there it was! It was a big old nasty-looking cock roach crawling out of the water that I had just spit out. Yuck!!! There were so many roaches and water bugs everywhere, so much so, that even our pet turtle living in the basement, couldn't keep up with them.

It's because of this one incident that I literally turned into an overnight NEAT-FREAK! I instantly become, "OCD" about everything. The next day I began cleaning the basement from top to bottom, including the cobwebs out of the floor joists openings where the joist over-lapped the concrete exterior walls.

Afterwards, I sprayed bug spray everywhere and hung sheets to form walls around my small space, which was my bedroom. I even went upstairs and cleaned out the rest of the house. I threw everything away that appeared worthless and to this very day, I still cannot stand a dirty or filthy home and it must be kept clean.

In fact, when I first met my wife, I insisted that she keep her bedroom area, also located in the basement next to her sister's bedroom... clean, if she expected me to visit. What is strange though, is that their rooms too, only consisted of sheets as did mine. Well, she did and even until today; we're both neat freaks.

My area was really a neat little pad where I had an old recliner setting next to the bed where I could sit and watch TV any time I wanted. Having all this free space and spare time got me into trouble though. I was able to have friends coming and going and we had the ability to sneak in and out of the house during all hours of the night. It was easy; the basement windows were removable and I seemed to go out and get into all kinds of trouble, but always managed to elude being caught.

I kept the Basement so clean and nice compared to the rest of the house that my sister started inviting her boyfriends, into my room. It was more convenient and private as they watched TV while on my bed. I was always told to turn around and watch TV or get hurt. I was only twelve at the time and she was thirteen. I really didn't know what was going on, although I had my ideas; and six days after Donna's fourteenth birthday, she gave birth to a healthy baby boy, named Kenneth Robert Thornberry.

One day while I was in the 8th grade, five or six of us kids skipped school. We went to my house because it was a nice warm and safe place to hide during those cold winter months, with no adults. Only, my unwed sister was home with her baby, who was fast asleep, so we all played games and watched TV.

We were all in the living room when Donna called for me to come see what she had found in my dad's closet; hidden on the top shelf.

At first, I thought it was a toy, but she said, "No it's not! Look", as she opened the gun's chamber, revealing it to be loaded with 6-bullets, which she dumped into her hand. She said, "Here, feel". She then said, "You know what?" I said "What?" as I gave them back to her? I watched as she inserted one bullet in the chamber. Then she slang it shut and spun it with the palm of her hand like someone playing Russian roulette. As the pistol carriage was coming to a stop; in one Simultaneous sweeping motion, she placed the end of the barrow directly into the middle of my chest and all I remember hearing was, "click."

I knew then that my sister had some sort of real issues. She could have killed me. It must have been from having all the pressure of being left in charge and having a baby at such an early age. She had never seemed this enraged before, but she yelled, "You and your friends better get out of the house." Well, she didn't have to say that more than once. We all scrambled to our feet and frantically, bailed out the front door. As we did, she came down the hallway holding that gun. All I remember was the spinning of the chamber, and the sound of "Click!" Thank God, for watching over us and protecting us.

Yes, the Lord really does protect us, all of us, but do we ever stop and realize his intervention and say thank you, or do we just consider ourselves lucky? Well, all I can say is Thank you Lord!

In fact; it's because of my sisters actions that I have refused to have or own a gun in my own home until after our children were grown and out the house and it's only to be used as a deterrent to head-off any potential dangerous encounter, as a means to protect us, so to speak. Even then, I have no real desire to use it, unless absolutely forced into a crisis situation where I have no choice, but to use it only in a life and death situation.

Poor Ole Dad

One thing my dad did though was to make certain that there was always plenty of food. One summer he literally filled our deep freezer, which was approx. 36"wide x 78"tall x 30"deep. He filled this thing to the max with a whole side of beef. I don't think my dad expected us to do this, but when he wasn't home, my brother and I would eat this for lunch. We would cook it on the Bar-BQ and used wood in lieu of charcoal with gasoline to get it started. The wood we had used, come from my buddies backyard picked fence. We snuck out at night through the basement window to get only one single slat at a time. We didn't want it to look, too obvious that they were being removed, so we stagger the removal of each slat, sporadically.

One day my dad said, "Douglas, I'm having company over today (meaning another girl friend) how about bringing up a couple of those porterhouse steaks, off the third shelf." I opened it up and yelled; there isn't any." He said, "There has to be, that's where I put them." Then he said, "What about the next shelf." I said, "Nope, There's nothing here but three roast." He said, "That impossible, unless you kids have been selling the meat to the neighbors." I said, "No dad, honest! Dennis and I have been eating it for lunch." I thought he was going to lose it as he stormed down the steps to see, so Pot Roast it was.

As went upstairs he said to me, "I swear Douglas, when you and your brother get older, and on your own; you're going to have to have two jobs. You're going to need one to support you and your families, and the other... to support that gut of yours."

I remember another time too; when my dad said to go down stairs and to get him some potatoes and I told him there wasn't any... that time either. My dad said, "Sure there are son, I just bought a fifty pound sack of potatoes Friday night, remember?" I said. "Sure dad, but they're gone!" He said, "What do you mean they're gone?" I said, "We ate them yesterday." My dad said, "How on earth could you possibly eat fifty pounds of potatoes in one day?" I said, "We learned how to make French fries and we used the can of lard you bought and the new bottle catsup, too."

Needless to say, my dad was beside himself, but I remember him putting clothes in layaway for us boys earlier in the summer so that we would have something to wear when school started. We even tried them on to be certain they would fit loosely in case we grew a little; A little... I was 5'6" but when he brought our cloths home come the end of August, just before school started; he was amazed, they didn't fit. Both my brother and I grew seven inches over that summer. It must have been all that protein we ate. I think my brother was able to fit into my new clothes, which were in lay-a-way, but as for me? Well, the clothes originally intended for my brother were too small and were used as an exchange to buy something much bigger for me, so things worked out. My dad always told me Dennis would outgrow me, which I didn't believe, but eventually, he did. I began the 7th grade at 6'1 wearing a size 13 shoe. We were some of the biggest kids in the neighborhood. My brother & I eventually hit 6'-6" for me & 6'8" for him and were like twins.

One day I was going up to my buddy's back door as I always had; calling out to him to come out and play? I noticed his dad was at the back edge of their driveway; gardening and tilling around his peach tree he grew from a seed. I felt a little uneasy, as he kept looking toward the fence along the back yard. I asked if Eddie could come out and play. He said, if his chores are done.

It was then that Ed came out and said he was finished, so his dad said alright, as he looked up back toward the fence again. As he did earlier, stopping Eddie and asked him a question, as he pointed at the wooden picketed fence. It was missing so many slats that it looked like a piano keyboard and Eddie's dad asked, "Eddie, do you know what the heck is happening to our fence?" As they spoke, I slowly turned around and walked away, as if to be waiting on Eddie. Ed said, "NO sir!" But I knew, exactly and turned away to hide my face and to keep from laughing. His fence actually looked like a piano key board by sporadically missing wood slats. How sad. As I said, "I knew exactly what happened, but I never had the nerve to tell Eddie. Again, he was my buddy, but then again, Dennis and I had to eat.

As, I look back at it in life, I come to realize how terrible of a friend I was back then. I believe too, this to be the reason Dennis and I grew so much over that summer. This too, is probably the first signs of me putting eating at the top of my comfort list, but I've come to learn, that it is the Lord... that must come first, above all things, including food. I also believe when you're without adult supervision and there's no one to cook, you compromise, with what you have available. No wood? No Food.

Eventually, I have I turned to God to help me control my appetite. Unfortunately I got up to 317 pounds wearing a size 15 shoe and only now, slowly losing weight and have gotten down to the low 270's, having hopes of reaching 250 or less. The one thing I am thankful for though, over this whole event; is the fact that we didn't get lead poisoning from eating all that BBQ meat, using lead painted wood fencing.

What I did was wrong, but the Lord must have been, watching over us. We both survived that event, to live and see another day, thank God! I think too, that Eddie's dad would have stepped in between our friendship if he had learned the truth about his picked fence disappearing and I didn't want to do that. Eddie was like a brother to me and I wouldn't want to have our friendship ended over my stupidity.

CHAPTER 3
"God is Always Watching Over Us"

Cave In

There was this one summer day when a bunch of us were playing in a small cave that we found, which some other kids had carved into the clay hillside. We crawled inside to investigate and as we were crawling out, the tunnel totally collapsed. It could have buried us alive and nobody could have helped us, yet someone was watching over us. Thank you, Lord.

Playing Tag

There is 0ne Week-end; 6 or 7 of us were wandering around looking for something to do. It was cold and snow was on the ground and we were just out, walking around near a wooded area where there are these long lean, but straight and tall, Hickory Tree's. They're fun to climb and to skin a cat on, which means as you climb to the top of the tree, it will sway... way over, and the higher you climb the more it bows down to a point where it almost reaches the ground, depending on the weight of the individual. If it bows into another willow; you can even switch trees and climb up a different one, which is a lot of fun, especially when playing tag. Kids really do not know what fun is or they are missing today by staying indoors.

It's really neat and a whole lot of fun when the trees begin to bow a little more than mid-way up the tree. The higher you climb, the more the tree bows, so much so that you have to un-wrap your legs from around the tree trunk and hang by your hands, 20 or 25 feet above the ground, but don't let go... you might just break a leg, if not worse. So, hang-on and continue your ascent to the top of the tree which requires you to hand walk, one hand over the other, until the tree bows enough to allow you to wrap your legs around it again, only to descend to the top of the tree, now reaching downward, toward the ground.

You just keep your legs wrapped around the tree and slide downward... close and closer to the point where you will be at a height, where you feel safe to let go of the tree and drop 5 or 10 feet to the ground, unless you choose to ride it to the ground. It literally bows down much faster when the first person dropping, is being chased by another person wanting to tag you. You just have to decide; do I drop now or later, but you always warn the person chasing you by yelling out; hold-on... I'm letting go.

What happens when you do let go, is the person still hanging on will be catapulted upward in a violent surge of energy due to the sudden release of weight distribution. He'll either say, okay... I'm ready, as he wraps his legs around for security and he better do just that... his well-being depends on it. So, he is literally hanging on for life and without his legs wrapped around the tree, he may be in trouble. So, as the lead guy is being chased and gets to that point of release, you just holler and then, let go; all you'll hear is... S W I S H and a scream of pure joy and delight as he tree sways back and forth, before coming to a stop. Man is that ever fun. Sometimes the guy... who is it, will try to fool you and tag you but when you let go, they scramble to hang on; screaming whoopee; S W I S H... SWISH... Swish...

Well, it was getting dark and we were getting tired of playing tag, so we started to head homeward but we notice a clearing in the woods. So, we went to investigate and a Construction Co. had cut into a hillside leaving approximately three feet between the fence-line and the edge of a cliff leading down to a clearing, to layout foundations to build a new apartment complex below, from where we were standing. It was not shored-up and there were dirt hills and embankments leading up to & down from this cliff, and being kids? We saw a challenge and began playing tag all-cover again, running up and down, and all around; beside and beneath this 40 or 50-foot high cliff that was a couple hundred feet long or longer. This cliff was actually an embankment, over-looking an area that had been hogged out, to clear and make way for a new construction site. The cliff we had been running on, raced across, playing tag suddenly... gave a little tremor with a slight rumble and then stopped, as quickly as it started.

Then it rumbled again, only a bit stronger and just enough to tell us something wasn't right, and to run. As we started running to get off the top of the cliff, I looked down, yelling to Dennis, my little brother, who was at the bottom. He was unaware of what was going on or about to happen. So I yelled to him, "RUN, there's going to be a landslide" but it was as if someone held back the landslide just long enough to allow all of us, to get clear. Then the rumbled suddenly gave way, and perfectly timed as we turned around; we watched in awe as the hillside collapsed. This incident would have killed my brother for sure and possibly injured, if not killed the rest of us. That three foot clearance from the residential fence-line was now only inches away from the cliff edge. We never played there again, but I drove by years later and saw the apartments with reinforcement railroad ties. My only concern was that of termites. Again, The Lord must have been watching over, all of us. Thank you, Lord.

Frozen Nightmare
....

One cold winter day, I'd swear we were in the middle of a blizzard and I wanted a sled to ride down the snow-covered hills. I had seen one earlier, which I priced at the local five and dime store in the shopping plaza, approximately a mile from my home. It was perfect, being red and white, long, and brand spanking new and only cost $12.

Ever since my first vision of showing me the stacks of coins, I knew what I had to do to get the money. I made it the old fashion way; I earned it! I learned to run errands and cut grass, pull weeds and to rake leaves during the spring, summer and fall, and in the winter, I shoveled snow and my buddies and I even pushed cars up icy hills that couldn't make it. I managed to save enough money, so that on this particular day, I would be able to buy that sled, so I thought, and I walked to the store. It began to snow that morning and about halfway to the store, it was coming down really hard. I was so excited about the snowfall and wanted this sled, but I come to find out at young age what taxes are. So, I came up short and headed back home, empty handed.

As I stepped out of the store, I noticed a city bus being stuck in the snow. It had snowed so hard that it must have been about 16" deep or more and was really coming down harder than ever.

I started playing around in the snow and I finally realized I'd better head for home or I might wind up like the bus and those riding in it that were stranded at the store. So, I began wading through the snow as I crossed the schoolyard in an attempt to take a short cut home, but I managed to get disoriented, lost and a little worried. I couldn't see a thing. Everything was whited out! I looked down at my gloved hands to be sure I wasn't blind or that everything was okay. Yep! My hands were still there and I found it easier... to just crawl on top the snow because it was almost waist deep. By the time I had reached the other side of the field, I was crawling over some snow drifts where the snow was actually above my waste, near chest high and then I felt something hard with my hand, as I was crawling. It was the top of a picket fence and I knew exactly where I was! I was at the last house, at the end of the field and I followed it until the roadway came into view. As I got back out onto the street, I headed for home again, only a few blocks away.

The snow on the road was about 24" deep, where-as the area where I had been at was apparently deeper because of the way the wind had been blowing across the open school field; creating deep snowdrifts. I was glad to be back on the road, but while heading home I noticed the retention pond being iced over and decided to play on the ice. About half-way across the ice, it gave way on me and I found myself neck deep in freezing water and the ice kept breaking, as I tried to climb out. Something inside me told me to put the back of my legs up onto one side of the ice hole and both arms onto the other... while facing up-ward, and then to straightened my body horizontally. This lifted me out of the water and then I felt led to roll over and over until I reached the edge of the pond. I was wet and freezing. It had to have been the Lord, who helped me. Face it; I was just a kid and had no knowledge of what to do and my cries for help would have probably gone unnoticed and I more than likely would've died.

I was out of sight from passing cars, but I did make it out and struggled up the embankment, finally making it home. I stripped and took a cold shower and slowly adjusted the temp to warm. Otherwise, a warm shower was unbearably Hot. Once again however, if not for the Lord's intervention, I honestly believe I may have not survived or even made it home. Thank you Lord.

Sole Saved

As I said before, in the summer, I cut grass, pulled weeds, and raked leaves in the fall. Once, while cutting a yard... the blade managed to come loose and fall onto the lawn. I was totally unaware of the event and stepped right into the path of the whirling blade. It was then that I felt something hit my foot hard and fast. It startled me as I looked down seeing the blade buried into my shoe. I thought the worst but felt no pain. Maybe it had cut me like a razor and I just didn't feel, as of yet. So, I sat down immediately to investigate the damage. It was then I realized that it had only slid between my foot and the sole of my shoe. My foot was without a single cut, scratch or mark. It could have been much worse, but once again, someone was watching over me. Thank you, Lord!

No Where to Turn

Yes, the Lord has really been watching over me all the days of my life. He's always been near to protect me. One of the few buddies I still had as a friend while growing up after the divorce was Jimmy-D. His parents let him put an opening into the back of their garage wall for an entry into a homing pigeon pen he built inside their garage. It was big and reached from the floor to the ceiling and was about 4 feet deep and 7 or 8 feet wide with cubby holes but he only had a couple pigeons and wanted more. He offered to allow me keep a pigeon or two in his pen, so we saved our money and decided we had enough to buy our birds.

We needed to take a trip to downtown St. Louis via bikes. He took his and I had a brand new one with a book carrier setting over the front fender which was perfect for carrying our pigeons. So we began our journey that was at least 20 miles one-way. It looked to be a great day and the sun was out.

While Jim and I were on our way, we witnessed a large gray squirrel get run over by a passing car. One his legs were broken. He began flopping around; spinning in circles before settling down. He just laid there panting in pain and we felt so helpless. But then we saw a by-passing law enforcement officer and began yelling and jumping up and down as we waved frantically to get his attention and he came to a stop. We then explained what happened and he got out of his car to size up the situation. We asked if he could call the humane society or something. He then asked us to step back up onto the curb; that he would take care of it. So, we stepped back up onto the sidewalk away from the curb as he asked, he got back into his cruiser. Much to our surprise, he put his cruiser into reverse and ran over this little helpless squirrel and squished the life out of him. Then he put his car into drive and drove away. I even think I saw him wave good-bye to us. This episode should have been a sign, as to the things to come. All we could do is scream... "No", as he did this terrible thing before driving away. We were extremely up-set with him, but what was done... was done. So, we continued on our journey and as we did, a cloudy over-cast began to move in.

Finally, we got to where we were going and spent forty-dollars on some homing pigeons and put them into a cardboard box and secured it to my front fender's book rack. As we headed back home; wouldn't you know it? It began to rain, and it only increased with each passing moment. We had only gone a few miles toward home and the rain was really come down. The box was getting soaked. We feared it may get soggy and fall apart, so we peddled fast toward a major intersection that had six-lanes in each direction. We were within a 100-150 yards of the intersection and the light just turned green, in our favor and we were going down a pretty steep grade on a flooded paved street.

It was so wet and slippery but we figured the green light should last a couple minutes, so we peddled as fast as we could. We felt as if, we were flying. We were sailing on this open road without any traffic ahead of us, except for those waiting at the red light in the opposing direction. We were fast approached the intersection and within a hundred feet or more where we would be crossing an extremely heavily trafficked rush-hour roadway, and wouldn't you know it? Because of minimal or no traffic on the road in which we were traveling, the light went from green, to yellow, to red, almost immediately! This caused us to stop peddling immediately as well and to apply our breaks. As we did; my chain came off leaving me without any foot brake. It was bad enough that the light that had turned green in our favor, only to turn red was beyond belief, but to have no brakes? I hollered to Jim, "HELP!" He said, "What wrong?" I explained that I lost my chain when I stopped peddling and didn't have brakes. I asked him to take hold of my hand and to use his brakes to stop me, but and he couldn't or just wouldn't; for fear of his own safety. We were nearing the point of entering the intersection. So, I panicked and stiff-armed my handlebars screaming to my buddy again, help. He yelled at me to slow down, but I explained I couldn't. He said, "Put your feet onto your front tire" but my tire was shielded. I quickly explained that it wouldn't work because my new bike had splash guards. As I explained, my buddy had to brake and come to a stop but I was unable to. All I could do was screamed, "Help" and I entered the inter-section where the traffic was already speeding through the intersection from both directions, right in front of me. I could have put my foot into the spokes and flipped the bike, but I knew that I would have crashed and lost or killed our birds, so I decided to take a chance. What else could I do? It was too late, anyway. I was already there; speeding through the intersection. It happened so fast, but it was as if I was riding my bike in slow motion. I was afraid that I was going to die. As I passed through this intersection stiff-armed out of fear; so much so, that I couldn't even weave in and out of traffic, if I wanted to. As I did, I passed in front of and behind speeding cars coming and going in different directions. All I could do was yell Help.

I don't recall one of those cars slowing down, speeding-up, or even honking a horn or slamming on their brakes. I don't even think they seen me or realized I was there, but every one of them missed me. If, they had seen me at all, they must have thought I was crazy and that I was just an accident looking for a place to happen. Either/or, it doesn't matter. I was under His protection and went through that intersection; completely, and unharmed! I may not have been aware of His presence at the time, but the Lord was definitely there. Now that was a Miracle! I could have died like the squirrel but was spared. Thank you Lord. I'm so undeserving, but I did ask for help, and Jesus... Never Fails.

Sheltered With a Friend
....

This same friend, Jim had a new family room added to the back of their home and we had planned to spend the night in an enclosed crawl space. We'd slept together before in the Boy-Scouts, but this night we'd be camping under his home instead of out in the woods in some tent. No campfire or cookouts but we played tag or hide and seek with other friends until it was dark. Those were the usual games to play in the evening hours but then we split and headed for home. As we went back to Jim's, we ran into an old stray dog that was growling and whimpering. Personally, I didn't want to mess with this stray, but as for Jim?

Well, Jim went over to the dog showing the typical concern, as one would have toward someone or something that might be hurting. So, I followed behind him, over to the dog. As I did, he bent down to pet the dog for a minute, asking him ever so softly, "What's the matter fella?" Afterwards, we decided it best to move on toward Jim's house where we were supposed to be, and as for this dog? Well. he began following us. As I recall, I'm sure it was because of Jim's coaxing him to do so, and Jim already had a Labrador retriever named Rex. He must have run away or got picked up by the pound. He was gone and his yard wasn't fenced in, so any animal had the freedom to come or go as they chose and as for Jim? He liked this sickly, looking dog.

When we got back to Jim's house, we opened the hatch to the enclosure beneath the family room where we had intended to spend the night, and crawled in. After we were in our sleeping bags; the stray dog was just outside the door, so Jim coaxed him in and then latched the door behind him. He did this so that we would be safe from intruders. I wanted him to put the dog back out because he kept whimpering and growling, which told me something wasn't quite right, but my buddy insisted. My buddy coaxed this dog to lie between us; closer to him obviously, which made me even more uncomfortable. Eventually though, the dog got up and went over into an adjacent corner and stayed there.

My friend called out to him several times, but the dog ignored Jim and stayed to himself. He whimpered and growled throughout the night. When we woke up that next morning and the dog was quiet and wasn't growling any longer, so my buddy crawled over to him. As he did, he spoke to him, asking him, if he's okay. He said, "Maybe the dog needs to go out to do his business." But he noticed the dog didn't respond when called. So, Jim reached over to pet the dog and said, "He's cold! I think he's dead." I said, "Grabbed his tail and pull it to one side to see if he pivots around." Sure enough, he turned around looking right at us, but he didn't move. I explained that the dog must have just died and that rigamortis must have just set in. I don't really know what was wrong with the dog, but he definitely was sick. Whatever the case was, he kept his distance from us and did not attack or even attempt to bite us, though he could have. It makes one wonder why he didn't. He was obviously sick, hurting and upset. He may have even been mad with Rabies. God only knows for certain, but it leads one to believe, that someone was with us and watching over us, yet again, and I believe this someone, was the Lord. Thank you, Jesus.

> **Isaiah 41:10** *Fear thou not; for I am with thee: be not dismayed; for I am thy God: I will strengthen thee; yea, I will help thee; yea, I will uphold thee with the right hand of my righteousness.*

Leap of Faith

That same day after we disposed of the dog, we planned on shooting target practice with some of the blunt target arrows Jim just received for Christmas along with his new bow and arrow set. Jim lived on a big hill that led down to a creek bed which was perfect for setting up the target. Jim's new bow was a 45 pound bow and came with a target and numerous target arrows, so we practiced hitting the target for quite a while... shooting into the embankment before Jim started shooting some of the arrows straight into the sky above our heads. They went so high that they would disappear and then come back into vision just in time to see where going. We were just kids trying to have some fun by entertaining ourselves, without any adult supervision. The keywords are... "WITHOUT" and "ADULT SUPERVISION!"

We obviously, didn't have enough sense to know better, using our own heads as targets, so to speak. All this stupidity caused Jim to have another crazy idea, as we were calling it a day. Jim had been shooting a 15 pound bow for years before getting his new 45 pounder, and had actually become quite a good shot. He was very good at hitting the target and when we were thru shooting that day, I decided to head home for a late lunch. I was going to cross the creek bed that separated Jim's home from his back-yard neighbor's home, which also had a hill going up to their house from the creek. In reality, Jim had no business with a bow and arrow! He obviously didn't realize how lethal they could be. As I turned away to go home saying good bye, Jim said, "You'd better run." I turned back around to face him and said, "What?" He said, "I'm going to shoot you" and repeated himself and said, "You better run." I was in total disbelief and couldn't believe my friend would do this. Surely, he was just joking, right? So I said, "Get out of here." in disbelief. Man, was I a bad judge of character! When we had about a hundred feet or more between us, he called out my name and I turned to see what he wanted. He said, "Start running" as he started to make his move to take aim on me. I yelled at him, "You better not"... thinking he wouldn't really, do such a thing.

However, I was wrong and I was beside myself out of fear, not knowing what to do, as I watched him place the arrow. Then I watched Jim pull back the bow, aiming the arrow straight into the sky, as he would do when shooting at the target and then he slowly brought the edge of the arrow down, as he trained his sights on me. The arrow was pointing directly at me now and I really got up-set. I began yelling at him with the sound of fear in my voice, begging him not to shoot me; telling him that I was his friend and asking how he could do such a thing. He said a third time now, "You better run." Somehow, I come to realize that he was serious and then he did the unthinkable, he let go of the string. I wanted to dart for my life, but I didn't know which way to move out of the way and it was then, as if someone inside me told me to leap as high as I could and to turn sideways, so I did! I had just enough time to do, just that. So, I leaped as high as I could, turning sideways to prepare for the inevitable. No doubt about it, he's a good shot and the arrow hit its target, me. I was hoping it wouldn't and that it would miss me. Wrong, again!

I yelled out his name in fear of losing my life, as I followed through by jumping and turning sideways and then Bulls-eye! The arrow had hit me right in the center of my body, waist high. The arrow had more than enough force behind it to penetrate my abdomen area or chest cavity, but by leaping and turning, as I did; it saved me from serious injury, possibly even death. Was it just by coincidence that I did the right thing or was I truly told from within, what to do? I believe God was watching over me that day, too. By doing as I felt led to; by leaping into the air as I had to dodge the arrow; it prevented me from serious injury or possibly even taking my life. So, it was the Lord that saved me.

Granted, the arrow still hit me, but by leaping... the arrow hit me on my thick leather belt, which actually cushioned the impact where it covered my right hip-bone. The skin and the hip-bone alone may not have stopped that arrow, but by adding the additional thickness of my belt, as a cushion; it stopped it. I never so much as received a single mark or a bruise of any kind.

Jim screamed with a shrill in his voice, fearing the worst, as he ran up to me, saying how sorry he was after realizing what had just happened. He thought I was hit, and really hurt. He said he was just playing as he checked me out and didn't know why he did what he did. He said that he didn't really think he'd hit me, but I knew he could because I saw how good a shot he was earlier, which is why I yelled. Again, he could have possibly taken my life. There is absolutely no doubt in my mind that someone was watching over me. Thank God! I know that I know that I know that I know, for the Lord is truly with me, as he's with you, always. As unbelievable as it is, I walked away from this little episode without any harm, but the loss of a friend.

Trying to Survive

Let me step back in time for a moment to where my parents were still happily married during my early years in grade school before I go any further. My sister had failed and had to repeat the second grade, which cause me to be held back a grade because of her failure to advance. So, I was destined to repeat the first grade. The problem came about because this was a new school and had only one second grade classroom. Donna and I obviously, didn't get along well even back then, and by sharing the same classroom would have been a nightmare. This was because Donna could not accept being around her younger brother, so I was forced to repeat the first grade even though I actually passed. My mother did her best to explain to me that my being held back was done to prevent my sister and me from fighting, but she never really knew how much this one small event hurt me. It changed my whole attitude for years to come. I didn't deserve being held back, but what could I do? This situation was out of my control. I was just a child and so discontent and discouragement followed me for years as all my school buddies moved up a grade and become friends with my sister while I was forced to stay behind. It was then I learned the meaning of flunky by those who had moved up. My peers considered me to be stupid for failing, which wasn't true.

I knew the truth and always considered myself to be smart, but who'd believe a flunky? I was set up to be ridiculed and teased by all my friends for many years to come, because of the lies told by my sister. I was told I'd get over this, but I didn't for years and as the years passed, the school grew larger and larger.

It was in the beginning of the fifth grade that I learned some kids were actually moved up a grade for being gifted, so I was told. It was then that I met a new friend on our first day back to school. I explained my desires to him and he too, wanted to do the same. So, we tried to excel together, as we raced through to complete our classroom's annual mathematic workbook. We did this on our own time after school and it came so easily, because we loved math.

We completed this task; finishing the workbook in just weeks, before the end of September. We were so proud of ourselves. We had high hopes of being recognized and maybe even be moved up a grade. By doing this, I thought that all of my old friends would recognize that I was as smart as they were and that this would put an end to all the lies from my sister, when in fact she was the one who failed which caused my pain and suffering. All I wanted was to put things back as they should have been where I would be in the sixth grade, where I rightfully belonged. I just wanted everyone to recognize me for not being a failure, but my hopes were in vain and our reward was not forth coming. In fact our teacher said, "Very good, but now what are you going to do for the rest of the school year?" We asked, can't you move us up a grade? He said, "NO... you're going to have to just sit there like the rest of us and watch the rest of the class catch up", which we did. So, our dreams were shattered and to top that off... my parents divorced and my interest in school declined.

What an incentive, but I tried to keep kept faith and worked hard, maintaining good grades into the sixth grade! Eventually though, my grades began to fall and I developed a... "Who cares attitude", my actions started to become hostile toward everybody and everything.

I did manage to make it through the seventh grade with decent grades, but the eighth grade was almost a total loss and yet, somehow I managed to get promoted into the ninth grade. This, I did not deserve. More than likely, it was because of my size and being nearly 6'-6" tall. I should have been held back because I failed at nearly everything, except for gym, which I Aced with flying colors, but no family recognition! I even broke the High School Record in the One Mile Run, but the ninth grade; turned out to be something special. I had so many problems with being bounced around between parents and hearing nothing but negative statements; it gave me nothing more than a perfect straight "F" attitude. It was nothing to be proud of because I was nothing more than a failure. All I ever heard was the negativity at home and at school that just added to the situation. I was so unhappy and between all the scraps and fighting with my discontentment; not knowing what to expect in the future... I had no desire to go forward. What I did know is that I did not want to become like my parents, seeing where it lead them and yet, like them; I even stopped going to church and any love I did have was set aside for survival. That's all I understood! Survive, at any cost! Live or Die! I was not going to fail, though it couldn't be proven by my grades or my lack of interest in school. School was extremely boring to me and I had no one to love or encourage me, so I loved no one and almost made an enemy out of everyone, whether I want to or not. No one liked me, so I played the tuff guy, hiding my feelings and sought comfort in eating, but because of my activity level, I was never over-weight. It's the one thing my dad was right about and I still have problem with, and that's eating. I'm constantly eating. I suppose it is for comfort, as so many others say even though I am happily married. I've tried making sense of all this and it's sad how things happen but as for divorce, it truly does affect people, especially a child throughout his childhood years. It got to the point where I just didn't care anymore and even my friends had gotten to the point, where I had no friends. It appeared to me, as if I had no one or nowhere to turn, but God never left me. I was blind by my foolishness and misguidance, but my eyes and heart were unable to comprehend my future.

What is Family?

My friends were limited. I was taboo and shunned by most; having no real family. This explains a lot about kids today. It gives good reason why kids today, cling together as gangs; as family! They do so because without them, understand this; there is no family, no love, no hope or trust in God or anybody, because where there once was commitment? Now, there is none, or any knowledge of God or Salvation, or love, peace or support.

These children cling to whatever comes along... just to escape and to survive. Imagine this! There are only two people that a child should have to look up to for guidance. If, these two people; mom and dad abandon each other and their commitments they once made to one another with little or no regard for the children, what happens to the children? There is always that cop out used, in telling children; "You're too young to understand, but someday when you're older, you'll understand then." Well, I am here to tell you; I'm 70 years old now and I still don't understand, fully. Put yourself into the Childs mind and answer this question. If love becomes hatred, then does God still love me? This was but one of the many questions, I once had? How can one hate... the ones you love? We're all made in the image of God, yes? Well, I wonder if parents ever really thought this through, about the real change or damage they create in their children's lives, or do they even care or consider the many questions their own innocent little children may have that will go unanswered? These questions may be shrugged off as being resolved, but are they? Only, time will tell, and God does say to love and pray for our enemies. So, not to love or to be loved... doesn't equate, and this type of love can, and does cause much disappointment and confusion to the young and innocent at heart, which are broken.

How can marriage between a man and woman in love, turn into so much hatred and rage, and then disguise it as just the opposite? Where can one escape... through God? If, no one is there to show the way to God, then God is out of the picture and morality is gone, which is why gangs flourish without morality. Yes, God hates divorce and He must have a broken heart because, I as you, are made in His image and as for my heart? It too, was broken, and because of such, I promised myself and the Lord, never to divorce my wife out of my love and respect for her and for our children's sake. Not to forget, I too, fear the Lord... who loves the children dearly and calls them unto Him, and said unto the His disciples that actually applies to all people:

> ***Luke 18:15*** *But, Jesus Called them unto him and said, Suffer little children to come unto me, and forbid them not: for of such is the kingdom of God.*
>
> ***Luke 18:16*** *Verily I say unto you, Whosoever shall not receive the kingdom of God as a little child shall in no wise enter therein.*

All I can say is, thank God for Bobby Grammer and all the Bobby's, Peggy's and Sue's who are out there; reaching out to help those of us, in need. Especially, to the children like I once was. It's because of these types of special people, like Bobby and his wife, Sue; who made a difference in my life and why I claimed them, as my "Adopted Family."

This family is the only reason I am saved today, because without them, I would have been abandoned, completely! They helped guide me into areas that my mother and father failed. Thank you Jesus, for sending them my way, for you... as always, have been watching over me, which has become more obvious and clear, through the years.

What is truly sad though, is how many others have to suffer before we realizes the damages we cause not only to ourselves, but to our children and their pure sensitive hearts, including the very heart of the one who created all of us? Have our hearts hardened so much that we too, become blinded from truth? We are to love and pray for one another, including those who are our friends and even those who are our enemies, and are not to curse those with the same mouth we use... to give praise unto the Lord.

Blessings-N-Prayer
....

One thing I know without any doubt is that I've been blessed throughout my entire life. Primarily, because I know that I know... that I know that I know... that Jesus Christ is Lord, and that He loves me. His Holy Spirit dwells within me and He too, has always been with me, even before I was born, when I wasn't even aware of the Lord's presence. I know too, that He is with me... even now, as I reminisce and write these events, as they come to mind. It has become evident to me, from as far back as the vision of coins and the mirror. Yes, He knew me before I was created in his image, as were you, before you were created, as it is written in the Word of God, where the Lord says:

> **Jer. 1:5** *Before I formed thee in the belly I knew thee; and before thou camest forth out of the womb...*

I am, as you are, as we all are... a miracle created in the image of God. Know this. Not only, is He with me, but He is with you always, and there is nothing better than a quiet moment in prayer, especially when you're in total seclusion and it's just you and the Lord. You may even want to turn off the lights and want to be in an area where there is almost complete seclusion and total silence. Now, Shhh... be still, and just listen; deep within, where one goes into one's most deepest, most inner thoughts... from within the heart and soul, and then whisper unto the Lord, pausing on occasion. Leave your spirit open to Him and then, feel His presence; the presents of the Holy Spirit, like flutter wings all around you. What a feeling; a sense of love and comfort. Know too, that God does love you and as you listen... He will speak to you, in a way that words cannot say. You may even tremble, and moan and groan; for God is in you... through His Holy spirit. God is Love and Love is life, and Life with God is truly A Mighty Fortress of Strength, and Greater is He that is in you... than he that is in the world. Trust in Him and you'll never go wrong, for Jesus loves you and "JESUS NEVER FAILS." Praise God... and thank you Lord Jesus for loving me!

CHAPTER 4

"From Home, To Home... To Homeless"

Rejected by My Step-Father

Through the years I've come to realize that the majority of my intelligence must come from my dad, only because he was a caring and a committed individual toward others and obligations; financial or otherwise. My mother also cared, but more about herself and taught me how not... to do things. The only thing I really learned not to do from my father was something I don't really blame him for, and that was for the day he abandoned me.

My parent shuffled us kids back and forth but I seem to be the one that was shuffled the most. I would make new friends and lose them almost immediately, as my stepfather moved all across the country as an engineering design consultant, from company to company. It was exciting to see new faces and new places but the results were always the same; no stability. I soon realized, this type of life-style isn't intended for a child... or most people.

Eventually, I become more of a nuisance to my stepfather, the older I became. I can only assume that this rejection must have come from him having to raise another man's children when he himself, also came from a previous marriage. I can only remember him seeing his own children twice while growing up and they were... straight "A" Students. Their visits only lasted a few days. So basically speaking, he never saw his kids and was in a situation where he had to accept us, as his. I didn't like this arrangement, so I pulled a lot of shenanigans on him shortly after we met, but again, he tolerated me to a point. When we were in Cincinnati, Ohio I tried to share Jesus with him once. What happened next was very clear to me. He started yelling and screaming at me profanely and what followed next, offended me, greatly! Something to the effect: "Don't you ever... mention that man's name in my house again." I only had to be told once. So, I didn't mention Jesus to him again until later in another chapter.

Gil and my mother did have a child between them, Andrea. We called her Candy for short. She was my little sister but she was never little. She weighed 11-pounds and 13-ounces at birth and at two years of age my mom passed her off as a five year old to get a head start in kindergarten.

Note: My wife first met Candy when she was only eight years of age. She was five inches taller and outweighed Joyce by a hundred pounds. Today my little sister is 6'1 or 6'-2 and weighs 400+ pounds. I'm as proud of her today, as I ever was and she may not know it or believe it, but I really do love her, as I always have and I miss her, too. I haven't seen her for years though.

My mother always swore that Candy is actually, my full sister because my mother and my dad made one last attempt of getting back together for us kids, but it wasn't meant to be. Gil had no knowledge of this and as far as he knew... Candy was his little girl, which I suspect is why they married, not to forget, the love they shared and had for one another.

Anyway, Candy was two years of age right after we arrived in Chesterfield, Virginia from Cincinnati, Ohio. I just started school and I met Susan, who was my first kiss and my first love in life. I've never kissed another before her. There was this one particular evening though, after diner where Gil was sitting down watching television and enjoying his night cap, so he would call it. It was getting late and Gil called Candy over to him to give her a kiss good night. When he did, Candy kissed him with a big ole' henpeck of a kiss, as she always did when saying hello, good-bye or good-night. I'm not sure why, but during her kiss, she apparently noticed something on Gil's breath or lips. So, while Candy was kissing him, she decided to stick her tongue out, possibly to taste whatever he had on his lips or in his mouth. Needless to say, because of this action and with me being the fifteen year old step-child; I was automatically accused of teaching his daughter, my sister... the unimaginable; how to French-Kiss! I couldn't believe it! He started swearing and threatening me, accusing me of making out with my own sister!

He then told my mother, "I want him out of here"! So my bags were packed and I was on my way back to my dad's again, up in St. Louis, Mo. I'd only been in Virginia a couple months and learned about love and being introduced to the pain of having to say my good-bye's to Susan, which broke both of our hearts. My heart had been broke before, but never felt like that.

Arrival in St. Louis
....

As I arrived in St. Louis by Grey-Hound Bus, I was in for a big surprise. I saw my dad standing next to a woman, whom I literally despised. This was because of the abuse she had shown toward her own son, and a good friend of mine. His name too, was Doug and we were class mates in the 5th or 6th grade.

One day, I went to visit another friend named Joe and he lived next door to Doug, which I was unaware of. When I saw Doug taking out the trash, I said, "Hi Doug." His head was hung low and he took a quick glance to see who said hi and then looked back down toward the ground, as he quickly headed toward the house. I stopped him though, to speak with him and made the statement, "I didn't know you lived here." He said, "I can't talk and got to get back in the house" but before he could finish, his mother was already out the door yelling at him for stopping to talk, after being told to ignore those boys next door. She reminded him that he was told to take out the trash and get back in house immediately because he had chores to do, as she was smacking him for misbehaving. She nagged and harped at him all the way into the house. She didn't know me back then, but I remember thinking; I'd hate to have a mother like that and then?

It was a pleasant surprise to see my dad as I was arriving at the Grey-Hound Bus Station. He obviously, had been standing there for a while waiting on me. He was wearing a big smile on his face, as if he were really happy to see me coming back home. At first he appeared to be by himself, but not for long. My dad stood 6'3 and he said to me, "Douglas, let me introduce you to my new wife", which caught me... completely, off guard.

I didn't even know he was thinking about getting married, yet there he was, claiming to be married. The realities, of both parents getting back together now, were next to impossible. Deep inside, I was screaming in disbelief and then this small framed woman hiding from behind my dad... stepped out into view. My smile became an expression of surprise. I thought to myself, "NO, not that woman!" Thank God, our thoughts could not be heard; my dad would have knocked me for a loop.

She greeted me with a big smile, but I was already set in a standoff mode remembering how she had treated my friend. I said, "I already know her; "She's Mrs. So-N-So". It was then I was immediately corrected by her saying, "Oh no! I'm Mrs. Thornberry now, but you can call me Wilma... or you can call me mom, if you like." I was naturally offended and immediately said, "No! You'll never replace my mother, so I'll call you Wilma." She said, "Alright!" Now, I know we didn't really get off to a good start and it was my fault I suppose, but I was really blindsided and totally unaware of the changes that had occurred in just a few months. I asked my dad, "What happened to Bonnie; who happened to be his last girlfriend just a couple months earlier. I was informed that there is no more Bonnie. Obviously, I was trying to be a troublemaker, but it didn't work.

Rejected by My Step-Mother
••••••••••

When we arrived at her home I was given a room and informed by Wilma, while my dad wasn't present; that the home I was raised in was given to my older sister, Donna and her husband, and that my dad and I now live in her house, and there are rules that will be followed. I was told I would be expected to take out the trash (since her two boys were already kicked out of the house.) I could handle that. Doug was my buddy and my age and Danny was his older brother and was the same age as my older sister, just a year old than I. Doug and Danny had two younger sisters; the oldest was Mary and she was 13 and Donna was 10. My brother, Dennis lived there too, and was 12 at the time. I had just turned 15 and already deemed the problem child. I was quickly told to watch myself and informed my chores included cleaning the bathroom, doing the dishes, sweeping and mopping the kitchen floor. Well, to ask is one thing, but to demand is another, and I already resented her, so I said, "That woman's work; I'll cut the grass and clean the bathroom." Wilma said to me, "Woman's work, Huh? Well, I'll tell you what! You will do your own laundry and not here, but down at the laundry mat!" I didn't mind because I did that all the time while staying with my mom, so that wasn't a big deal. So, I was dropped off at the laundry mat and she would drive by and she seen me enjoying my peace and quiet. Next thing I know is she decided, she'd do it at home. She wanted complete dominance and I had attitude as did her sons and I didn't care if I stunk or not. I told her okay, that I didn't care and that she'd have to live with me. It wasn't wise thing to say and eventually I apologized.

I also, started getting harassed at school again by the same old friends that thought I was a flunky. "You know, "Looks whose back." There was also, this girl whom I was quite fond of, but she accused me of coming over to her home one evening and causing a fight between her mother and father, just days earlier that had caused them to be getting a divorce. All I did was to stop by her home when I first came back into town to give her a mole-hair sweater as a Christmas gift, which she accepted. She thanked me, saying I shouldn't have with a big smile on her face, which put one on my face. I didn't know that her folks were divorcing and I had absolutely, nothing to do with it. She knew it too, but needed someone to blame and with me coming from a broken home... it must have rubbed off! You think? She used me as her excuse for being angry and I was hated by almost everyone because of her popularity. I was constantly running away to keep from getting into fights with all her male friends that wanted a piece of my hide. There were so many that wanted to get at me that I skipped school regularly. I skipped so much school that my grades were off the chart and my dad told me I should just consider quitting school and getting a job, so I did. I was only fifteen, so I lied about my age to get my first real job as a dishwasher. I was making $1.10 an hour at minimum wage and managed to save $50.00 from my couple checks in a bank.

I held a little back for myself for smoking and such, but then one day, my dad got a call from school and they wanted to know where I was. When he came home from work, he asks me, "What's going on?" I reminded him that he said to quit school and to get a job, so I did. He said, "Oh no, you don't... you're going back to school, tomorrow; I'll write you a note and you will... get back, into school!"

So, so be it. I began going to school again, only one morning soon afterwards, my dad over-slept causing him to be about a half an hour behind schedule. He had to use my allotted time frame in the bathroom to get himself ready for work. He hurried as fast as he could to get in and out, but it wasn't fast enough. When he finished, Wilma walked him to the front door, as I took off for the bathroom, just as quickly as possible. I knew I had to hurry because her oldest daughter, Mary would need to get in there too, and I was already infringing on her scheduled time frame, as my dad had done to mine. Pressured for time, I didn't even take a shower and only used the toilet and was in the process of rinsing out my mouth from brushing my teeth. It was then Wilma yelled at me, "Get out of the bathroom; you're in Mary's scheduled time!" I said, "Just a minute, I've got to comb my hair and I'm done." She demanded, "Get out here, now!"

She then began banging on the door with something that was so loud, it sounded as if she were coming through the door.

I opened the door rather abruptly to see what the heck was going on and why I couldn't even have an additional moment or two to comb my hair, and there stood Wilma. She apparently began making sandwiches' and was holding a Miracle Whip jar over her head, as if she were going to hit me. What I did next was out of natural instinct and fear. Now, I didn't really know this woman personally, except through association; knowing her son and now, as my dad's wife? I didn't know her well enough at all, except she had real attitude and I knew too, how she had treated her sons, which reminded me of my Sisters bullying. It's because of my experiences in past years from my sister that I became concerned about her holding a jar over my head, as if she was preparing to hit me with it, as my sister would have. To me it was a nightmare all over again, only now she had the authority, but to do what? I honestly thought the worst; that she would hit me? So, as I stood there in the doorway wondering and not knowing exactly what to expect; remembering encounters with my sister, and what she would have done. Knowing my sister would have clobbered me and with Wilma in that pose reminded me of my sister banging on the door. I wasn't sure, except that Donna was truly that abusive and I wasn't sure about Wilma in that pose. So, what I did next was to visualizing the worst all over again, only coming from Wilma this time, as she was holding a jar over her head, in what appeared to be a threatening manner.

So, as I opened the door, she stopped yelling and just stood in that pose looking into my eyes with rage and l did the natural thing and panicked. In self-defense, I automatically reached out grabbing both her wrist to keep from being hit, so I thought. As I did, I very slowly backed her out of the doorway, ever so gently, as not to hurt her. It was out of respect for her and out of fear of the consequences from my dad. I said to her just as polite as I could, "I told you... I'll be out in just a minute. I just need to finish combing my hair... thank you." Then I released her and closed the door to finish what I started and went to school.

I was to report to work later that evening, but I was unable to do so, thanks to Wilma. I don't know exactly, what she had said to my dad and I never had an opportunity to discuss it with him or explain myself, not that he would have listened, he never did. It was an open and shut case. I walked in from school and was told to a sit down and not to get up until my father got home.

I had hoped he listen to reason, because he loved me, so I thought. Man, was I in for a rude awakening. When he came home... he physically grabbed me and slammed me into the wall. I wanted to talk to him but he wasn't in the mood to listen and he took his index fingernail and poked me hard and fast, right between my eyes. His words were, "If, you ever lay another hand on my wife, I will put a bullet right between those GD eyes of yours; do you understand me?" GD didn't mean: gosh darn. I was shocked! My Dad never spoke like that and he could have care less about my side of the story, but then again, why should he? I was seen as just a child and she was the adult that just happened to be banging a quart size glass jar on the bathroom door, which I'm sure she did not mention. She was the one out-of-control, making demands in here high pitched voice of rage, as she hollered at me with lack of understanding. She just wanted me out of that bathroom at that very moment and I had been in there, only 3 or 4 minutes, if that long. It was without wonder... why my step-brothers no longer lived at home and something wasn't right. Who bangs on a door with a jar? Had she put a hole in the door, I would have surely been blamed for that too, as in the past, so I stepped out... in fear of being hit.

Abandoned for a Reason

I believe, after this event, he went into speak with Wilma, as I went to sit in the living room, hoping things had settled down, but Not! My dad marched into the living-room where I had gone and said, "Come on!" So, I followed him into my bedroom where he packed up an old army duffle bag with what few clothes I had. Then he took me down to the bank where I was told to withdraw my $50 in saving's, which was all I had. It was after that, he took me on a trip to down town St. Louis, where we drove through town, right-up to the front door of the Greyhound Bus Station. It was there that he stopped the vehicle and got out. I really don't recall much conversation taking place during that whole trip, except for one thing he did say as he headed to his trunk. He said, "I don't know what you want to do. You can always go back to you mothers", but what he didn't know is that Gil and my mother had abandoned me too, just weeks earlier which is why I came to be with him, but now I was abandoned yet again. Only now, I would be homeless. He reached into the trunk, grabbed my bag and slung it onto the curb and said, "Well, Douglas, You think you're a big man? Let's see how long you can survive!" Then he got back into the car and drove off. He abandoned me. So, there I was; all alone, so I thought.

What I didn't know, until years later is that God was with me and had other plans. At first I thought this was some kind of joke. So, after a couple cigarettes while standing on the corner on that that cold wintery night, waiting and wondering, I came to realize... he wasn't come back. I thought what the heck? You don't just turn your back on your own kid, someone you're supposed to love, unless you really didn't have any love for them in the first place. He chose his wife over me is what went through my head and I was just a kid, barely fifteen. The more I thought about it, the more I was in disbelief, thinking: Well, forget you! I decided to change my name to Dion and had no intentions of returning to what I once referred to as home even though it wasn't mine; not then, not ever, and I didn't see my dad again, for the next five years.

I accepted the fact at that time, that I was destined to be a ninth grade graduate and even to this very day... I still lay claim to that, including the fact that I am blessed. Yes, very blessed, by God. You see; there I was... abandoned by my dad at a Grey Hound Bus Station, of all places, but I was not alone.

Now, this is the kind of place... where one can get a real quick overnight education and this is what some would more than likely refer to as a reality check. The reality is that there are all kinds of people inside and outside of a bus station; from sweet little old ladies and young people traveling from Point-A to Point-B, to local drunks and wino's, to punks, perverts, prostitutes, and those who were once referred to as bums, but more commonly referred to today, as homeless people. In reality, I too, had joined the ranks of the homeless, so young, innocent and naïve and became the perfect target for others. Not all, but some of these people actually were there looking for the young and innocent; to take advantage of them. I'm sure I was seen as one of those less fortunate, an opportunity that wanted to know who I was, along with other questions. Why, I didn't know, but I was on guard and approached by some, as if they were my friend or just wanted to say hello, and I was frightened.

I did see this young man in a uniform of sorts passing through the bus station though and I asked him about the uniform he had on. He told me about a new program that provided him a place to eat and sleep with a roof over his head, and it was all free of charge. He could eat any and all the food he wanted, any time he wanted, which got my attention. It sounded, almost too good, to be true. All I could do is sit on the edge of my seat and drill him, saying, "Who? What? Tell me more, I want to know" and he said, "You'll get to go to school and be paid to learn a trade or skill and get a Gold Sealed Certificate upon completion. They guarantee to help you get started by finding you a job and giving you money they set aside for you upon graduation."

He said, the money they give when you graduate is money in addition… to what they pay you while you to go to school for living expenses, to buy personal items. You'll get uniforms too and a clothing allotment to buy clothes to wear out in public including a Navy Blue Blazer. They'll also give you an all-expense paid, round-trip, week vacation, for each year you attend up to two years maximum, until you graduate or you drop out. This is something they provide to all who people who sign-up. It was then that I interrupted this young man and said. "This is just what I need! What's the name of this place and where do I sign up?" He said, "It's called the Job Corps." Thank you Lord! He was definitely looking out for me… you think? I mean, here I was, abandoned… with nowhere to go, and then along comes this person I'd never met before, to speak to me, just at the right time and right place. Was this by chance or coincidence? No way! I know our meeting each other must have been that of the Lord, who sent him my way. He was a real God send, thank you Jesus!

Learning Forgiveness

I wanted a future for myself and wanted to be successful in life. What I didn't want to do is live on the streets. I also, wanted my dad to see me become successful and not the no-body that he once stated... I would be, just to prove him wrong.

So, I called my mother in hopes that just maybe, Gil would find it in his heart to forgive me; for what he thought I'd done; knowing that I hadn't, but I was hoping that he would reconsider. I explained my situation and who I had met, including my intentions, which was to join the Job Corps and take up drafting. This must have hit a soft spot with Gil, because he took me back in and he was happy knowing that I had a plan.

To my surprise, Gil supported me and wired me money to buy a bus ticket to join them in Virginia, and I arrived just in time to help load up a U-Haul. Gil just landed an Engineering Design Drafting Consulting position in Florida. So, we were moving again. I had just enough time to stop in and say hi and good-bye to my girlfriend who was so excited to see me, but again, so sad to hear I was leaving just as fast as I had come, back into town.

I told her about the Job Corps and that I would be back. We promised to write each other which we did until she became pregnant many months later by a boy next door. She told me how sorry she was, and I was too, but she wasn't meant for me.

Last Chance

After we left Virgin, we were on our way to a little town called Lakeland, Florida. I told my mom and Gil all about the Job Corps and everything the Corpsman had told me during our trip to Florida. I told Gil too, that I wanted to be a Draftsman, just like him. He was surprised and gave me encouragement, which really surprised me. So, when we arrived in Lakeland, Gil went to work while my mother took me down to the Florida State Unemployment Office to sign-up for the Job Corps. I really wanted to and had to make this work because this was my last chance to prove to myself and to everyone else that I could be, and would be... successful in life. I only had one setback. I had to be 16 and wouldn't be, until September. So, I had to wait, or did I? I knew Gil might get up-set, but what else could I do?

So, when they asked for an address where I was staying to receive a notice when I become 16, I said that I didn't have one and that I was living on the streets because I was, though it was relatively, only for a very short time. She questioned me about that and I told her my step-dad had booted me out and sent me to my dad's but my step-mother did the same and I was abandoned at the St. Louis, Grey Hound Bus Station. I told her that I just got into town and had heard about the Job Corps and was hoping to join, but thanked her anyway.

Well, sometimes there are exceptions to any rule and with me being abandoned and living on the streets, changed things. It was Friday and she said, "Let me make a couple calls. Come back on Monday and I'll let you know, if I find out anything, so I did. Well, come Monday morning, she told me that I was given special consideration to help get me off the streets.

It was then I learned I would be flying out of Orlando into Indianapolis, Indiana where I would be reporting to the Atterbury Job Corps Center. I was to stay there until a drafting position opened up at Gary Job Corps Center, in San Marcos, TX

Note:I want to say this about the Job Corps; I know it has changed somewhat and it may not be for everybody or just anyone, but the Job Corps still exists today. It's a tremendous program for those in need! I can't recommend this program enough, to anyone between the ages of 16 and 25 that may be seriously struggling and looking for hope... and a chance to climb that Ladder of Success shown on the Job Corps Emblem.

The Job Corps really works and I am living proof of that! I believe this program was created by those guided by the Lord to provide those like myself, or those in worse situations; a means of hope. A program with the necessary provisions that will lead them into a more successful, productive and happier life. To get those living on the streets or in a helpless situation... a place to call home and to receive a first class education with on the job training that they may not have otherwise, had the opportunity to receive elsewhere. I can't recommend anything... any better.

The Job Corps Training Programs was generated primarily to take those as myself that had nowhere else to turn, and to train them. To teach them how to have a sense of self-worth, self-respect and to be self-reliant, as well as to assist them in so many other ways. They will even go as far as to help them land their first job upon completion or may even help open doors to a university should they elect further their education.

The sky is the limit and the Ladder of Success will help you reach those heights of success that you desire, but only at one rung at a time. So, go ahead and take a chance. Grab the rungs of opportunity and climb as high as you desire and should you slip and feel as if you're falling? Just hang in there... and hold on! We all bang our chins a time or two in our lives, but whatever you do... do-not give up and don't let go, because there is but one-way up that ladder and again, it's one rung at a time.

All I can add to this is; thank God... for such a great program By President LB Johnson: as Job Corps, including all those who really care and are the professionals, who are more than qualified and specialized in making sure you succeed. Give them the honor and respect they deserve and they'll push you as far up that latter you want to climb, but only you have to make that decision. Well, do you? Check it out at your local unemployment office and expect a waiting list but don't worry. All good things come to those who wait and reach-out for what they want but personally, I've learned to trust in the Lord, so best wishes.

CHAPTER 5

"Learning to Love and Forgive"

Home Away from Home

Job Corps allowed me access to their facility in April of 1966, almost six months before my sixteenth birthday. This took me by complete surprise but was done in order to get me off the streets, because this program again was established to do just that. To get kids like me off the streets, especially those who were destined as failures and possibly a burden to society. By taking me off the streets; I now had a place to live where they would provide housing, food, medical attention, clothing, and a quality education; teaching me a trade and even prepared me for my GED exam. I was happy and knew this was what I needed to be independent and to be ready to tackle life.

In order to make sure our personal needs were met, such as toothpaste, shampoo, soap, cigarettes, etc., each corpsman was given an allowance that would be increased by merit, so we could concentrate on our studies and not want for anything. We were in; a live-in, on the job training Facility. This program consisted of an eight hour day, five days a week to prepare us for what to expect, in a real job environment. It was as if we were performing real job functions...

in a real place of employment, as to prepare us for what would be expected of us, on a real job.

We didn't need to worry about graduating. The Job Corp put aside each month, a certain amount of money into a personal account for each of us that we would receive upon graduating. This was done as to help us venture out into the world, not just educationally, but financially. As I said earlier, they even help place us into our first real career job we trained for. What a plan! What a program. This program truly made it feel as if, one were in a home away from home, which is what I told anyone that asked me where I lived. I'd say, "The Job Corps is my Home." and I'm sure many felt the same way... for it was all we had.

Camp Atterbury

Orientation was truly the toughest two weeks for most of us kids coming into the Job Corps, but we all had to go through it. Some just couldn't handle being alone and away from their families. These were the ones that would break-down and cry at night. They kept to themselves and didn't fit in well with others. Most would come out of it, but some went home because of this kind of pressure. Then some like me had no choice; it was a do or die situation. I had to make the Job Corps work for me and to refuse and accept... defeat. Those of us who stayed... were tested, to see what skill, trade or profession we best qualified for.

I elected, like my step-dad; to sign up for "Drafting" before I was taken into the Job Corps and was told to put in for a transfer upon entry, which I did when I was asked what I wanted to take. I was told that "Drafting" was being taught in only one camp; in San Marcos, Texas at Camp Gary, so I put in for a transfer. I was forced into taking a secondary trade until then, which I chose to be heating and air-conditioning. I did this only, because I had to do something. I had absolutely, no desire to learn this trade but made do with what was available, expecting to transfer within a matter of weeks that turned into months and eventually turned into well over a year later. The Drafting Course in itself was a 24 month course and by waiting meant that I'd have to work twice as hard, if not harder to complete, should my transfer even come in. I was so discouraged and depressed; I skipped classes... months at a time, and may as well, not even been there.

After 8 or 10 months of waiting for what appeared to be false hopes; I began thinking about quitting Job Corps. I even stopped returning to camp on Friday and Saturday evenings, to stay away and to have time to think about what my options were. In truth, there weren't any options! I didn't see a future in staying or leaving; only hope. I just wanted to leave due to there being little hope or time left for my transfer. So, come one week-end I decided not to return and took refuge in the alley ways and wherever there were vented roof tops that were blowing out heat.

Tomato Soup

That morning after I failed to return, it was so cold that I was freezing. It snowed that night accumulating about four to six inches and I was out and about, crossing through a railroad yard in town and heard a train passing by. As it did, I could hear the steel wheels screeching and squealing, ever so loud. As they cut through the snow; the heat melted the snow away from the tracks leaving a path where the rails laid. I remember learning about friction in the Boy Scouts and how it could generate heat by rubbing to objects together like two sticks that could start a fire. So, I knew by the sounds coming from the steel wheels against the rails, that they probably generated a lot of heat. After the train passed, I went out to checked it out and sure enough the tracks were nice and warm; almost, hot! So I laid down on the snow beside the tracks with my back up against one of the rails to absorb the heat, to warm up my back. I folded my arms and it felt so good; I just wanted to lie there, if only for a little while.

As I laid there, three strangers walked by in front of me, looking down at me as they passed by. The last one stopped to check me out. They were all bundled up and I raised my head as I watched the first two walk over to the side of an old building and then they set down on some cold concrete steps. One of them pulled out a flask or bottle of sorts from the inside of his topcoat and then sipped from it as they stared at me. They're friend stood over me. He appeared to be as the other two; a bum of sorts; a homeless person, possibly in his mid-fifties and he spoke as if, he was an educated man with some style of mannerism. He said, "Hey there young fellow! I looked up at him. You shouldn't be laying on those tracks." I said, "Man, a train just went over these tracks and they're nice and hot; come on down and feel... they'll warm-up your hands." All I know is that these three guys came by, just in time to prevent my demise or at least one of them did. He was the guy standing over me and he said, "Well, you don't want to be laying on these tracks because you may fall asleep and there'll be another train coming through here in about ten minutes and it'll run over you.

He said, "If you're cold, come on, I'll show you a place where you can get warmed up and get a free meal." So, I jumped up and we were off while leaving his two buddies behind. We walked a few blocks or so down the street to an old railroad dinner car, which was actually a beautiful sight with the aroma of breakfast that filled the cold crisp air. It smelled so good and I didn't realize just how hungry I was. This Diner Car was well lit and was made from an old passenger railroad car with lots of windows covered with frost from the steam condensation that filled the air, as did the inviting aroma. There was a set of stairs leading up to the side entrance, which we began to climb.

As we walked up the stairs, this gentleman took off his gloves and put them in his pocket. Then he removed his hat and dusted the snow from his topcoat, with his hat. He then removed his topcoat and like a gentleman, he folded it over his forearm, followed by his scarf and stompped the snow from his feet, as we entered, onto the entrance rug. He still had other garments on like an old worn out ragged sweater over a sweatshirt, which he left on that made him appear to have somewhat of a protruding belly to go with his beard. As we entered, he nodded toward the waitress as if to gain acceptance and quickly glanced for a booth; first to the left and then to the right. I couldn't help but notice that some people stopped what they were doing to watch us, to see what we were going to do next or possibly concerned, as to where we were going to sit. In fact, in all honesty, I think they were looking at my newly found friend more than they were me, do to his attire, but he acted, as if he could care less.

The waitress had her foot propped up on a footrest at the end of the counter where it divided into two for passage. She was talking with a customer with his back to us. As she looked up, I could see an expression of disgust come across her face, as we stood in the doorway. There was a certain attitude that could be felt in the atmosphere, but it didn't bother him in the least. Without saying a word, he turned toward the right and started walking down the aisle, passing the waitress heading toward a booth. I watched the waitress lean into the customer and softly say sarcastically, "Oh brother, look what the cat drug in!"

This didn't appear to bother this fellow though; whose name I don't really recall, but Jim seems comes to mind. He appeared to be a man with a sense of pride and attitude. The kind that one would have while holding his head up high, as if to say, "I'm an American and I have the same freedom and rights as you do, to come and go where I please, just as much as anybody else."

He then sat down facing the entrance and I sat directly across from him with my back to the entrance. After we were seated the people turned around to continue whatever it was they were doing. It was only then that the waitress stopped talking to this guy at the counter whom she had been flirting with or whatever, and then put her cigarette out. She wandered over to our booth saying, "May I help you?" As I said, I don't really recall this man's name and this was the only time, we actually spent time together, but I learned a lot in this short visit. He was a nice person, a Godsend so to speak; teaching me..."How to survive."

He said, "Ah, yes, water? It's still free, isn't it?" The waitress said, "Yes," with a puzzled look upon her face. He then said, "Fine, then my new found friend and I would like to have two cups of hot water, if you would please." She asked, "Is that all?" "Yes, thank you," he said and to my amazement, she left to fulfill our order of two cups of hot water and once again, free.

Then he proceeds to share some of his finer-tips in life with me, such as: "This is a public restaurant; everyone has the right to come in and to be served." He then nodded toward the end of our booth beneath the window and said, "Do you see that?" I said, "Yes, it's one of those little red and white push button juke-boxes that play records on the big jukebox over there." He said, "No, no, not that; taking my mind from the juke box. He said, "Do you see the basket beneath the jukebox?" I said, "Yes sir."

It was at this time the waitress returned, setting down two saucers, each with a spoon and hot cups of water. The waitress asked, "Will that be all?" This gentleman again, says very politely, "Yes, thank you." as he nodded, as if to say, have a good day. As she was leaving, she turned her head to peer over her left shoulder, to see what in the world we were up to.

Then he continued, saying "These items are what is referred to as condiments and they're free", as he reached over to pick-up the catsup dispenser. He removed the cap and turned it over, placing it above his hot cup of water. He then squirted a generous amount into his cup and picked up his tea spoon; placing it into the cup, and began stirring as he placed the catsup back onto the table. As he was stirring, he looked up at me with a smile on his face and said, "Hey... Hot Tomato Soup and all the free crackers you want". I looked at the basket and it was just plumb full of crackers. What a guy! He was like an angel that was sent there... to get me off the tracks, but he not only prevented me from being run over by a train, but taught me the means of... how to survive. Thank God for sending someone my way, to come along and to keep me from getting a bad start in life. He taught me a lot. I thanked him after we finished our tomato soup and we went our separate ways. I'm sure he's long gone by now, but it helped me to decide that I didn't want this type of life style, which reminded me of what I wanted to be; successful in life. So, I returned to the Job Corps pickup Center.

Remember the Homeless

To this day though, I still have a special desire in my heart to reach out and help these people. That's what they are! They're people, just like you and me. Some have class and some have attitude. This is what gives them their spirit. What is sad though is that whether or not they are in their situation by choice or just by circumstance. It doesn't really matter and it doesn't mean that they should be treated with any less respect, as a person. They're created as you and I; in the image of God. What's really sad though is that there are some people in this world that are really worse off than the homeless. For they have such an outlandish outlook in life and have so much that they can't even be bothered with these people. They're blinded and look down on them, as if they were the scum of the Earth; beneath them. May the Lord have mercy on them.

A lot of homeless people are humble, gracious and caring toward others. Some are loners and somewhat stand-offish while others would do whatever they could to help another, yet while they have little or nothing, but themselves, and time. Some are even our military hero's just trying to fit into society, after a war.

Let's not forget the story that Jesus told, of all the governors and dignitaries that were invited to a party in which not one came. So, the master sent his servants into the streets to bring back the poor and the homeless for they came and did appreciate all that was given unto them.

It is for this reason; it is better to give than to receive for it makes for a merry heart and it is written that if you do it to the least of one of these, then you are doing it unto the Lord. Well, these people are one in the same, and if the Lord is willing to go the extra distance for them, then we all should reconsider, if we have ever had any doubts.

For again, they too, are made in the image of God as we are, but whom... do we serve?

Yes, not only do they need a helping hand, but in the eyes of the Lord, maybe we too, need a helping hand. In short, we all need each other. Let's not forget to have respect for the less fortunate. For we too, at one time; may have, or could have been where they are now or even worse. Remember to give thanks and remember too, before Jesus came, we were all outsiders, without a future or any hope. So, beware! Give thanks to God; the Father, the Son and His Holy Spirit. Who knows for certain, but the person you may be entertaining, may well be, an Angel.

I waited until the following year, in February 1967 before my transfer came in. By then I had learned how to work on HVAC, how to run the movie projectors in a theater including splicing films, and play the Guitar. I was even being trained by a second place, Silver Medalist in the Breaststroke competition for the United States who had won in 1964 World Olympic, swimming competition. I don't remember his name and at first he was beating me by 12 or 15 body lengths. He said I was a good and strong swimmer and encouraged me to join the team which I did. I was a natural swimmer, having a set of size-14 flippers for feet.

So, I had somewhat of an unfair advantage, so to speak besides being so long and lanky at 6'6. As such, I was pushed to swim at least a mile or more, which seemed to be nightly.

This was done to provide me the strength I needed to compete in the breaststroke competition in the 1968 Olympics. I was getting bigger and stronger with each passing day and it got to the point that my instructor was only beating me by only a half a body length. I was so preoccupied with swimming and training that I almost forgot about my transfer that I was waiting on, and then it came in one night, and I had to make a tough decision.

The coach said I had gotten a lot stronger and would even be stronger by qualification and that I had a good chance of winning at the Olympics. I was really excited and wanted to go and it meant so much to me, but it wasn't meant to be. As I said, the transfer came in; placing a fork in the road, so to speak. Well, sports did not pay back then, as it does today, so there was little to decide on. I elected to pursue a career in drafting. After all, this is why I had joined the Job Corp; to learn drafting. I wanted to succeed and be someone that my parents would be proud of.

What I did next though, was terrible. I packed my bags and slipped away into the night without stopping in or saying good-bye to my coach, because I knew he may have persuaded me to stay, but my mind was already made up. I was determined and was really forced into making, only one decision. I wasn't afraid of being rejected or discouraged from doing what I knew had to be done... to be successful in life as a businessman, a husband, and a father. I just wanted to prove to my dad that not only could I make it on my own, but I wanted them to know that I could do it without his or my mom's help. I wanted to be a better man too; a better husband, a better father with a family that would stand together, no matter what! I promised myself a long time ago never to reject my family when I decided to marry and to have only one wife and however many children we would be blessed with. I'd never turn my back on them, or denied them anything within reason. I would have sacrificed all to salvage everything if need be, which included... winning a Gold Medal.

So, in doing so, God has blessed me well in all things and I'm really undeserving, but then again; are any of us? God loves each and every one of us and the sooner we realize just how much he really does love us and that his desires for us are to make us happy and prosperous in life; the more likely we will recognize His intervention in our life, because He is; right here, right now, waiting on you to surrender your life over to Him.

Camp Gary

So, I was transferred and relocated to Camp Gary in San Marcos, Texas the very next day giving me that night to pack and to catch an early flight that next morning. I had to go through orientation and more tests all over again. A complete waste of time in my eyes because when all this testing was done, I had approximately one year to cram in and a 24 month drafting course. I was told that this would be possible, if I worked at it really hard and that it had been done once before by another individual in a little more than 9 months. I figured, if he could do it, I can do it, too. Think positive about everything! That's always been my motto. All things are possible through the Lord!

While at Camp Gary, I joined a Junior Citizens Achievement Club and because of my size, I was asked if I would consider the position as Sergeant of Arm, which I accepted. The club was a good experience. While in the Corps I learned how to wine and dine with proper mannerisms. I learned correct table placements and settings for each dish and piece of silverware and how and when to use them. I was also, taught how to speak on a telephone properly, especially during phone interviews. They taught us how to file our own tax returns so we could take care of ourselves after we graduated and become successful. I even went through a drivers' educational training program and got my first state certified driver's license scoring 100 and given the opportunity to be an Assistance Driver's Education Instructor.

The Job Corps also prepared me to take the GED test, as well as any additional education needed to fulfill my desires and/or requirements to achieve my goals. I even went through a speed-reading course and I have always hated to sit down and read anything, but at least I know how to glance over papers quick enough to find what it is I'm in search of, which has become very usefully in my professional career.

There were a lot of things to do during our spare time. We had laundry mats to wash our clothing and lounges to watch television or libraries to sit down, relax and unwind while we sat around reading. We also, had to keep our personal living areas clean before we were allowed a pass to catch a bus into the nearest township for some R&R, (Rest and Relaxation). There was a Job Corps Activity Center in town where we were encouraged to bring our dates to the dance floor. All the girls' were local girls of course and if you didn't want to dance, there were always refreshments and pool tables, Ping-Pong tables and so much more to be entertained with. If, one elected to stay on the base or just didn't merit a pass, there were still a lot of activities to take advantage of on camp. There was a swimming pool and a place to race 1/12 scale cars on a huge racetrack. There were so many other things to occupy our time with what I won't even try to mention, for it would take away from my point.

My main issue is that they had a pool hall with approximately 24 billiard tables in it and a bowling alley in the same building with 12 lanes. All the pins had to be manually placed though in a drop box that would be lower to set the pins on the alley before the automation era. I loved bowling and this is where I spent most of my spare time in competition; winning, with trophies.

Worst Thing... I Ever Did

One of the worst things I've ever done... No! Not one of, but absolutely, without a doubt, the worst thing I had ever done was the following. First, let me add this; "Please, do not judge me."

Satan, is truly a very powerful being and can and will deceive us in any way he can and it is up to us; you and me, to know right from wrong; truths from untruths, and good from bad. In my case it was a test and I blew it! I mean, I blew it big time! This is what I come to refer to as my personal trial or tribulation.

Had I not been so far away from God after the divorce and being abandoned at fifteen, I may have seen what was going on. But, I was a teenager who was abandoned and gotten off to a pretty rough start in life. I was however, somewhat content in my own little world, so I brushed off the event, as if it were nothing. By the time I realized what was done, it was years later, which I'll share in the chapter six, but first I'll want to say this.

Reader: As you read this… Please, do not judge me for what I am about to share with you. For I was once judged by a man of God who had given me reason, to seriously take my own life before intervention came. Personally, from Jesus Himself. It's because of this man's judgment though, that I have a better understanding of what it means; where it is written, "Judge not, lest ye be Judge." God still loves me and He forgives me and I am saved… thanks to Jesus, who has personally intervened. I know this to be true from personal revelations and a personal relationship, which Jesus had shared with me where He literally came into my room for more than just a visit. Let me first share the experience of why He did this for me and then I'll share the event and how He intervened to save me because, He loves me.

As I stated earlier, I played pool, but I loved to bowl. So, I spent a lot more time in the bowling alley. Especially, after joining the bowling league! As a kid, I had over a 200 average and even thought I may even go professional one day, which never took place. I had bowled as many as seven consecutive strikes in a single game and had a 742 High Series. Since bowling was free, I average 5 or 6 games each week-night and bowled even more on weekends. There was a lot of competition and trophies to be won for the best, and the silliest of things such as who'd knock down the most 6,7,10 pin split… in 10 frames.

Very rarely would I ever get a split when bowling and if I come up short on the strike, I could almost guarantee without a doubt, to pick up any spare, except for that 7, 10 pin. It rarely happens and I have picked it off before, but I usually miss it.

One Saturday while practicing for a tournament that evening, I thought myself to be alone, but unknowingly, I wasn't. In bowling my first game… I bowled my worst game ever. The game I bowled, to me was totally unacceptable. Nobody would have ever believed that I could bowl such a lousy game, not even me. In fact, I had never bowed this score since my first game ever, which was my first attempt at bowling with my mother at the age of 8 or 9. It too, was a 99, but now after all these years while practicing for an up-coming tournament; to bowl a 99, again? Ouch, that hurt! I couldn't believe it and was so up-set. Why or how this happened was beyond my comprehension and I was so frustrated that I blurted something out. I'm not sure exactly what it is that I said, but I made the statement in the form of a question; "What the heck is going on around here?" As I said, I was alone and I did not expect a response to my question.

So, there I was; all alone practicing for an extremely important game that evening. I knew that this poor performance was unacceptable, which is why out of frustration... I simply blurted out the question about what was going on. I hadn't had a score this low since my very first game, as kid and haven't done this poorly since, until then. I didn't understand and wasn't expecting an answer, especially being by myself in the alley. So, to hear what I felt to be an audio voice, speaking out of the clear blue, caught me totally by surprise; saying, "God is testing you".

In my disbelief, I said, "What!?" I expected a response, but there was none. Then I asked God directly as I waited for my ball to return; "God, Are you testing me?" Still, there was no answer. So I said, "God, if you are testing me, I don't need this right now... I have a really important game coming up tonight. I want to win." I thought to myself, I can to do better than this; remembering the first game I ever bowled where it too, was a 99.

Then I asked, "Let me know if you're testing me? If you are, let me bowl a strike, then I'll know." Believe it or not, it wasn't until just now, while writing this story that I've come to realize; that the strike I ask for wasn't a strike, confirming my question. It was yet another near impossible split in a series of many splits.

So splits were all I could bowl and I couldn't even pick up the spares. That's right! I can't remember picking up a single spare. So, there was no strike to confirm my question about God testing me, because of my inability... to make even one. Believe me; I tried desperately, but to no avail. I was obviously in a slump which I have never experienced before and didn't need with the up-coming tournament that evening. Therefore, I don't believe it was God who was testing me and if so, I failed miserably.

So as I said, I didn't make that strike, and I missed the split, but while I waiting for that ball to return, I spoke to God again... saying, "Please, don't do this to me. I really need to do better than this." Then I said, "Let me try, again" as I reset the pins. My next statement was, "I'm going to make a strike this time." I took my stance and made my approach as I have thousands of times before, and then I released the ball. It's going its going and it looks perfect as it swings into the pocket, as it always has, but then again, SPLIT! "Split? Again, I say, "What the heck"?

I'm saying to myself, I know I can do better than this! That is when I asked God, again. "Are you testing me? It is the next statement I made that was the worst mistake I had ever made and Thank God for having so much love, mercy, patience and understanding with such an arrogant teenager. I said, "God, if you are... you better not be, or I'm going to stop believing in you." I said, "I'll try once more time" and yet again, I got another split. I recall saying, "That's it God, you blew it. I'll never believe in you again", as I left the bowling alley. I'm not proud of what I did, but I washed this event out of my mind until years later. I hadn't been walking with the Lord, as I should have and because of such, this event came back to haunt me.

I was so foolish and what was I thinking? This is something I can, in all honesty say, that no one should ever do. This was a terrible thing for me to say and I can only say; if it hadn't been for the Lords intervention some years past, I may have taken my own life then. By rights, God should have slapped me down and taken my life, but again, God loves me. He had plans for me and still does or I believe I wouldn't be here. It's because of the following stories in the next chapter that explains why I still live, to this very day. For what Jesus had done and given me has shown me the love and mercy God has for all sinners, even a sinner like me. For He has forgiven me, and has confirmed it personally, in a way... that only, He could.

My statement to God was not only foolish, but also that of a paradoxical statement. Imagine! Here I am, telling God that I'm not going to believe in Him, but to whom, am I be speaking... if I didn't believe in God? My disbeliefs indicate that I still believe and thank you Jesus, for being so Patient, Loving, and Merciful as well as, Forgiving. Praise you Lord, and I do love you so.

CHAPTER 6

In Search of Love"

Graduating from Job Corps

Upon graduating from the Job Corps, I was placed in a little town outside of Galveston, Texas called Freeport. This was provided through the courtesy of the Job Corps placement program for graduates. It was there that I was to start work with DOW Chemical, one of the largest chemical companies in the world, which had a policy that required a physical exam for all prospective employees. After the exam, I was informed to have a bad back; a birth defect that caused me to be rejected. Had I stayed, I was to start working in a machine shop as a journeyman, but fortunately I was passed over, which forced me to seek work elsewhere. Had this not happened, I like others before me may have settled in on that permanent job, as a machinist instead of following my dreams of being the draftsman which my heart had desired. So, I went back to St. Louis and started working with a small firm. It was during my second day on that job when I received a call offering me, yet another job paying 150% more money. So, I quit that job and began my third job, all in one week.

My stepfather, Gil was impressed with the fact that I had managed to settle down and apply myself toward accomplishing something in my life. It was in the Job Corps where I had gained the initiative to do something to improve myself. I really had no choice and just a young man at 18 and thank God I was denied that first job. It's for that reason only, that I went back to my home town; St. Louis, Missouri and found my second job, but as for Gil? He really surprised me and went the extra mile for me by sticking his neck out to help land me that third job. Actually, this job Gil helped me get was at Emerson Electric and put me into the position of landing my first, real professional job which would launch my career into some 40+ years and was the beginning of a new found respect for one another.

Personally, I believe in the trinity: The Father, The Son and The Holy Ghost, as one God; consisting of three. Now, know this; the number three is not a superstitious thing with me, but I have noticed that the number three does seem to play a very significant role in my life. It begins with the Lord always being near, as God in the Trinity. Also, there were the three stacks of coins in the mirror that I mentioned earlier, which I believe was an indication that I would be living a blessed life; a life of not just prosperity, but a life blessed in so many other ways. My life has continuously been blessed and protected from harm. I may not always be aware or know of such at the time, but when I look back, I can see that the Lord was with me. He's always been with me, especially during my greatest times of need. Don't ask me how I know... I just know that I know that I know that I know; the Lord is with me always and He loves me. As it is, I've hardly ever want for anything that I did not have.

As I look back, I can only marvel at what has taken place around me, in awe. The Lord has always been here to protect me or lead me into a direction which I should follow or given me a little nudge in a direction I should be going. I had three jobs leading into my professional career and they are just another example of trinity. You'll also notice, as I said that the number three comes into play quite frequently in my life. Such as, my wife; the third person I asked to marry me. The first two young ladies I asked had not proven to be as serious or faithful, as I had hoped. It was after them, I met my wife to be. Thank you Lord. Next to the Lord, Joyce is the best thing that ever to happen to me. She and I, as my parents before me, have had three children. Our three children were born three years and three months apart. Joyce comes from a family that was double the size of my family. There were six children in her family, which brings to memory, the six stacks of coins from three.

Gil, was quite a guy; a Sr. Design Engineering Consultant having an Engineering Degree. He was the man in whom I looked up to and hoped to follow in this great profession. The only thing I did not care for about Gil, was that he was an atheist.

He didn't believe in God and God was the farthest thing from his mind or heart. I wasn't even allowed to mention God or say the name of Jesus while in his home, or in his presence. Only he could and only did so, through his profanity, but he did take me back in when I first arrived in St. Louis. There I stayed for a few weeks and then Gil helped by getting me a head start in life.

It was my dad that gave me the desire to succeed by telling me that I would never amount to anything, but it was Gil who encouraged me. He's the only one to give me direction on how to be financially secure, but the know how to make it on my own without seeking help from anyone, or so I thought.

Lonely and Searching for Life

As I said, I wasn't walking with the Lord, as I should have been at that time and being on my own was not good, because I was lonely, which would not have to be as such, had I been walking with the Lord. Not realizing this at the time though, caused me to be in search for someone or something, because of my loneliness and being unhappy. I was so lonely that I started looking for a room-mate to share my time with and hopefully a female. It was then; I remembered this one young girl that I grew up with in school and attended church with, which I liked very much. She was a very cute gal and somewhat frail, only because she was so, petite. I had always been attracted toward the small and petite. In fact, this is exactly what I married, an extremely cute and intelligent gal who matured into my lifelong sweetheart; lover, buddy, pal, friend and help mate... Joyce.

Diane however, is a gal who I had grown up with and was spoken for at the time and destined to be with another, but that didn't stop me. No, not me! I knew we went to the same church as children, so why not? That's when I began going to church again in hopes to woo her away from another. What happened though is that I had apparently forgotten where I was; in the house of the Lord and by hearing the Word of God; conviction set in and was so strong that it began eating away at me inside. Conviction was so strong that it overcame my desires to be with Diane or anyone or anything. Something wasn't right and then I remembered what I had said to God in the Job Corps. It was definitely a mistake, a big mistake and it was killing me. Either, I had to quit going to church and continue not being right with God or quit believing in God altogether, which I could not do because I knew the Lord and that He was very real and very much alive. I also knew that if I quit going to church that Diane would be completely out of reach. I didn't want this to happen and knew what I had to do. I needed to go forward in church and seek God's forgiveness. So, I went forward and even got Baptized. Now, this was my third time of being Baptized, but this time I knew why and I wanted to be baptized, expecting all to be well. My first Baptism was as an infant and I can't even recall doing so, for I was far too young. My second Baptism took place, only because I was following my sister's example. So I really didn't know the true meaning of Baptism at that time, but I knew it this time; the third time and I really wanted it. It wasn't much later after this though... that there was something inside that still didn't seem, quite right! So, during a late night service alter call, I went forward again and asked the pastor quietly, if we could speak in private after the service, for what I had to discuss would take too long at the altar, and he agreed to meet me with me.

Lost and Rejected

After services, when everyone had gone home; it was late but the pastor still made time for me and invited me into his office, offering me a seat. As I sat, I began to explain my dilemma and the conviction I was feeling. As I did, he just sat there listening to my accounts as they unfolded and then when I finished, I asked for him if he would pray with me and help me by asking God for forgiveness. It was then that he sat up wide-eyed with a look of rage and anger on his face from behind his desk, which could have been from being there so late that evening, after services, but that wasn't the case. He was preparing to nail me.

He sat there as if to gather his thoughts and then just spewed out his judgment against me. We had known each other for years, since I first began going to church there as a three year old, but what he said to me next... completely caught me off guard. He said, "NO! I won't pray with you! There is no reason to pray for you! You committed the unpardonable sin! You Blasphemed God, boy! You're going to straight to hell! There is no hope for you! Praying for you is a waste of my time. Please leave, as he pointed toward the door and seen me out, where I began to weep and as we left, he locked the doors.

Jesus says in Matthew 7:1 *"Judge not, that ye be not judged."* and I was not only judged, but convicted and condemned by a man; not God, but by a pastor without further ado. This happened that quickly and this wasn't just any ordinary man either, but a man of the cloth, ordained by God. Only God knows, but when he spoke in church and preached from the word of God... I was brought up to trust and believe what He says... to be Truth. I also believe... who am I to question Gods authority?

God is surreal, but as for me? I'm just a man... a condemned man... that's going straight to hell, without any hope of salvation. The pastor said it, he's a man of God; I believed it, and that settled it! I did the unthinkable! The unimaginable! The unpardonable! I sinned against God! I'm destined to go to hell! The preacher said it, so it must be true! I'm going to hell is all that ran through my mind. Wow, talk about the pits! I literally cried almost 10 miles or more, all the way to the house where I called home; praying and pleading to God... for my forgiveness.

Destined for Hell

My home was really nothing more than a room that I rented, which was one of the two bedrooms located up-stairs in this family's home. I had kitchen privileges and shared the up-stairs bathroom with their oldest son, Steve. It was late when I came home and everyone was already in bed, so I slipped in quietly.

As I went up the stairs, the bathroom was to my left and Steven's room was to my right. I slipped by quietly across the floor looking into Steve's room and he was fast to sleep. Then I quietly went to my room and got ready for bed, turning off the light and sat on the edge of my bed and buried my face into my pillow to muffle the overwhelming cries, as I cried out to the Lord. I was having a serious discussion; begging and pleading for forgiveness. I felt so un-alive and dead inside, as I cried. I asked God, "What's the sense in living, knowing that when I die that I'm going to go to hell? I might as well get it over with... I might as well be... dead!" It was only then; I questioned living, as I lay down, to go to sleep. Life, no longer had any importance or any meaning. I felt dead, feeling so all alone and there is no feeling like the absence of the Lord... especially, for an eternity!

As I lay in bed tossing and turning because of my uneasiness, I was so restless, and I had such a tremendous, heavy heart. I lied there just saying over and over again, how sorry I was, and that I didn't know. I kept saying, I didn't know what I was doing and pleaded with the Lord... saying, Please-e-e-e... forgive me? I love you Lord. I'll never say anything like that again.

I'm sure my words turned into mumbles that muffled into total silence, as I drifting off, but as I did; I heard a squeak and popping coming up from the floor, as if someone had just come across the hallway floor... up to the opening of my bedroom door. I thought it was Steve. He must have heard my crying and praying and I thought to myself; I must have awakened him, so I got out of bed and looked in on him, but he was fast asleep.

I didn't see or hear another soul up and about, so I went back into my room and crawled into bed and covered myself, nestling in hopefully for a good night's rest. As I lay there, I thought to myself, "It must have been this old wood frame house settling, so I closed my eyes again while still speaking to God, saying "I'm sorry Lord" asking for forgiveness over and over again. I began to drift away deeper and deeper, as I was falling asleep.

Now, this old wood frame house had genuine hard wood flooring and I'd lived there for months. I knew that when I changed clothes or walked from one side of the room to the other, that there were certain noises that would take place, such as creaks, squeaks and popping sounds coming from the floor that would occur, especially when one weighed as much as me. In fact, I lived there so long that I knew where to step cross the room to minimize the noise, as not to wake anyone when I got up to use the rest room. So, there I was, lying in bed, falling asleep, but a little on edge and restless, but slipping away and just before... I completely slipped out of it, falling into a deep sleep; I heard: SssqqueeeaaakkkKKK.... Ssnnaapp. Popppp... Ssnnapp. CrackkkKKK! This annoying noise disturbed me.

As I was lying there, I began to come out of this sleeping mode into an awareness of someone's presence, realizing that I'm no longer alone and someone else had just walked across my bedroom floor. Then it happened... I'm wide awake, and I jerked myself into an upright, sitting position, as to see who was in my room and as I did, I come to realize that no one was there.

I really expected to see someone, anyone, but no one. as I looked down toward the end of my bed and across to the other side of my room. Yet, No one was there. So simultaneously, as I looked across my room and I literally leaped to the floor and darted to the stair-well but didn't see anyone. Afterwards, I looked into Steve's room and then checked the bathroom including behind the shower curtain and again, no one was there. So, I looked back into Steve's room to make sure he was still asleep. He hadn't moved, but I just had to ask him. So, I shook him and said "Steve, are you awake?" and he said, "I am now." I asked if he had gotten up to use the bathroom or anything and he said, "No!" I apologized for waking him and went back into my bedroom... thinking to myself that I must be hearing things.

As I lied back down, I wondered to myself... what's going on, as I closed my eyes and just laid there, as I tried to go back to sleep... sleeppp... ahhh! And I began drifting off, a third time.

As I lay there, drifting-off, deeper and deeper, and no sooner than I began to drift off; I began being pulled back out of my state of sleep into reality, yet again by this constant, annoying noise. It was as if someone were standing at the end of my bed. It was as if, this person were just rocking and swaying, back and forth while standing there, as if someone were trying to maintain their balance. I recognized that squeaking sound as the same sound I would hear coming up from the floor, at the end of my bed where I would stand to put on my socks or pants on, one foot and at a time.

All I could hear was this annoying noise; Squeak... Squeeeakkk. Squeak... Squeeeakkk. My eyes were heavy and it was a strain to open them, but as I did, I did so, ever so slowly. I tried to lift my head to see who or what was going on. I tell you the truth and the Lord knows, I'm speaking the truth. At the end of my bed in a white garment, not a glaring bright white, but an off white garment, possibly a robe... stood a man. The room was dark, but He wasn't, and I could see his face. He had long hair, and wore a beard and mustache, and didn't say a single word. I have absolutely; no doubt who this person was... it was Jesus.

As Jesus was standing there, he began lifting his arms, spreading them apart to open them, as if he were inviting me to come... come and join him, but I was so tired. All I remember is trying to raise my head to get a better look at Him, but it was as if, someone had put the palm of their hand onto my forehead; applying pressure, forcing me to lie my head back-down onto the pillow. I fought to sit up but out of exhaustion, I passed out into a deep sleep. All I remember is passing out as my head was falling; collapsing into my pillow, and then I was out of it. This is when I entered into a deep, deep sleep, where I entered into three separate, almost unbelievable, but absolutely beautiful... dreams. There was such vivid detail, it was as if though, I was actually there, and I will try my very best to describe these dreams, as best I can, which I believe the Lord would have me do though they were intended to show me... that God Loves me.

Dream #1 – Place of Rest
....

My first dream was surreal. It was as if, I was actually there. I found myself to be standing in a strange place and as to where, I did not know, and wasn't really sure, why? I didn't notice any climatic change, but I did notice a light had begun to fill the room that soon began to take on the shape of an elongated cavern of sorts. I noticed too, that to my immediate right, was standing the figure of a man, whom I recognized again, to be Jesus.

Jesus appeared tall, approximately 6'2 or 6'3 and we didn't exchange any words at that point, but we slowly began to stroll forward. To my left was an outer wall of what appeared to be a corridor, like that of a tunnel or cavern. As we walked, my arms swung ever so lightly and it was then that I lift my left arm, just enough to allow the back of my left hand to brush up against the wall. I looked down as I did out of curiosity and found the wall to be cool and dry to the touch. My eyes followed the wall to the ceiling, and then across the ceiling to the adjacent wall on my right where they joined, at a rounded corner too, where I saw shadows. I looked down between Jesus and myself to find the source of this light. It was coming from an old style lantern Jesus held. It was there for my benefit, as to allow me to focus on why I was there. This lantern swayed back and forth as we walked in somewhat of a slow stride, as if He wanted to share something with me. It was then that I noticed shadows reaching to the ceiling along the wall, just to the right of Jesus and were set back approximately eight feet. These shadows swayed back and forth and appeared to be dancing projections from what I thought to be rocks or stalagmites, and Jesus knew my thoughts.

So, we stopped walking, and simultaneously turned to face the wall on the right, and as we did, Jesus lifted the lantern to reveal people lying on their backs; fully dressed in suit and tie but without shoes. Their hands clutched together resting on their mid-drift and the souls of their bare feet faced us, as they laid on a 3" thick, 7' long x 3' wide stone top, setting on a 2' high altar. These altars were spaced 6' apart and as far, as the eye could see.

I remember, vaguely seeing the figure of a person laying on a separate altar to the right of the man in front of me and possibly another beyond him, but I really don't recall seeing much other than that at a glance beyond that point, for Jesus was on my right. I do however, remember looking off to the left of the person in front of me and there was a person lying next to him, and then another next to him, and so-on and so-on, as far as the light from the lantern would allow me to see. As I turned back around to face the man in front of me, I didn't understand, so I asked Jesus, "What am I doing here with all these dead people?" It was then Jesus said, "They're not dead... they are, but asleep."

Now, I really did not understand the meaning of this dream and I should have asked. It was years later that I come to realize; those who passed away in the Old Testament are referred to as sleeping, where it states many, many times over and over; they slept.

It also says, in the New Testament that "The dead in Christ shall rise first." However, there was one of the thieves on a cross to the right of Jesus, in Luke 23:43... And Jesus said unto him, *"Verily I say unto thee, To day shalt thou be with me in paradise."*

This caused me to wonder what exactly, was the meaning of my 1st dream? Could it be that I will rise on a particular day when the dead in Christ will rise first, or do we actually rise and go straight to heaven... or paradise at that very moment as we pass on, as did the thief? Either/or; it's a bit confusing because it also says that Jesus will be returning like a thief in the night and that the graves will be opened which I would think to mean that those who are sleeping will be awakened and where there are two standing in the field; one will be taken and the other will be left, all of which shall be done in the twinkling of an eye. Maybe this is that point in life, when those sleeping and walking among the dead, who are in Christ, shall rise first into life ever-lasting.

It's for this reason I believe Jesus was showing me the resting place where I may be when I pass on... to rest among others, living in Christ until that day; "the dead in Christ shall rise first."

> *<u>1 Thess 4:16</u> For the Lord himself shall descend from heaven with a shout, with the voice of the archangel, and with the trump of God: and <u>the dead in Christ shall rise first</u>:*

> *<u>1 Thess 4:17</u> Then we which are alive and remain shall be caught up together with them in the clouds to meet the Lord in the air: and so shall we ever be with the Lord.*

> *<u>1 Thess 4:18</u> Wherefore comfort one another with these Words.*

It is for this reason I share this dream, to share the good news that Jesus Christ is alive and well, and with us, always. Only, if we accept, trust, believe and receive Him, as our Lord and Savior. I also, see this as proof, where Jesus states we... will be asleep (in our resting place) until we shall be raised up, upon that last day.

> *<u>John 6:39</u> And this is the Father's will which hath sent me, that of all which he hath given me I should lose nothing, but should raise it up again <u>at the last day</u>.*

> *<u>John 6:40</u> And this is the will of him that sent me, that every one which seeth the Son, and believeth on him, may have everlasting life: and I will raise him up <u>at the last day</u>.*

> *<u>John 6:44</u> No man can come to me, except the Father which hath sent me draw him: and I will raise him up <u>at the last day</u>.*

> *<u>Daniel 12:1</u> And at that time shall Michael stand up, the great prince which standeth for the children of thy people: and there shall be a time of trouble, such as never was since there was a nation even to that same time: and at that time thy people shall be*

delivered, every one that shall be found written in the book.

Daniel 12:2 And <u>many of them that sleep</u> *in the dust of the earth* <u>shall awake, some to everlasting life, and some to shame and everlasting contempt.</u>

Wow! I was so blind, but now I see! Jesus didn't come right out and tell me. I think He wanted me to realize it for myself, that I have been forgiven, and that I'm saved. Thank you Lord.

However, because of my questioning my existence and my very purpose for going on in life, including my not having the understanding I needed, to understand the Love, Mercy, Grace and forgiveness of God; He blessed me again, with a 2nd dream.

Note: Much thanks to the Artist depicting Jesus carrying a lantern, on the Internet Domain who is "Unknown" but found... and used to reflect the Lord who I seen, in my dream; Dream #1.

Dreams #2 – Though the Eyes of Jesus

I believe Jesus was well aware, that I would not have believed anyone else but Jesus himself, because He alone... is the Lord. After all, it was a Man of God who convinced me I was going to Hell, no questions asked. Also, I did not immediately grasp the meaning of my first dream and thank God for His patience and understanding with me, and because of this? He blessed me graciously, and out of His love for me; he did allow me a second dream immediately following the first, without any time lapse.

It was after Jesus had spoken to me, I found myself transformed into a situation where I was in somewhat of a seated position; straddling some sort of a bench, or a log that I was actually resting upon. This seat caused me to be elevated above the ground, approximately eight to ten inches. The bottoms of my forearms were resting upon my knees, as my hands dangled loosely in front of me and my chin was pressed, lightly into my chest as my head hung low. It was as if, I were in deep thought or possibly a prayer. I heard many voices and I slowly lifted my head, not being sure of my surroundings, to see where I was. As I did so, people came into view and were held back by Roman Soldiers that were around me. I was sitting there alone and not sure of where or why I was there. Being alone; I was somewhat curious as to what was even happening and why I was there.

What happened next though, caught me off guard. I was quite surprised, because there wasn't anyone directly in front of me, yet at that very moment, as I set up to see where I was; it was as if someone had placed the palms of their hands in front of my shoulders and upper chest with their thumbs resting in the middle of my sternum, just beneath my collarbone. The fingers of each hand, ever so lightly rolled upward passing over my collarbones with the tips of fingers slightly curling over the top of my shoulders. As I felt these hands, they ever so gently began applying pressure; pushing on my chest, forcing me to lay back onto my back.

At first, I thought I was going to fall, but much to my surprise, I didn't. It was as if the hands of God were laying me back, ever so gently. I realized too, that this bench continued behind me, as I come to rest upon it in a lying position. Then one of the Roman Soldiers began approaching me on my left.

I remember while being laid back, I swung my arms outward to catch myself to keep me from falling backward; holding up my head as not to hit it while looking to my right, as I come to rest upon this bench. I then rolled my head over to face my immediate left. I was in the hands of God. As I did, I looked across my left shoulder and down my arm to where my left hand rested in an open position. It was then that I realized what my arm was resting on. What I was seeing was the Crucifixion of Jesus Christ, but not through my eyes, but through the Lord's eyes.

This soldier, who had approached me from the left, was now kneeling on one knee at the end of the cross. He reached into a leather pouch hanging on his left side and pulled out a spiked nail; tapered from end to the other, about four inches long. In his right hand was a mallet. Now, this mallet appeared to be made from, of all things; wood that was wrapped completely in leather? I say this because; it appeared to be about eight inches long and about five inches in diameter. This mallet was literally strapped to a wooden handle that may have been two inches in diameter and eight inches in length. There were straps tying the two together with what appeared to be made from drawn leather. The mallet was belled out with frayed edges on both-ends, and rolled over from being used, so many times before.

Now, this soldier was dressed just as one would expect a soldier to be dressed. He was wearing the complete wardrobe of a Roman Soldier; with his sword and a skirt with shielded plates of steel, including breast, back, shoulder and arm plates of armor, a helmet and sandals laced up the calves, and wore gold plated wrist bands. Speaking of wrist; this soldier had extremely large wrist with forearms to match, so big and meaty, with a fist like a big ham hock wrapped around that mallet. What a warrior!

He had my attention and it frighten me, knowing what he was about to do. Again, I was witnessing the crucifixion of Jesus; watching it unfold through the eyes of Jesus, as if they were my own, knowing the pain I was about to feel was going to kill me. I was about to die and I knew where I was going... I was going to hell! A man of God had told me so, and I believed him. So, I screamed out aloud, "MY GOD... I DON'T WANT TO DIE!"

All this took place, as the soldier was drawing back his arm to strike that mighty blow. It was when his arm started to come forward when I screamed. It was because of my fear of dying that the Lord saved me from that moment of feeling anything; not even the first blow. It was then; Jesus blessed me, yet again.

Yes, Jesus lifted me up from that scene into a third dream to help me realize... that I am saved! Oh how the Lord loves me. Isn't the Lord, absolutely wonderful? He didn't even allow me feel a thing. What I did fear though was my fear of dying. Also, another thing I feel though, even to this very day... is the thought of the pain one feels deep within one's heart, knowing what the Lord suffered on the cross, for you... and for me. He loves you!

Jesus truly suffered a tremendous amount of pain and anguish; more than words could ever explain or describe. He did so, out of the Love God has for all of us; you and me; who have repented from sin and accepted Jesus Christ, as Lord and Savior.

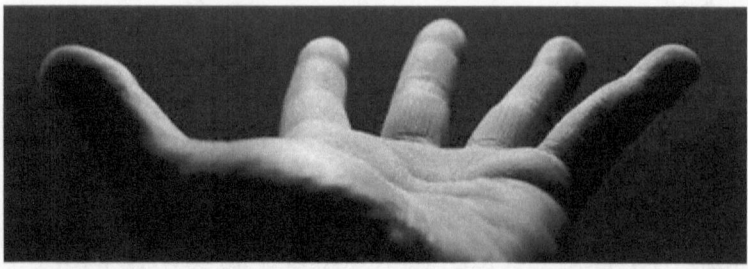

Note: This is by an "Unknown" Artist, who depicts an open stretched forth hand appearing to be as if, receiving something, showing the free will and acceptance of Jesus, before His Crucifixion on the Cross in my Second Dream; An absolute beautiful concept of God's Precious Love.

Dream #3 – Life is so Short...

Now, in this third dream, immediately following the second, I'm literally standing in the middle of the universe. I mean literally, in the middle of absolutely, nowhere. There was no need for a space suit and there wasn't an atmosphere to distort my vision either. What I was seeing was absolutely, crystal clear.

As I'm standing on what, I don't know, because I can't see anything of substance, beneath me. Yet, it was as if, I was standing on a rock, but there was nothing there, but space. In fact, that's all there was all around me, just space! An eternity of space and of course, standing to my right, was the Rock... Jesus!

I couldn't see Jesus' body or His face but what I could see, was the silhouette of His image. He had an aura about Him that made it appear, as if he was like that of an eclipse... with the sun directly behind Him, but there was no sun to be seen. I know this, only because, I didn't see one. I remember stepping forward with my left foot, bending my left knee, as I leaned forward to take a peek around Him. There was no sun, but there was an aura emanating around Him. Jesus appeared to be clutching the top of His garment, holding his right hand over his chest... where his heart would be.

There was darkness. Yet, there was light. There weren't any particular planets or solar systems or galaxies to be seen. No Milky-Way, No Big Dipper nor Little Dipper; not even the North Star was seen. What there was though, were countless billions upon billions, if not trillions upon trillions of stars and Galaxies, everywhere! There were so many that they alone lit the heavens.

I noticed too, that when Jesus moved ever so slightly; His garment glistened and rippled all about him, surging with energy that could have, if He allowed it to do so, just burst forth... in all His Glory. I believe too, that He clutched His garment for my benefit, similar to what someone would do, simply by turning down a dimmer switch, as to adjust the lighting in a room.

I believe it was His way of holding back His awesome Glory to keep His Radiance from filling the universe, which I know He could have done, if He wanted to. However, I believe He did this, as to allow me to see something, to learn something, and had He not done so? I may have been so overwhelmed by his presence that I may have missed it. I might not have been able to see or to understand the meaning, of what He wanted me to.

I do believe in Jesus Christ and yes, He is my Lord and Savior, and I truly know now.... that I know, that I know, that I know, that I know... that Jesus Christ is Lord! Praise God!

As I looked out into the universe, He spoke unto me and when He spoke, I turned around to look upon Him. This is when I saw that His robe or garment was blacked out to match the darkness of the universe, but as for His garment? It just rippled with energy everywhere; trying to burst forth, as He spoke. What he said unto me, was that of a question, where. He asked, "Why fear death, for life... is so short, compared to all Eternity?" It was then that I heard His voice roll throughout all eternity, as it literally filled the universe as He said unto me "B E H O L D!"

As Jesus said this, He had stretched-forth His left arm... in a long sweeping, but graceful motion, from right to left and as He did, not only could I hear His voice expanding and rolling throughout all eternity, but I could also see the Awesome Power of God glistening beside me; trying to burst-forth, from underneath His garment, that would have filling eternity, itself. It was then I found Salvation and Eternal Life through Jesus Christ, my Lord and Savior. Praise God! Thank you Jesus.

Truly, had He not been grasping His upper Garment with His other hand, as to allow me to see and experience all eternity with Him, I may not have seen it. This is because, by His presence alone,

He could have filled all eternity, as I said... if, He wanted to, but all the stars would have faded away in His Magnificent and Majestic Glory, and I would have missed what I was to find; Salvation! I'm truly saved! Thank you Jesus and Praise God!

I wish everyone could see the visualization of the awesome beauty and creation of God, for there is no place on earth that one could ever begin to capture the beauty that is in store for us. It was only, after this dream that I knew, without a shadow of doubt; that Jesus died for me and that I am Saved! Glory to God in the Highest, for Jesus Christ is Lord... Halleluiah and Amen.

Eternal Gift of God

So Imagine, if you will; from the knowledge of knowing where one may be resting until the return of Jesus, to seeing the crucifixion of Jesus' through the own eyes, as our Lord and Savior, and then witnessing all eternity before you, as no man has ever seen. Jesus literally, laid down His life for man through His own personal sacrifices to show the Love of God, which He did for all of us, and it's only after these dreams that I come to realize the true meaning of salvation. All Glory... to God, Amen.

I know now, without any doubt; that I am saved and I too, am Born Again; into a new being. God really does love me and Jesus suffered and died for me, which He tried to show me in my second dream. It was only in the third dream however; that it was confirmed to me... not to fear death, for death... is defeated.

<u>1 Cor. 15:55</u> O death, where is thy victory? O death, where is thy sting?

Death is inevitable, for God hath said, "Ye shall surely die." It's because of sin, that man was separated from God, but God has provided us salvation through Jesus Christ, to save us from death and provide us eternal life, to live in the hereafter in the presence of God. Hell is the second Death; the absence of God, which is intended for Satan and his angels, and not... for man.

Hebrews 9:27 For it is appointed unto men once to die, but after this the judgment.

The second death for man is that of a free will choice... made by man who walks among the dead and the living in Christ, while on Earth. We have the choice to choose: Heaven or Hell. We either accept the Gift; Gods only begotten Son, Jesus Christ as our Lord and Savior, or we will die, which means; to die in our sins, unto a judgment which ends in the second death. As for me? Once I feared death because I was lead to believe that I was destined for Hell without hope; like that of the walking dead.

I even considered taking my life; a life, so precious to my Lord and Savior that He personally, showed me the sacrifice that He has made for me, and that He loved me and saved me! So, I need not fear DEATH any longer... for JESUS has personally saved me in a way that no man; not even, a man of the cloth or a minister, could ever convinced me of otherwise, because I know.

Thank you Lord for saving me! This is why I know, that I know that I know that I know, that JESUS CHRIST IS LORD; Lord of Lords and King of Kings, the Bright and Morning Star, the Alpha and Omega; God's Mercy, Love and Grace, and the Righteousness of God. Also, "God will... Never Abandon You."

It was after my Third dream... I felt led to write the following poem, I once referred to as Space, but have rename it to, Eternity.

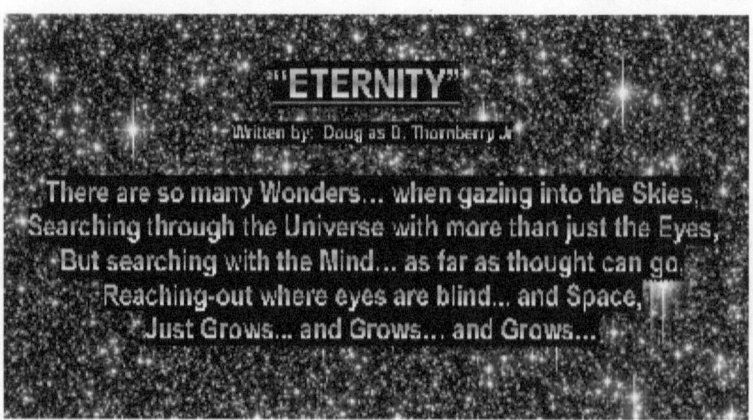

God is Love

....

God is Love and the best thing we can do, as a man or a woman, is to love one another. We should love all people; be they alive in Christ or not, or of any color, or creed. We all need each other and we all need Love. For Love is of God and God is Love and we all need God, and He abides in each of us and does so, through His Holy Spirit. Therefore, like Jesus that loved even the harlots and beggars; we too, should love them. If we claim to have the love of God in us, then we should be as God; full of love and compassion. Believe me! It's Hell to be without God; this I know! When one knows that God lives and then feels lost, as if they are no longer a part of God's family... due to something questionable, such as something they may have said or done? Well, they come to know... the real fear of God, and that of banishment, forever! They may feel cursed and as if it was impossible to find forgiveness from God. It may be from something they said or done causing them to believe they committed the unpardonable sin. This I didn't do and the Lord knows it and intervened. Thank You Lord... for loving me and saving me, and being with me, always... as my Lord and Savior.

Rather than to reject someone that is in search of God's forgiveness for what they think they've done; the unpardonable sin? Maybe one should offer support and prayer to this person. Because, just maybe, the Holy Spirit is working in that person; calling him or her to repent. But, how can one repent, should that person... end their life, due to depression? They can't! Also, how can one come to repent, if a person of God refuses to help comfort and pray for those in need? Isn't that what prayer is for; to turn to God for help; to find comfort and forgiveness? How can one be led to prayer and/or forgiveness, if shun. By shunning them, would be like standing in the way of Salvation when Gods Spirit is calling them and who are we to do so. The question is: who's at fault? Could it be the one in search of repentance, or that of the person refusing to help another seeking repentance, due to one's, personal judgment? Rejection may very well cause the one in need, to fall. So, judge not, for there is, but one judge, and for us to judge is to be judged, so be wise.

Do let the living water flow, and be glad that you know salvation,and that you are saved. Love one another and share the Lord by letting your candle shine and being a light in a dark world. May the Lord be with you and in all that you do, and may your wisdom and knowledge of the will of God, grow as you help others come to know the Lord. Again, I say Judge not for there is but one judge, and judges we are not, but we are; Saints.

> **Luke 6:37** *Judge not, and ye shall not be judged: condemn not, and ye shall not be condemned: forgive, and ye shall be forgiven:*

Keep your eyes open and have an open heart, and an open Spirit unto the Lord, and love one another, as the Lord Himself loves the Church. You know, it is because of the Love Jesus has for us, that He has gone out of His way, to save you and me; like that of a lost sheep. I believe there are more important issues in life than being born and dying. Jesus really does love us; all of us. You don't need a dream to prove it. You can feel him in your heart, just by inviting him in; into your life. I didn't need a dream either, except I was judge and condemned unjustly, by a man! I needed the Love and Forgiveness of God where I once was truly lost, but now, I am found! I pray to God... to have mercy on this man of God, who judged me. I pray too, that he hasn't done this to other individuals, and if he has; that whoever they are... that just maybe, they may not have been so weak or heartbroken to have taken their own life, as I once considered.

Only God knows for certain and may the Lord have mercy on them, as He had on me. Thank you so much Jesus, for loving me, and forgiving me, washing away all my sins, as far as the East is from the West, including others depending on you, for Salvation. It's in Jesus name I give thanks and all the Glory... to God the Father. Amen.

CHAPTER 7

"Unity of One"

New Beginning

As I stated earlier; my first place of employment was with Emerson Electric Company in St. Louis, Missouri. It again, was because of my step-father, Gil who had pulled some strings from being within the profession and helped me land my first position. I was so excited and thankful, and Gil really surprised me. Gil wound-up being the guy I looked up to even over my own dad, and it was his footsteps; professionally speaking... that I wanted to follow. I did my best on this first job, as not to disappoint him or my mom. I finally become something that would make them proud, including me. This was the beginning of what I had hopes of being... a successful, professional life, as a draftsman.

It was when I returned to St. Louis that I ran into an old school buddy of mine, Benny Lane. Benny was a very close school buddy and he had been in numerous bands which he started throughout high school and college. He was telling me he had just started up a new band and asked me if I wanted to come along and watch them play that very night at a night club. It was their first night together as a band; "James Brown Body and Soul". So, I agreed and wow, was I impressed! This was an 11 man band counting the singer who was quite a gal. They were great! Benny played lead Guitar and there were other playing guitars as well, including a man on the key-board, quite a few on the horns, and then there was the drummer. Combined, they sounded a lot like the group called "Chicago" and played their hearts out. As I sat back and listened, I was excited just being there and listening to an old friend doing what he did best. I'd been out of town nearly three years and lost complete contact with everyone and this was the beginning of getting back together. After their gig that evening I helped load up their equipment and Benny said to come on by his place in the morning.

So, I went by Benny's that next morning and was invited in. As I entered, I noticed a piano which was directly behind Benny and he turned around and walked over to it, as I entered into his home and he began playing some tunes. As he played the piano for me and began telling me how much he had improved, and how musically inclined he had become; telling me how music ran in the family. In fact, his cousin is Bobbie Gentry who had just released a recording earlier called, "Ode to Billie Joe". He said he hoped to do the same. Benny then proceeded to tell me that there's not an instrument he can't play; that is, all except for one. Out of curiosity, I asked Benny which one and he said, "The harmonica." He began telling me how he had tried numerous times but was just unable to pick it up; that it was too complicated. As he was telling me, I pulled out my harmonica from my hip pocket and showed it to him; saying, you mean this? Much to his surprise, he asked, "Do you play man, and I said, "Of course, I do." He said, "Well, play me something." So, I asked what would you like to hear and he asked me, "Do you know the song; Sonny?" So, I began playing and he said, "Man that was great! How would you like to play in my band! We need a harmonica." In fact, he said; "We have a birthday party coming up this week and I'd like to have you play with us." I asked are you sure it'll be alright with the others and he said, "Yeah, don't worry about it." I said, "Okay, I'll be there."

Afterwards we went down stairs to where his family room was, which also had an area where they practiced playing music. He showed me how well he could play the drums, and he was good but not as good as Ronnie, his little brother that was only 12 years old. He yelled up stairs for Ronnie to come on down and play us a beat. Benny was good at everything, but when it came to the drums... there was no doubt about it! That kid brother of his... blew the socks off Benny.

Well, Come the night of the party, I showed up and took a back seat and until Benny nod for me to step up to the spare microphone. I don't think anyone else was aware of Benny's decision because some seemed surprised when I stepped up.

Well, I played Sonny flawlessly and it felt really good to be a part of the band and I'll never forget it. Thanks Benny. I began playing the harmonica after my dad gave me a Chromatic-12 made by Hohner at the age of 12 for Christmas. Finally, all that hard work paid off. It wasn't your standard run around toy. Hohner has always been the leader in the industry for making harmonicas. It was through the years that this became something I learned and loved to play, especially during those many times of loneliness and solitude, which I faced often in the Job Corps. As most, I loved music and found it very peaceful and relaxing when playing, especially when sitting in an area that had harmonics like that of an echo chamber, such as an enclosed stair well. To this day, I still love playing when I can.

I met up with Benny later in the week and Benny told me the band split up. I was shocked and couldn't believe it. I was hoping that it wasn't anything on my account, but Benny told me he was getting drafted, so he enlisted in the Navy. Benny also said that when he signed up he had requested certain privileges because of his background and knowing too, that there was always a need for a band at all the officer clubs when in port. He requested to be allowed to be a part of this as a stipulation when signing up, because he was so musically inclined and gifted; playing lead guitar or any other instrument. Much to my surprise then... he signed up and got his wish and actually did play in all the ports at the officer clubs. It sounded great, so I signed up as well, knowing I would probably get drafted too, sooner or later. I mean, why wait to get in the Army to be on the front lines when I could join the Navy. Ben said, to sign-up on the buddy system, which they supposedly allowed and we'd be able to get together, but what I didn't know is Benny signed up a week earlier, making this almost impossible.

Since I am a Christian and there was a war going on, I didn't really want to fight; especially involved, with killing someone. One of the Commandments says, "Thou Shall Not Kill" and this was reason enough for me to avoid the draft but knowing the inevitable would happen; joining the Navy... looked pretty good.

The recruiter agreed that I could transfer and catch up with him, but only after completing boot camp. So, I signed up and it was shortly afterwards that Benny received his papers to report to the Great Lake for Boot Camp in Chicago, Illinois. I was disappointed because I hadn't even received my physical, but only days later; I receive notice to report for a physical in downtown St. Louis. One of the questions on the form was, if I had ever had a bad back or a back injury. I recalled jamming it when I was a child doing some silly stunt where I had to go to a doctor (Chiropractor) to relieve the pain. He also, helped me to get back on my feet and walking again, with the absence of any pain. With a few adjustments; a snap here and a crack there, I was back to normal. So, I answered, yes on the paperwork.

Afterwards, I got into line for my physical and all recruits stripped down to their skivvies and did the normal routine. The final thing was a simple question. There was a guy in front of me and he was asked, "Do you have any physical problems?" This guy said, "Yes, I have a bad back." They asked, "What's wrong?" He said, "I have Scoliosis"; curvature of the spine. It was after this that he was asked to turn around and bend over, as if they could really see something, but sure enough; there it was! Even I could even see it... definitely, curvature of the back.

They thanked him for enlisting, but that the Navy would not be requiring his services at this time. Then I heard the words, "Reject... next" which is when I stepped up. I stood 6'-6 and towered over this guy and was asked the same question; "Do you have any problems?" I looked him straight into the eyes and said, "Yeah... I've got a bad back, too." He pushed me through without even checking my papers; saying, "Get out of here, next!" So, I went into the next room, joining a group of 20 or more guys and we held up our right hand and took an oath, received a ticket and next, we boarded a train to the Great Lakes.

After reporting, I was fitted up with the proper gear and attire and assigned a barracks. Next, was inoculation day? After being inoculated, I was asked to step aside and report to a naval doctor.

He questioned my answer referencing to the "Yes" comment on any back injuries. I explain to him what had happened when I was younger and he sent me in for x-rays. Come to find out, I really did have a back problem and I wasn't even aware of it, so I was being discharged. I served 35 days in the Navy as a Seaman Recruit and I received an Honorable Discharge. My DD-214 indicates the same but it claims my enlistment as erroneous, and cannot be changed, as I have tried numerous times. The only thing erroneous about my enlistment was the man conducting the physicals. He did not listen to me or verify my statement. So, I was inducted into the United States Navy. This is not my error, but the error of the one pushing me through without fulfilling his personal responsibilities by following-up my statement or even checking out my paper work, as such. The most important issue here is not the Navy, as much as the person whom I met in the navy. His name is Terry and he came in and set down in front of me in the mess hall. There was just the two of us at the table. He placed his hand on the table, holding it up like a dog standing on four legs. His middle finger began to bob up and down as he made noises that sounded like a dog sniffing, as he walked his finger toward my dinner plate. He had this middle finger held up-right as he held it over the top of my mashed potatoes and then he dropped it into my potatoes; squish! As I grabbed him to smash his face, he held up the palms of his hands between the two of us saying, "Woe, wait a minute! Hi, my name's Terry." He apologized and explained he just joined the Navy and had no friends or knew anyone, so we become friends, but it was with the promise... Never to mess with my food again, or die! He went on to explain that he was getting a medical discharge, saying he had palsy in his back and his eye vision was 200 in his left eye, so he was rejected, as was I. So, we hung around together and departed for the airport and waited on our flights. I was returning to St. Louis and he was going to Akron, Ohio. Terry said that he'd like to come to St. Louis and visit, if I didn't mind, but I never thought he'd actually come. Then one day he did, wearing a patch over his left-eye. He was quite a likeable character and a knowledgeable friend, a little strange and slightly wacko, but a lot of fun to hang around with.

Meeting and Courting of My Wife

I didn't have a vehicle when Terry came into town, so we walked everywhere until a buddy of mine; Joe Wells, drove by and offered us a ride. We brought each other up to date and come to find out; he was getting married. He wanted us to meet his fiancée and offered to set all of us up on a triple date.

So, later that week, Joe picked us up and we headed over to pick up the girls; first it was Joe's fiancée, Sue and then Terry's Date was next. Terry and I were sitting in the back seat and I was to the left of Terry and he was blinded from seeing me due to the left-eye patch. I'd been picking on Terry a lot in horse play as we become closer friends, but now, here we are in the back seat waiting on Terry's date. Then the front door opened and this good looking young thing came out the house, down the stairs, ditty bopping across the yard with one heck of a strut.

As I said, Terry couldn't see me on his left side due to his eye. I said, "Wow... she's a cutie! Is that my date?" Joe said, "No, that's Terry's date." This is when I backhanded Terry in his shoulder with the back of my knuckles saying, "You lucky stiff." as he grasped his shoulder while turning to face me, saying... "OW!" Before we could really exchange any other words, his date swung open the door, looking at my other friend, Joe and said, "I presume this is my date" as she pointed her thumb toward Terry. Both, Joe and his fiancée agreed and then she embedded her left knee into the seat, as she semi-crawled in. As she did this, she reached across Terry with a clenched fist and hauled off and slugged me, a good one; right in the arm after seeing me hit Terry. Now, I hit Terry out of jealousy, but as for her, she was such a sweet-heart; a real knockout, and I was hoping that she was my date! However, as she was punching me, she was wearing a big smirk of a smile; telling me, "Keep your hands off my date... you big bully! It was fire-works time!

Well, when I was young and got into trouble; I'd get a whooping and sometimes my parents would say, "I want you to know, I'm doing this because I love you." So, she loved me!

Yes, you may call this is sick, but as soon as she hit me, I knew right then and there; she might be Terry's date, but she loves me! My date wound up being this tall gal named Sherry until Wood Stock came into play. You know; "Wood Stock", the place to be! Well, Terry was determined to go and under no circumstances, did he want to miss out. I on the other hand; was working and needed the revenue, so I bowed out. He was gone for many months and the door was open for me to go by and pay Joyce a visit. So, one day I took off and rode up to the curb on my motor cycle, a Honda 305 Scrambler. It was a good bike for street riding but much better on the dirt, because that was what it was made for; climbing hills and such, which I enjoyed, but it was too early to introduce her to dirt riding, just yet anyway.

Much to my surprise, I didn't even have to go up and knock on the door. Joyce was already out the door and on her way down to see me, as I set at the curb taking off my helmet. I asked if she'd like to go out for a spin and she surprised me by saying; let me ask my parents first and luckily, I had another helmet. She came back down just as fast as she had gone up to the house and we were off. We stopped off at a place down the street called the Chicken Shack or something like that, where we grabbed a bite to eat and spent some time together to get more acquainted with each other.

She asked a lot of questions and the one of her many questions... I had lied about, which regarded my dad. I lied and said that he was dead; not explaining that he had abandoned me, which I wanted to keep private, at the time. She seemed to have accepted that and then went on asking about my mother and then she wanted to meet her. I asked her if she wanted to go right then, and she said, "Yes?" So, we left and headed straight to my mother's where we visited for a while and then my mother slipped up and mentioned whether I had gone by my dad's yet or not. I was taken back and caught in a lie and I believe this is when we said our good-byes and prepared to leave, beside it was beginning to get dark and I needed to head out and get Joyce home before night-fall.

I explained that I had an electrical problem on my bike that would not allow the battery to charge, which I intended to get taken care of, but hadn't had the time to do so, as of yet. I also explained that if I turned on my lights, it would drain the battery almost immediately, killing the bike where I would be unable to ride it or even take her home. So, we headed out to the bike and I climbed on first, as Joyce was saying good-bye and putting on her helmet. As she did, I began backing up the bike to turn it around to take off, but as I did the chain literally fell off the bike's back sprocket and just hung there... unable to engage. I leaped off the bike in disgust and disbelief that this even happened and as I did, I noticed the master link lost its pin which held the chain together.

Joyce asked me, "What are we going to do?" With it being so late and there wasn't much else, I could do. I couldn't really call anyone and didn't have any tools. So, being an engineering design drafter and having a creative mind, I made like MacGyver would do; I compromised. I assessed the problem and realized I just needed a pin to replace the one lost, so I looked at Joyce and asked Joyce, "Do mind if I have one of those hairpins that you're wearing." She looked at me with this puzzled look and asked why, as if this was going to help. I explained the situation, and that it should hold as long as I drive slow and easy without any sudden jerks that could shear the pin and she said, "Alright" and she gave me one of her hair pins. She must have thought I was nuts, but it worked, until I could fixed it later.

In the meantime, Joyce and I headed for her place and it was getting dark so I decide to take a shortcut. I turned on what I thought to be a road I had used once before, but I mistakenly turned down the wrong road. As, we progressed down this road, I actually found myself to be headed in an area that was one of those, less than desirable area's to be in, especially at night. There was a group of guys or a gang of sorts that saw us easing down their street and they began yelling profanities at us and lifted old car tires of all things, up, over their shoulders and slug them forward, trying to slam them into us, or scare us.

I couldn't believe these guys were trying to knock us off the bike and they probably would have beaten us for being in their neighborhood, but I managed to swerve back and forth enough; giving it, just a little more gas, knowing anymore could have snapped that pin. Joyce was afraid and squeezing me so tight, but I felt better knowing we cleared the area, as we continued on down the road. It was only moments later, when I realized it was a dead-end; finding ourselves at a public neighborhood school.

All I could think of is... now what? There was no place to go but to turn around in the direction we just came from and I could see those guys were expecting us, but first, we came up to an intersection separating us which I drove through the first time. So, I turned to the right without stopping at the stop sign. Afterwards, and headed over one block and turned to my left, which put us running parallel to their street, which we were trying to avoid. As we continued to work our way back to the street we had originally turned from, these guys appeared again, passing through the yards to head us off. They were running toward the street, with their tires on their shoulder to toss at us again, but I managed to give the bike just enough gas to pass by them without any confrontation or without breaking that hairpin... thank God. By this time, it was already dark and I had to drive without any head-lights because my bike would have died had

I turned them on, as I said earlier. It was scary, but we rode that whole adventure without any head-lights across town including on the interstate; back to Joyce's mom and dad's place. Thank you Jesus for protecting us, and getting us home safely.

After I pulled up to let Joyce off, she took off her helmet and as she did, I thought to myself; Man, I blew this one, but I'd never really know, unless I asked. So, I started out with an apology for taking the wrong turn and then I said, "I don't suppose you would ever consider going out with me again, would you?" Much to my surprise! She said, "Yeah, but only if, you don't take me for another joy ride like that again... and get those lights fixed." I agreed and called it a night and went home.

It wasn't too much longer after that when we began seeing each other on a regular basis. I wanted her to know where I was going if she was expecting me, so I stopped by to explain that I was going dirt riding. I just wanted her to know where I'd be, not expecting to take her with me, but she seemed disappointed, So I did the unthinkable, I invited her, not expecting her to say okay to something she had never done. She didn't have a clue, as to what she was getting into. I should have explained it to her in more detail, but I just assumed she knew without a second thought and if not? Well, I'd just have to take it nice and slow, and real easy with the two of us, riding double. We fastened our helmets and were off, heading down the highway, making a turn off the main drag where we came up to a clearing in the trees with a path leading to where we were going.

The place we were going was off Mo-Bottoms Road, which was right next to the Missouri River leading toward the Mississippi River and I am positive it is still there. These hills are hidden by a wooded area that run right along the side of the Missouri River and are some of the biggest dirt hills in the area with jumps where you literally fly through the air with a hang time that was a blast, depending on how fast you hit the jumps. These jumps vary from small to huge and begin along the path leading down to the big ones! So we exited the off the road into this little clearing and preparing to enter into this wooded area having a very narrow path with lots of trees we would have to dodge, to keep from running into them. Also, there would be small jumps or dips in the pathway, as well as obstacles, like fallen trees or branches which we may be able to go over and if not; go around... to avoid them, but that was part of the fun. I mentioned... she may want to hold on tight as we entered into the woods. I wasn't worried about a thing and new these woods well at the time and besides; I was proud of this bike and knew it would make the trip, just fine. We headed down the winding paths of trees and went up and down and all around as we went deeper and deeper into the woods. The trees cast dark shadows all around us and the sun-light tried to break through, giving us just enough light to see the path and obstacles as they came into view, such as a tree... lying across our paths.

There was dirt piled up against the downed trees on both sides, so we could leap over tree trunk. Most jumps were small and easy but it was then I realized that there is no such thing as easy, if you're going to make these jumps. They had to be hit some of them hard and fast, if I was going to clear them.

Some of these obstacles were easy while others were not, as were the dips that immediately dropped off, only to lift us back up onto the path again, but finally we come out of the wooded foot hills into a huge clearing and we weren't alone. There were probably 10 or 12 other bikers there at the base of some of the biggest hills around; reaching 100 to 200 feet high and having an incline of 70 to 80 degrees; almost straight up; a real challenge. Some bikers were already at the top and coming back down.

At the very top of these hills... they drop-off almost straight down from where the ledge was, which ran the full-length of the hills. They appear to be sheared off all along this top edge. This hill again, drops almost straight down and runs along-side the river without any transition along the top and was very dangerous. So, dangerous that someone... either by hand or by using a shovel; carved or dredged out a passage that rounded-off the ledge. This was to allow the bikers to have the means of following through to the top of the hill and to prevent their bike from flipping back, landing on the top of them; crushing them.

This dredged out area eliminated one problem, but because it was such a narrow passage, it created another. It created a wall with only 8 or 9 inches clearance on either side to pass through and this passage was 8 or 10 feet long along the base as it passed through the walls of this cliff. Most people are good enough to ride through the passage without any problems, but one day a guy named John wasn't so lucky and didn't make it, which is why they call this particular hill, "John's Coffin." He had actually clipped the side of the dredged out area's wall, while passing through the cliff with his handle bars; dis-engaging the clutch that slowed down his momentum; killing the engine. This prevented him; from make it to the top nor gave him the ability to turn around.

He was trapped within the dredged out confines of an area and to keep from rolling down-hill backwards, he did the unthinkable. He hit his back brakes; flipping his bike over on top of him; crushing his chest and dying from his injuries.

I shared this story with Joyce and she wanted to know what I was going to do and I said, we're going to the top, so you better hang on as I hit the throttle. I couldn't open it all the way because of a dip at the base of the hill but once we were over it... I opened it up all the way and everyone must have thought I was crazy. It's hard enough doing this with one person on a bike, but two? Unbelievable! They all watched, as Joyce and I leaned so far forward, I was lying across the handle bars in a standing position and she was standing on her pegs hanging onto me for dear life screaming... "I want my mommy." But we made it all the way up there and she said, "Okay, I'm ready to go home now." I asked, "Really?" Okay, but there's only one-way down... Zooomm. Actually, I took the long way down for her sake. This must have been when she decided this bike had to go.

She obviously forgave me and must have loved me because eventually, I was invited to have dinner with her and her family one Sunday, and this too, began being a regular event. It was nice to just sit there and listen to the family converse and burst into laughter, without any yelling or fighting. This is truly something I do not ever remember experiencing growing up or even having family dinners, except for once or twice, like the time we ate my pet chicken, Peaty.

As the conversations continued, I just sat there listening and taking it all in. There was Joyce, her mom and dad, two sisters and a brother always together for dinner. Joyce told me that she had two older brothers too, but that they were serving in the Navy and then I mentioned to everyone that I was in the Navy too. They wanted to know more and I explained to them that I was released early because of a medical condition. It was something to do with my back that I didn't even know about it and it didn't bother me, because it got me out early with an Honorable Discharge, as a SR and only after serving 35 days.

They wanted to know too, where I worked and where I lived; whether I was on my own or still living at home with my parents. I told them I was 19; knowing Joyce was just sweet-sixteen, but a real sweetheart; so innocent and pure and I just wanted her in my life. I was hoping they wouldn't hold my age against me and I'm sure they wondered about me dating their daughter who was three years younger than me, but they themselves were three years apart. Joyce's mom was actually three years older than her dad, so I suspect, I was acceptable. Plus, I may have impressed them with the fact that I was part of the Aerospace Program; working at McDonnell Douglass Aircraft, which is now owned by Boeing Aircraft. I told them that I had been working on the Skylab Orbital Space Station, as an Engineering Design Draftsman, and had worked at Emerson Electric prior to that. I mentioned that I have basically been on my own since I was fifteen and spent two years in school taking up Advanced Drafting; receiving a Gold Sealed Certificate upon graduating. I also, finished my high-schooling in the Job Corps by acquiring a GED. I mentioned too, I have been on my own for years and was room and boarding with a family, I come to know from church.

They asked about my parents and I mentioned my mom and dad had divorced and that my mom remarried and that I didn't have a dad, and Joyce jumped in and said, yes you do! So, I apologized and explained to them why I said what I did, and explained my past. What they didn't know is that Joyce and I were getting pretty serious and discussed marriage among ourselves, so after dinner, Joyce insisted on meeting my dad. So, we set out to see my dad which had been almost five years since I had seen him last. So, there I was on my way up to my dad and Wilma's front door with Joyce beside me. I knocked on the door and we waited and waited, and finally Wilma answered the door by opening it. She obviously recognized me standing there and without smiling, saying or nodding hello or anything; she just closed the door in our faces with a blank expression on her face. I said, "Well, so much for that" and took Joyce by the hand and headed for the bike. As I did, I explained... that was Wilma!

I explained, I'm not welcome here and my dad probably doesn't want to see me anyway. So, as we were preparing to put on our helmets, my dad walked out from the side of the house and said, "Yeah Doug, what do you want?" I said, "Well, this is Joyce, the girl I plan on marrying someday and I came by to introduce you to her and visit for a while." My dad said, "That's nice. Well, today's my birthday and Wilma invited over some friends and is throwing me a party, so I've got to get back inside." After saying that... he turned around and left. Now, I don't recall a good-bye or anything else being exchanged, other than that of a cold shoulder. I apologized to Joyce and said, "This is why I say, I didn't have a dad." I had no idea... what day was my dad's birthday. I mean; how would I possibly know? I was an outcast and he had a great way of telling me. I may have said Happy Birthday, but it didn't cross my mind, especially after what he had said, only to turn around and walking away, as if I were a stranger.

Joyce was nice to me about the whole incident and said that at least, she did get to see him and that it was okay, just knowing that I have made an effort to reconcile with him. Personally, I think she just wanted to see what I'd look like at that age. She did tell me that though that she like the name Doug over Dion and decided to stop calling me Dion any longer, a nick name I'd taken on to distance myself from my dad. So, so much for that part of life that I was clinging on to and eventually, my dad and I did get back together, but not before Joyce and I were married. Joyce's mother and dad, as was my mom and Gil... were invited to our wedding, but as for my dad and Wilma? They wondered why they weren't invited but I think they were smart enough to figure it out. Besides, I wanted our marriage to have a positive start and it did after 11 months of dating each other and the Lord has truly blessed both of our lives, even up to this very day. Think about it... destiny united us as one, and had I not hooked up with Benny, I would not have joined the Navy or met Terry, whom I took for a walk in St. Louis, getting a ride with Joe, who introduced Terry to Joyce, who then left town for Wood Stock; opening the door for us to date and then getting married? WOW!

Benny even did me the honors at my request of buying me an over-sea's; "Blue Diamond – Engagement and Wedding Ring." The set was much less than I could buy in the states, and as for God? I really believe our destiny was planned for the two of us.

You may not know it yet, but in this great big Universe, so massive and so ever expanding; God is right here with us, and we don't have to... or need to worry about tomorrow, or what it brings. For I believe in what the Word says;

> **Matthew 6:34:** *Take therefore no thought for the morrow: for themorrow shall take thought for the things of itself. Sufficient unto the day is the evil thereof.*

Another way to look at it is; there's no need to worry, because God is already there and has everything under His control and He's always with us, as he says; "Lo, I am with you always."

Families Beginning

After Joyce and I married I continued working at McDonnell Douglass in St. Louis and the money I brought home weekly was pretty good at $52 weekly. All I could afford at the time was a basement apartment which we called home that cost us $25 a week and I remember the very first dinner she made me on our first night together. We had Pork Chops, mashed potatoes, green beans and biscuits. The Lord truly has blessed me with a wonderful wife and she's absolutely beautiful; inside and out, and she's smart, caring and a great cook! What a treasure she has been to me and I'm sure she feels the same way toward me.

Joyce did not start birth control pills until after we were married, so nine months into our marriage, we were expecting a baby. We both decided to quit smoking at that time to protect the baby, but she was still smoking... secretively, and I had heard smoking was unhealthy for the baby. This is why we were to quit smoking, but when I come home; I could smell tobacco.

When I questioned her about it; she lied saying "No, I haven't been smoking." But, on this particular day when she made that statement, something come over me and led me into the kitchen where I went straight to the silverware drawer. Now this apartment only had a living room, bedroom and kitchen with a small dinette area plus the bathroom, and the chances of me knowing exactly where to look were pretty slim. As I said though, I felt led to march into the kitchen. I then opened the silverware drawer and what should I find in the very back of this drawer, but a packet of cigarettes? I pulled them out laughing and tried to scolding her for lying, as I crushed them in front of her; telling her, "no smoking!" Joyce sheepishly laughed as she asked, "How did you know... how, did you know?"

My answer then, as it still is today; is that I'm not sure, except that something inside me, told me to look there. It must have been the Lord and only then did she quit smoking. I'm glad she did because she gave birth to Valerie Lynn, a beautiful, 9-pound girl. Valerie was to be born on March 1st but she was moved forward in error, to Valentine's Day. Valerie appeared to be stubborn and a couple days later, the doctor broke Joyce's water bag and she was in labor for 36 hours; 32 of which, was hard labor. The doctor apologized and said he was wrong; March 1st was the correct date, but Valerie waited until the 19th. Immediately after her birth I was allowed to hold her and I was shocked saying, man she's ugly. They used forceps during delivery and Valerie's head was still malformed and collapsed, having a white thrush and blood all over her. I'll never live that one down, but she cleaned up nicely. I'd hate to think what she would have weighed... March 1st. Today though, she's as pretty as her mother and a far cry from anything, but beautiful. God has blessed her well, as well as her mother and I, who have been blessed with good looks, but more importantly, God's blessings.

Last Spin

Just before Valerie was born, I received a raise which was nice and then another after her birth. I also, just finished having my motor cycle rebuilt and painted a mid-night blue with white lace trim. It was so beautiful and I had someone we knew that wanted to buy it for the amount I quoted in jest and Joyce knew how much I loved this motor cycle, but a decision had to be made. It was our only means of transportation and to sell it would mean that I would be taking the bus or car-pooling with someone for a while. We both knew it was essential to sell, because the basement apartment would not do for a new-born, so I sold it with Joyce's approval and a promise that I could buy another bike at a later date. Of-course that time has never come, but the stipulation on selling the bike was, come that next Saturday, I was to take it out for one last run... and it was agreed.

This is why I told you about John's Coffin. Yes, this is where I went to have one last blast, running up that hill. Everything was perfect and the bike was like brand new and handled with perfection. As I went through the pass at the top of the hill, I too, like John... hit the left wall of the cliff and my clutch; disengaging it and my bike stalled as it re-engaging. I squeezed my legs around my 345 pound bike as it was dropping and I braced myself with my hands. All I could think of was; do not touch the brakes, as the weight of the bike fell with the handle bars coming to rest across my upper thighs. My hands were slipping, so I was forced to position my feet against both of the cliff sidewalls.

I knew what this meant and I looked down through my legs and could see the crowd gathering below and even the crowd couldn't help me, now. I was on my own and scared, but I kept my cool while trying to figure a way out of this predicament. I didn't have the strength in my arms to carry both my weight and the bikes too, or long enough, to release the bike which I didn't want to do. It was already sold and on loan to me one last time, so that idea was out of the question. Also, my bike was a kick start and oh, how I wished it were one of those electric starts.

My circumstances didn't look good, but then again, something inside me told me exactly what I had to do. So I went with it and rotated the throttle back twice, as if to be feeding gas into the engine. This was done, just to prime the engine before starting. Then I reached under my right leg, just beneath the handle bars that were resting on my crotch; carrying the load equally, onto each leg. With the weight being evenly distributed to each foot wedge into the cliff wall of the passage; allowing me to maintain balance. I squeezed the clutch with my left hand and managed to reach the foot lever with my right hand and used it to kick start the bike. It took two tries but it fired right up and my bike had knobby-tires that were made to dig into the dirt, so I opened up the throttle and the bike lifted slowly from my lap where I could now lay on the seat of the bike and used my legs to help me walk to the top of the hill. Wow! After that episode I went straight over to the owner's house and gave him the key and collected my money. Things could have turned out a whole lot worse, but worked out perfectly. Also, there is absolutely, no doubt in my mind that the Lord guided me through that little incident, thank you Jesus!

In Search of a Better Home

We took the money from the bike and signed a lease to move into our first apartment which was a single bedroom, but a good starter home and then one year later; a 2-bedroom apartment. We also, bought our first car, which was a 1965 white Pontiac Tempest convertible with a black-top, lite-blue interior and it had a small V-8 engine with only 215 cubic inch engine. Wow, it was super nice and just what we needed for our family and things finally appeared to be moving upward in a positive direction in our lives. We were happy and I was still working at McDonnell Douglass on the Space Shuttle Proposal Project at the time, and only so many people were part of the team. As the proposal date grew nearer; we had 4-weeks to complete and submitted the proposal to Washington DC. We were asked to work unlimited overtime with stress that was, almost intolerable.

Joyce was not happy being stuck at home with a crying baby and no help from my end and still being a new wife; less than 2-years. I was committed in doing this job, in hopes to continue having a means of employment with this company and I only came home to sleep. Once, after only 5 or 6 hours sleep; I got up dressed, had a bite to eat and prepared to leave, yet again.

Most people working on this proposal were working 120 to 125 hours a week and I tried to explain this to Joyce, but to no avail. We had no time for each other and maybe seen one another, for only 10 or 15 minutes a day when I wasn't sleeping. I was literally out of it and she was at her limits. I told her these hours would only last for a couple more weeks and then we'd have to submit the job and we either win this contract or we lose it and if we did? Well, this means I, along with thousands of others would be looking for a new place of employment.

Afterwards, I said my good byes and said, "I'll see you tomorrow" which was just a repeat of what she had been experiencing for the last couple weeks. She was so furious; she began screaming for me not to walk out that door, so I turned back around, to face her. I wanted to show some compassion and tell her I loved her, and to apologize, but that I had to go to work. It was then she grabbed our clock radio and hurled it at me and it was coming right for my face. I was so tired and exhausted; I just didn't care and stood there with my arms down.

I expected to be slammed in the face, knowing this would give me good excuse not to come in that day, but wouldn't you know it... it was plugged in. It was within inches from hitting me in the face and stopped dead in the air, and then fell to the floor. Joyce covered her mouth with both hands as she gasped in disbelief of what she had just done; thinking she had hit me. Now, Joyce is not a monster; I just had obligations as a husband and a father, and she was carrying on the load at home, all alone but Joyce came running around the bed in disbelief of what she just done, crying as she run up to me; apologizing and wanting to see, if I was okay. I wanted to stay home so much, but couldn't.

As most people, holding a job; I had obligations and not only to her, but to others depending on me. We hugged and held each other for a few minutes as we both cried together and kissed one another to make up. It was hard on her but sometimes I think it was harder on me, but I had to meet our needs to survive as a family. As much as I wanted to stay home, I just couldn't at this time. I was the provider, but wouldn't have been very good at it had that clock radio hit my face. So, I'm sure it was the Lord who helped with the specification on the clock's... cord length, because if it had an additional inch or two longer, it would have hit me. Thank you, Jesus and know this; I know that I know that I know that I know that the Lord... is always watching over me.

Well, McDonnell Douglas did lose that contract and had a major layoff, but I managed to find a temporary job, as an apartment maintenance man. I learned how to fix things that would save us money in the future by doing our own repairs, I wouldn't have otherwise known. One day though, Gill called me and asked, "Are you working, yet?" He was referring to the profession that I followed him in. I said, "No." He said, "Well, pack up and come on down to Florida... I have a job for you, working at the same company I'm with." I was surprised and I went home to tell Joyce that we had to pack up because we were moving to Florida. I explained that I'd be making more than twice what I was making. So, we agreed and packed-up everything we had into an 8'x12'x6'tall U-Haul and we were off.

Florida Bound
....

I had little or no choice, but to take I-55 Southward, toward Memphis but unable to do so safely, because it was near impossible to maintain the minimal speed limit posted at 45MPH on the Interstate. We were lucky, just to hit 40MPH on a straight-away while others traveled 70MPH or greater... putting us in danger. I tried going faster, but I just couldn't do it and I hadn't even hit the mountains yet. Then this crazy idea came to mind, which I decided to try. I wonder... from wince it came.

It was a means of going faster, but involved our ability to swing in behind an 18-wheeler, as it was passing by us. We had to do it quickly though and could only do this, if there weren't any other vehicles directly behind him. By doing this, we could catch the tail-wind that follows all big rigs when speeding down the highway, but you have to be fast or you'll miss it. You'll know when you're in the tail-wind immediately, because your vehicle speed will accelerate, as you're being drawn toward the back-end of 18-wheeler's trailer, and as for the driver? Well, he'll probably notice it due to your vehicle causing him to drag.

Needless to say, trucks get terrible gas mileage for starters. They tow such a heavy load and in reality, they can basically feel or sense the load behind them. This means sometimes they may feel the slightest deviation too, when something happens, such as when a tail-gaiter attaches to their tail-wind. They notice this because of the sudden drag and will need to accelerate, as to increase their RPM's; to maintain the level of speed they desire to maintain, which leads to less fuel efficiency. Some truckers don't mind or care while others do, and do-not like it.

Also, to maintain a good hold on the tail-wind that is coming from behind the truck; you have to be near their speed to swing in behind them and then hold on to that position, to maintain the drag. Otherwise, they can, and will break free from you; leaving you behind. So, as one can see; truckers don't like having a shadows following so closely behind, for obvious reasons. If not, for the fuel consumption... it's because, they can't see you, so beware of the dangers.

There's no guarantee that they'll notice the change, but because of insurance purposes, if they do? They may try to lose you, because of not knowing where you are or you're next move, which could prove to be dangerous for both of you, so you must be careful. To make this tail-wind work for you safely; you must maintain direct and constant contact with the trucks under-tow, which requires your total alertness, because should they tap their brakes; you better be able to stop and if they step on it; forget it.

You can try but when you feel the sudden surge in power that only grows stronger and faster.... they will pull away from you. You will need to react fast enough to accelerate from the sudden loss of power and need to hold the pedal down constantly and you cannot afford to be mesmerized, which can and does happen. This is why, you must be alert at all times and be able to break in a moment's notice or accelerate should they decide to lose you, or its... otiose amigos. The ride is over and the chance of catching another tail-wind may not happen anytime soon.

As I said earlier, I was lucky to hit 40MPH on a straight away and this is exactly what happened to me as I was being towed from trucks I had been following, which happen several times. My speed would pick-up and then, just drop off. Some truckers didn't mind and didn't try to break free except to exit, and then I was on my own again, in search of another. On our way to Florida in south Missouri, I took a chance on this slow moving flatbed hauling equipment. I swung in behind him as I had done before with other trucks and as I closed in, something didn't look right, almost as if something were loose on the flatbed.

It was then, at that very moment, almost as if someone said to me, "Move into the other lane!" So, I moved... immediately, and the object that appeared to be loose, bobbing up and down; broke free and come flying through the air off the back of the truck. Had I not moved; a steel plate about a 1/2" thick x 4 or 6 inch wide x 48 inch long would have come through our windshield, possibly killing, all of us. I also believe, it is the Lord who is protecting us and keeping us safe, as always. Thank you, Jesus.

It was then we stopped following trucks and exited I-55 to crossover the Mississippi River into Memphis and then take the Tennessee back roads. They crossed the mountains and were smaller, less trafficked back-roads and highways. They were mostly 2-lanes wide except for additional lanes added to allow for slower moving vehicles like ours, but primarily added for heavy loaded trucks; from blocking traffic. These roads went out of TN into MS and though AL into GA and due S on I-75 to FL.

We were heading into a little town East of Tampa on I-4 called Lakeland, where I had originally joined the Job Corps. Only by returning to Lakeland, I had made the loop; a complete circle which I had hopes of doing one day, by returning to Lakeland. What I didn't think about though was the effect it would have on Joyce. She had never been away from home before and she literally cried during the whole trip. I tried to comfort her but it didn't help. She was heartbroken and she was well aware that I wanted to return to Florida someday, but I don't believe she was expecting to do so, so suddenly.

This trip too, was a real test for our little 215 cubic-inch engine; that huffed and puffed all the way down. There were times though that I thought the car would stop dead in its tracks. I would hold the steering wheel with white knuckles and put the pedal to the floor, accelerating up to 70 or 75 mph down a long steep grade, hoping to God no one would pull in front of us and thank God... they didn't. It would have probably killed all of us, but it was the only way I could get enough momentum needed just to be able to get up the next mountain. As I climbed the mountains my speed slowly dropped, slower and slower to 65, 60, 55, 50 and then 45, 40 to 35; forcing me to drop the automatic transmission shifter into 2nd gear, and then it was 30, 25, 20 to 15 and then I dropped it into low gear and listened as my transmission whined, as hard as it could. My speed continued to lower yet again, to 10 and then to 5 mph. I was creeping so slow that even the slow moving trucks passed us, but finally we made it to the top, just to start it... all over again. We did this from one mountain to another, and so on, and so on.

It truly is a miracle that we even made the trip and God had to be watching over us. By all rights, this Tempest, really didn't have the right size engine or have a big enough transmission to achieve what I was trying to accomplish, but we did it. We kept that car for at least 2 or 3 years after the move, before trading it in and I still miss that car. It was one of the finest products GM ever made and was unbeatable. However, GM has since decided to discontinue the Pontiac line and others; a tremendous loss!

By the way, this U-Haul had no braking system and was so densely packed to the max, without any wasted space. Yet, we had so many other items that we took with us... that they over-flowed into the car. We filled the trunk and back seat entirely, including floor board space and the rear wind-shield; all the way up to the roof, except for one little small space where Valerie was lying in her pumpkin seat. Valerie was wedged into place, between items with her face only inches from the Convertible's canvas roof-top. We had other items stuffed between Joyce and me on the front seat and on the front passenger floor boards. We were packed so tightly, Joyce had to keep her feet on the dash.

It was a snug fit for the three of us as we were Florida bound and thank God, Valerie was not yet two. She slept most of the way, as I comforted Joyce; telling her she could visit her family any time, or they could come down and visit with us whenever they wanted to. She seemed satisfied knowing that this was an option. So, all appeared well, as we entered into Florida and we were greeted with plenty of liquid sunshine, more commonly known as rain. Eventually, the sun peeked through the clouds as we made it into what would eventually, be our permanent home; Florida! It's the state that is right next to being in paradise and we have claimed Florida as home, from that day forward.

CHAPTER 8

"Life Changing Events"

Hello Florida

So, it was February 1973 when we first arrived and moved in with my mom and Gil, and this was the beginning of calling Florida our Home. We unpacked and settled in and rested for a week before I reported to my new job assignment and Gil had mentioned this place paid well, so I met with them. I didn't want to appear greedy, but it says in the Word to ask and ye shall receive. So, I asked for a bit more than I made at McDonnell Douglas and thank God! I received exactly what I had asked for!

Gil said the three us could live in his place free of charge and to save our money, so we could buy our own place, which we did. We lived with him for at least 9 months and he paid for everything. I never knew Gil had such a big heart but my mom told me he had a lot of respect for me because I had decided to take up a career in drafting; following his footsteps. The only thing he did that we didn't do; smoke, swear and drink heavily.

Each week-end he would buy 2 quarts of bourbon which made some pretty potent drinks that lasted through the week-end and one more for week days. I didn't know why he drank so much, but his profanity was just as bad, which we didn't need to hear or have Valerie exposed to, but we couldn't really complain; we were his guest. It was free and only meant to be temporary. We saved as much money as possible and finally had enough put aside for a down payment on our first new home. It was a two-bedroom, one bath, 12'W x 65' long mobile home. All we had to do now was to wait for delivery that was going to take, too long; about one to two months to receive, so we waited.

Beware of "Ouija Boards

While we were still waiting on delivery on our trailer, Candy's birthday came up and she was turning 11 years old and with Gil being a drinker? Well, he stopped by and picked up his week-end supply of bourbon. He would refer to them as his girls and gave each of them names, but this time he was carrying Candy a gift. Gil fixed a drink and we sat down to enjoyed dinner as a family; topped off with a birthday cake. Then Gil excused himself to fix another drink and went into the living room carrying his drink and the gift. We finished and join him.

After we settled down and were all situated, Candy began opening her gifts. I'm sure Joyce and I bought her a gift as well, though I couldn't tell you what it was, if my life depended on it. This is because of the shock of the Gift Gil gave her; taking our minds off all other gifts. The primary reason is, as I've said before; Gil was a devout, hardcore Atheist, having absolutely zero tolerance on anything to do with God or Jesus. To mention either name... was strictly taboo, unless like him... we were to swear in their names and this is something we would never do, but he did regularly, when up-set. A good indicator that he was headed in that direction... was by the changing of the color in his face that went from a flush color into deeper shades of red until he was so beet red that his blood pressure would go through the roof. So, by being guest in his home, we honored his wishes to prevent any fights, for my mom's sake. Besides, our trailer's delivery was only days away and this was only a temporary arrangement as guest; abided by his rule, showing appreciation.

Well, I've had other encounter with Gil in years past and I wasn't about to start one now, so we all watched as Candy opened her gifts, saving the one Gil had gotten her... for last. When she opened Gil's, Joyce and I looked at each other in disbelief and somewhat shocked, as was my mother with a look of surprise. The gift she had opened revealed an "Ouija Board" of all things. I started to say something and Gil looked up at me and I could see that my mom knew what was about to happen.

She sat their quietly on the other side of Gil right next to him and gave me one of those looks like, what are you doing? It's just that knowing what the Ouija Board was, set with me completely wrong and I just had to ask or at least, say something.

So, as Gil was looking at me he asked me surprisingly politely, "What?" I made some comment question him saying, "A Ouija Board? Do you know what the Ouija Board is?" Now, I did it, and I could see that expression of disappointment in my mom's face; like, now you went and did it!

Well, Gil had been drinking, and with me questioning his knowledge, definitely put him in a defensive mode. This is when my mom began to ever so slowly, and quietly; lifting her hands and flagging them at me as she was shaking her head, as if to say, No, no... no; don't you do it, but my conviction, was so strong that I just had to say something. It was obvious too, that Gil was showing signs of anger and rage as his face began to turn to a flush color and this definitely triggered his defensive mode. It was obvious as he sat up on the edge of his chair in rage and anger, just as my mom had feared. Gil looked at me as if to say, you're challenging me? He then said, it's just a game!"

Now, this isn't reflecting what he actually said, something I can't and won't repeat. That's just the way he was and I hated to seem ungrateful for all he had done for us, but he needed to know or so

I felt lead to believe. So, I said, "No, it's not just a game, but it's a means of communication; spiritually, with spirits that are in hell." He said what I was saying... was a lot of bull, and that it was just a game. I said, "If, I were to prove to you that this is more than just a game then you will have to accept that there is a hell, because someone is going to give us the answers, to any question... you want to ask. He said all right then... then prove it to me!" as he flipped his cigarette case onto the table. "How many cigarettes do I have in here, smart ass?" In truth, that's just the way he said it and I know this will offend some of you but please, do continue. There is a reason this event took place and you will understand why I was lead this way.

I really appreciated Gil and liked him a lot for his interest in me, but I needed to prove a point to him, which may be why he was so unhappy and drank as he did. Gil just needed a reality check that there is a God! Therefore, there is a son; God's son, Jesus Christ... the only begotten son of God; the Creator of all things. How could he deny the existence of God or His son, Jesus Christ, if this would prove to him that someone somewhere would be answering all his questions, but from where?

Also, before I go any further, before you think I'm nuts, let me just say this. Earlier in life I had heard some pretty strange stories or testimonies from others who claimed some really weird events taking place, including the Ouija Board flying through the air and striking them, out of anger. I wasn't sure how this would turn out but I asked Joyce to pull up a chair in front of me and I placed the Ouija Board upon our laps.

I then summoned up some sprit that claimed to be a Native American only by her tribal name which I do not remember, so I began my questioning her asking, "Can you hurt us?" I was surprised to hear her say, "Yes!" Then I asked her, "Will you hurt us?" She said, "No!" Joyce and I looked at each other in amazement and I could see that Gil was now intrigued, watching us ever so closely, as we conversed. I asked what her name was and I believe her response was Hilda and then I asked her what she did while she lived here on earth and she claimed to have been a teacher among her people; teaching children many things in some strange land we never heard of before. She then said that she had died in the year of 1057 at the age of 54. I asked if it was hot where she was, out of curiosity and she said, "No, it's just dark." I then asked where her home was and she said some strange Indian sounding name again, we never heard of before. So I went on and asked her if she knew what it would be called today... in our time frame and she said, "Kentucky." It was then that I decided to ask her some questions and I asked her if she could answer them to prove to Gil, that she was real and that she was communicating with us and responded by saying, "Yes."

Now, for those of you who do-not know what or how the Ouija Board works or what it is, trust me... leave it alone! I can't stress this to you, enough. I tight roped or walked a fine line, like a child walking on top edge of a fence; a picket fence. I should not have done so, but I did this to prove to Gil without a shadow of doubt... that there is a God. I really loved this guy who took care of my mother and sister, including my wife, daughter and me. We deserve so little and had so much, and I had a window of opportunity and didn't want to miss it.

The best description I can give you of what the Ouija Board is, or what it looks like is this... and I'll try to describe it to you, as best I can. It looks like something you may have never seen before, for starters. It appears almost evil looking at first glance, yet intriguing enough, to draw you closer into it, to investigate. I believe this is why, so many people end up trying out the Ouija Board sooner or later and mostly, teenage children out of curiosity. It's this intrigue that causes them to investigate and once they realize what it is and what it claims to be; it becomes just a little, too scary for them, because it has become just a little, too close to reality. I imagine this is why you don't see or hear about many adults messing with the Ouija Board... or children. Most people have either matured enough and out grown it or decided that it's not worth messing with any longer; realizing exactly what it is; evil! Then again, there are those who have never heard about them or even seen one, especially in action!

The Ouija Board comes in many different concepts or forms. The one Gil gave Candy had a Large Eye-Ball in the center of the board. It also, had the word YES on either the upper-right or upper-left hand corner of the board and had the word "NO" on the adjacent corner. It also, had two rows of Alpha characters forming two separate arc configurations running parallel to each other, beginning with letters from A to M on the upper arc and N to Z on the second/lower, offset arc forming a frowning type curve, centered just above the eye... similar to an eyebrow. Just below the eye ball was a horizontal row of numbers beginning from 0 to 9, reading from left to right.

Together, the alpha and numerical characters appeared to form a border of sorts surrounding the eye that was located in the center of the board. It almost appeared to be as a frowning mouth with an eye-ball within this parameter, as best I can recall. I'm no expert and I'll have no intentions on ever touching another Ouija Board again and I strongly recommend that you never do so, either! It truly, is not a game but a very real means of communication with those that are not of this world, as unreal, as this sounds. Some are skeptical while others laugh it off, but in truth, it's a real means of communication with familiar spirits.

This board also comes with a detached, up-side down, heart shaped... plastic slide that has three pegs or post that drop down off the bottom for support with felt tips. Now this object is, the communications device which flows so freely across the face of the board as it locates each character to form a message or an answer to the question being asked. This device requires two adjacent people, to place four fingers from each hand on this object with the up-side down heart, pointing up-ward. One person is reading the board, up-right while the other person sits across from him; viewing the board up-side down, as their fingers rest upon this movable object. This object also has a clear plastic port hole in the center of it with cross-hairs, if I remember correctly and it allows the individual to view the numbers or alpha characters as they are displayed through this portal opening. As each of these characters is exposed, they will slowly reveal words, spelling out a message for you to read. As I said, you ever so lightly, press down onto this object and ask a question and then just sit back and watch the board do its thing.

At first, the slide begins moving slowly, almost so slowly with little tugs that you wonder if it is your partner moving it, and he claims that it's not him... and this thing continues to move on its own, it just seems so unreal and provides one, a very eerie feeling inside, but know this! This is real... very, very real; knowing that you're not moving this object and your partner swears that their not moving it, so then the question remains, who is? As crazy as this sounds; it's a familiar spirit.

It actually uses you and your partner's energy as the driving force, and the more you use it... the faster this object becomes, and more able to provide you a quicker answer to your question.

Children are usually the ones drawn to this board and are just that. They are children, so young; naïve and innocent, and they are intrigued by almost everything in life, until they discover what it is. In this case, they may rebuke it knowing it to be evil for what it is, never to return to it again. It could be something they tired of, out of boredom or it literally, just spooked the heck out of them and frightened them so much so they leave it alone.

The Ouija Board however, is actually different. It is a spirit driven device by familiar spirits and can cause them to do several things. It can and will draw them back to the board for hours, days or weeks and in some cases, even months, if not longer. They can even become so familiar with a person that this person will lose their fear of whom they're speaking to. So, what they have basically done, is befriended a familiar spirit that has no plans in leaving. This is not a good thing!

When this person comes to realize that this spirit is there waiting for their beckoning call each time he's or she returns to the board; they're summoning a spirit and not a friend and it will do whatever it can say or do, to amaze any one and eventually, their hooked. One thing is certain and that is when these spirits find a home, they're not easy to get rid of. You must rebuke them in the name of Jesus and preferably destroy the board.

Otherwise, as I said, each time this Ouija Board is addressed; familiar spirits attach themselves to the board and will still be there to pick-up the conversation with the person whom they were speaking to before. It will be as if, they were never away unless, another more powerful spirit should move in. It will lie to you and try to convince you that he or she is the same spirit you had been communicating with all along, but it won't take you, but a few minutes or so before you realize it isn't, because of the change in personalities, so just rebuke it in Jesus' name.

It doesn't take long to notice the difference in personalities' and the best thing you can do afterwards, is to literally destroy the Ouija Board, ASAP and the sooner, the better!

These spirits again, are very real and very dangerous; more so than most realize. It also states in the Word of God not to have anything to do with them or those who deal with them, which I didn't know at the time, so again the best thing to do is to leave them alone and rebuke them and destroy the board so you or anyone else will not be unable to communicate with them. This is because spirits really do follow these boards around to peer out of their world of darkness into our world of light through a porthole... on the face of the board.

There are those who would shrug or laugh this off as being a fake and then will not be willing to give it another try, maybe because in reality, they know something about it just isn't right and have enough sense to leave it alone, because it truly will draw you into its presence, if you allow it too, but don't! It is, evil; a form of witchcraft or sorcery of sorts; strictly forbidden in the Scriptures for a reason, and now you now... believe it or not.

I never claimed to be the brightest kid on the block and by not really knowing the scriptures then, as I do now is no excuse, but I didn't haven't enough since to leave well enough alone and wanted to prove a point to a man I admired considerably and wanted to open his eyes to the reality that there is a God and that God is very real and that there is a hell which I didn't really want him to be damned to, for an eternity due to a lack of knowledge. There is an old saying that says; you can't teach an old dog, new tricks. I suppose this is why the older people are harder to convince... than those receiving God, at an early age.

Now, that I have explained that to you let me finish where I left off. Joyce and I went ahead and asked this familiar spirit; Hilda, the original question Gil asked, as to how many cigarettes were in his cigarette case and she said she couldn't see them. I said, "Hey Gil, you're going to have to take them out of the case for her to see them." which he did objectively.

Then she responded by spelling out another statement saying something was keeping me from seeing them and again I said to Gil, "Hey man, you're going to have to open up the pack, if you want her to count them... she can't see them." By now Gil becomes real indignant swearing vulgarity at me, saying well then you'll be able to see them, but we couldn't because he faced them toward himself and yet again, she said she couldn't see them. After objections and our promises not to be looking; he finally turned them around facing the board where we could see them, if we wanted to, but we didn't look. She went ahead and gave us the answer, but Gil was still skeptical and didn't believe us, so I asked her another question. I asked why she couldn't see the cigarettes originally, when opened facing the other way, as I placed my hand over the eye in the center of the board out of curiosity. I also asked as I did this, if she could see when I did so, which was to cover the eye ball on the middle of the board. I then put my hands on the indicator and it went straight to the word, NO! I then knew what to do next.

Gill had witnessed what had taken place and watched as we conversed, after which I said, "Hey Gil, write a number down on a sheet of paper but do so, as not to let us see it and then hold the piece over paper up-side down over that eye." and he did. This board not only gave him an answer, not once or twice, but three consecutive times using a greater number each time for 2,3 and 4 or more numbers, which were correctly answered... without fail. I could see Gil was a little dumb founded in disbelief and I had to say something.

So, I said, "Well Gil, now that I proved to you that there is an evil realm; you have to believe there is a God, because as and educated person, you know for every action, there is an equal reaction similar to a magnet, or anything else. This should prove that there must be someone giving you the correct answers and if she's in hell then you know there must be a God. After that, he went straight to his bedroom swearing and cursing saying, "It's only a game." I figured that was another lost argument and never brought it up, again. I could only hope the best for him.

Years later though, my mom shared he died in the hospital and was about to leave this world and said he smiled, closing his eyes; saying, "Here he comes." And he passed away. She gave me his briefcase with all his professional belongings that I could use. Much to my surprise... was a New Testament. Phrase God! It blew me away! I'd like to think God used us to reach him, but Joyce and I, rebuked that Ouija Board and all evil spirits in the name of Jesus and will never touch another one... ever again!

In-Laws Visit
....

Right after the Ouija Board incident; our trailer deal finally came through and we moved out from under Gil and mom's roof into our own home, never needing their assistance again. We lived in a trailer park at first and then moved onto 2½ spacious acres within the Green Swamp, located on the out skirts of Lakeland, within Polk County, Florida. We were alone in the middle of the Green Swamp. I'd go to work leaving Joyce home with Valerie who wasn't in school as of yet. I noticed that Joyce missed her family and I felt really bad about taking Joyce from her parents. So, to help out, I flew her home to see her family just to prove to her she could see her parents whenever she wanted. Shortly afterwards, Joyce's dad came to visit us and fell in love with the climate and had Joyce's mother fly down to visit during his stay. It was in March or April and they both loved it. It was the perfect time of year for anyone to be introduced to Florida and they loved it so much that the next thing I knew was come summer; I flew one-way to St. Louis while her dad flew down. He was a disabled veteran and couldn't make the trip by car, so he flew while I drove Joyce's mother and youngest sister (Linda) down in a Ryder Truck with the car buckled down inside and both the truck and the car was fully loaded, inside the truck.

By then Joyce and I moved the trailer into a small community within Lakeland city limits on a lot of land that we rented just a half-mile from where I was working. We all lived in our little 2-bedroom trailer until they could find their own place. This was what Gil had done for us and we did the same for her parents. We even gave them the master bedroom while Linda bunked in with Valerie who was only three years old while Joyce and I slept on the sleeper sofa. It was like this for 2 or 3 months but everyone seemed happy, and as long as Joyce was happy, I was happy. Actually, everyone seemed delighted, just being together.

We wanted to start going to church and Joyce wanted me to become a Lutheran, so I decide to, but eventually I decided against it. I was willing when we first got married, but it wasn't working. We should have talked to one another first before we married, as should all people, before making the life-time commitment in marriage, but we didn't. So, we postponed church until we decided, we as a family needed to. So basically, we more or less, didn't bring it up during our early years in marriage and yes, we believed in, and loved God, but mostly, we ignored church, which was about to become... a real problem.

Joyce's mom and dad finally found the right trailer and bought it, which I help set up and landscape. Then Joyce was expecting again and that's when Veronica was born and note; I really do love both my daughters but I wanted a son so bad that I insulted Joyce in the recovery room, being so young and dumb.

I just didn't think about it or know any better, but guys; "Please, don't ever do this." As she was in the recovery room, I said to her, "Honey I'm sorry, but it's another girl, we can try again later." What a Jerk I was. That was a heartless thing to say, at the least. I didn't realize it or even consider how much she had suffered... and gone through, for me; for us! I know now, but I didn't know then how unappreciative and heartless I really was. It was always about me, me, me, as she had said, and she truly deserves better than me, but I have tried through the years to make sure she realizes that she truly is the love of my life, my queen and so much more.

Stress of Marriage

Joyce had been raised Lutheran and I was raised Baptist. The chances of us two even getting married to one another I suppose was off to a rough start. I had shared my experience with her about my past as a Baptist and she wanted nothing to do with the Baptist... and no, it wasn't the Baptist Church's fault. It was the pastor who was a little rough on the judgmental side, especially when we all know that there is really, but one judge only. For the record; I've forgiven this pastor, only he's never heard from me personally or seen me since. I truly would greatly welcome the opportunity to do so in person, but unable to locate him.

It was after Veronica was born, we made the decision to start going to a local Lutheran Church here in Florida; knowing our children needed to come and know the Lord. I even committed myself to attending their classes in order to become a member of the church, not knowing communion was a closed door policy.

So, I believe, it was during an Easter Service when they were having communion and I waited in line like everyone wishing to participate. I was happy and content being back in church. I had been going to church before Joyce and I married, but just drifted away for some reason. So, here I am next in line to receive communion and then it's my turn. I stepped-up in position and receive communion and moved on making way for the next person, not knowing better and never participating in this custom before, but the end result was good. I partook of what the Lord has instructed us to do in remembrance of him and I felt great.

When I went to the next class to study I had my bible with me and was asked by the pastor to step into his office for a moment, which I did. I sat down and was instructed that to keep from creating a spectacle during services that he permitted me to partake in communion. I wasn't chastised though, and instructed that I was not to do this again, until I receive confirmation of being accepted into the church, which would only happen, after attending classes.

I had a hard time understanding and didn't mean to be rebellious, but it is my nature and when I have a different point of view, and I'm not afraid to stand up on a soap-box and give my opinion when I believe I'm right. Especially, when I feel I'm in line... with the Word of God.

I opened my bible to where Jesus instructed the CHURCH! The church is the body of Christ; that's you and me, and He instructed us to do this often in remembrance of him. He suffered a great beating and shed of his blood for the remission of our sins and died on the cross for you and me; and rose again on the third day. He defeated death and took away all our sins. This was accomplished only through God's love, mercy and grace, so that by accepting Jesus that we would have Eternal Life. This was only made possible by the Gift of God; Jesus Christ, our Lord and Savior, and it is Jesus who truly was the Worlds very first Christmas Gift,,, to take away the sins of the World. So, by my acceptance of Jesus as my Lord and Savior, I am saved and a born again as a Christian, which I explained to this pastor. I was upset and gave him no slack and hit him with both barrows as I opened the bible to the precise passages just as I needed them to prove my case. Then it was explained to me that he understands, but still, I could not and would not be permitted to have communion, again. I was instructed not to make an effort to do so, until I was confirmed as a Lutheran, because he would not serve me.

I couldn't believe it and I said, "But I'm a Christian" and the Pastor said to me, "It doesn't matter... you have to be a Lutheran first." I said, "Well, you just put your religion above Jesus Christ and I'll have no part of this church and I stood up and kicked the dust from my feet and walked out... never to return, again.

I know this may sound somewhat harsh, but all religions seem to think they have a monopoly on religion, but not all saints attending their institutions are there because of religion. They're there because they want to be; to pay respect to God and honor Jesus with their love and praise, as they should. If, brothers and sisters in the Lord are doing this, then hallelujah!

We must understand too, that we are there for the Lord and not religion. Atheism is a religion, but as for me and my family, we will serve the Lord; the Father, the Son and the Holy Ghost!

I too, will call no man father as instruct by the Word, The Word... being Jesus; the son of God; King of Kings, Lord of Lords. He is not a religion. He is a person, the Son of God, the Alpha and the Omega, the Lion of Judah and greater is he that is in me than he that is in the world. In short, let me ask you this... Got Jesus? If, you don't; well, don't leave Earth without him, especially without his Holy Spirit... for, ye must be Born Again!

When I got home and explained why I came home early and what had transpired. I may as well have kicked Joyce in the face. She was furious with me. I tried to explain to her what I did, which according to the Word, and is totally acceptable, but she comes from a devout Lutheran faith family and as for me. Gee, I sure know how to overturn an apple cart, but I made a stand for what I believed to be true and in line with the Word of God. This however, appeared to be just the beginning of the end of our marriage and again, love is like a triangle; the Love Triangle, where God must be on top and we should be side by side. Otherwise, our marriage may fail and we were so far away from each other and God; our marriage collapsed and flat-lined.

SEPARATION
....

One may think separation is more than one sided, but sometimes... the partner may not even be aware of the issue. I'm sure too, that there was more to our separation than I'm mentioning but personally, I believe the major cause of separation between my wife and I was the lack of God in our marriage. I also, believe that Satan took full advantage of our situation and used it against us. The word says that I am the man of the house, which I hold onto, as a final judgment, if need be, but I've always tried my best to keep my wife in my eyes and in my heart, as my Queen. She's more than just a Wife to me.

Joyce is my lover, she's my ole' pal, ole' buddy, ole' friend of mine, in whom I share anything and everything with, for when we were married, I believe in what the Word says; that we are united as one and shall remain as such, until death do we part. Also, God Hates Divorce!

> *Matthew 19:6* *Wherefore they are no more twain, but one flesh. What therefore God hath joined together, let not man putasunder.*

It was a typical night one evening, but then Joyce caught me completely off guard, as we called it a night. We kissed each other good-night and settled in. Then as always, I said I love you expecting her to respond, but there was no response. So, again, I said I love you and she had always responded by saying, I love you too, but tonight there was a silence. I thought maybe she didn't hear me, so I repeated myself a third time, just a tad louder, saying I love you and still there was only, silence.

I then realized, she may have intentionally not responded, so I thought I'd try again, only a little louder this time to make certain she heard me because I expected a response, unless she was up-set with me, so once again, I said to her; I said... I love you?. I then paused, waiting for a response and still there was no response. So, I rolled over to face her and asked, what's wrong? I said I love you. Don't you love me? It was dark and I could hardly see her face and there were tears in her eyes and she said, I don't know. I said, what do you mean, you don't know? Of course, you know. You love me, don't you? She said, I don't know... Maybe we should separate for a while. I was shocked.

Come to find out, I hadn't been paying much time or attention to her as I should have and it wasn't just her, but, Valerie and Veronica too. I was hardly ever home; working and attending night school to obtain an Engineering Degree. I was obviously, spending way too much time away from home. She was doing everything alone and I needed, to make a change and quit school. So, I Quit college that next day via phone and come that afternoon; ten of us were laid-off, due to the slowing economy.

This loss of job and the economy being so bad, affected our area so much so, I'd be leaving town, yet again. She decided to move in with her parents and needed to pack up everything soon.

The only words that came to mind, were GREAT, like this is really what I needed right now. So, I went back to the mobile home. It was now, just a trailer, because what I knew as our home, was no more. It was broken, as was my heart and our marriage. What I didn't realize at the time was just maybe, this is where God wanted us, but again, we weren't serving God.

Joyce came by the next day to finishing packing and I was there to help. I explained what had happened with my job and about quitting school, but that didn't change anything. In the mean time she began packing and separating the girls things. I asked her then, so you'll be staying at your mothers? She said, yes, but going to stay with Pam; her girlfriend, in Georgia for a bit, whose husband was in the military. They just moved onto the base which was where Joyce would be staying and naturally, I was not happy about it, nor could I do anything to stop this.

As she packed the box's I secretly slipped in things to stir-up her memories that would prove to be, to no avail at the time. Otherwise, I would have trashed them. Thank God she had them. As she continued packing she began sharing her plans and idea's, which I didn't want to hear; hoping they wouldn't work.

I had become a Professional, Contract Engineering Design Consultant/Draftsman; taking on short term contract assignments and need to be able to pack up and report to a job, over-night in some cases. I didn't always have the luxury of time to settle in except during spare time, which is usually, very limited. This is because most assignments are rush jobs, which is why they pay so well. Sometimes the money is good and sometimes not, but usually over-time was mandatory to get the job out, up, and running. Seldom, would I ever have time for anything else, but...

I came from a broken family and the last thing our children needed was not to have a mom or dad to tuck them in at night. What would have even been worse than that would be to have them grow up not having a sister to sleep with or to share life with in general. I knew this because I have been there, which caused me to make myself a personal promise; never to divorce my wife, if for nothing else... for my children's sake. But, I happened to really love my wife and children... a lot, and have literally put them above everything, unlike my mom and dad did. However, we weren't walking with the Lord, as we should have been. We had been trying, but to no avail. Our Love Triangle with God was totally up-side down. The further we pushed God out of our lives, the further we grew apart as each of us unknowingly fought to be on the top, as our love triangle; our trinity of unity with God, widened so much so, that we were separated already.

So, because we were separating, and I didn't want the girls to suffer the loss of a sister. I believed that the Girls needed to be kept together, if for nothing else, just to have each other for support while growing up and throughout life itself, which the family I had as a kid... never really had. I knew there would be a day when they would need each other and I didn't want be the one... preventing that from happening.

We should have prayed about it but we didn't because again, we weren't serving God, as we should have been doing all along; my fault. In fact I hadn't spoke to the Lord in a long time, forgetting what he had done for me in years past... how sad!

One would think I would have turned to him and maintained some sort of closeness, but I failed God, yet again. How many times will He forgive me? All I can say is, thank God for his never-ending love, mercy, and grace, and always being with me.

Joyce and I obviously had issues and couldn't see eye to eye or understand what was going on at the time other than we were separating; not legally, but separation... never the less.

During this process of separating, Joyce loaded up the girls and getting ready to leave. I was not a happy camper but I was going to be leaving town too, more than likely with the job market being so slow. So, out of frustration I said, "I hope you get a flat tire on your way out of town." Now, be careful how you use your tongue. It truly is a mighty instrument and as stated in the Word of God, we are made in his image and whatever we ask, even if we tell a mountain to move; it SHALL move! For one; to say this, or to say that, can be done through faith and confession, using the tongue, according to James;

> *James 3:10* *Out of the same mouth proceedeth blessing and cursing. My brethren, these things ought not so to be.*

Now, I didn't curse at Joyce but I must have said something to her apparently and didn't realize the power of the tongue at the time. I'm sure you've heard the saying, "Be careful what you ask or say, because it may come true?" In this case it did. To lay claim to or speak out toward anything, as if it already happened or exist, is what is referred to as speaking out in faith; and faith is, believing, and believing is... expecting an action or event to take place. I made this claim when I said what I did to Joyce and I know that there are those who may not have faith enough to believe this can happen.

However, when my wife was departing with our girls, instead of saying have a safe trip; with me being so unhappy about the separation as I was; I said, "If, you get a flat tire... don't call me!" It was about 45 minutes later. Joyce called me from the other side of town and demanded to know what I had done to her car; reminding me of what I had said.

She thought I done something while she was packing, but I never left her side and she knew it. I asked her what she was talking about and she asked again, "What did you do? You must have rigged my car?" Then Joyce explained, "I have flat tire!" It was then like an idiot, I said well, you're on your own, and a big girl now, so you change it! Then I felt lead to hang up, so I did. I was truly amazed at what happened and then remembered.

I remember saying things to various local companies that have taken advantage of my wife or me in years past. The people that managed these companies along with their practices were up-setting. They knew I couldn't do anything. This is when I would tell them, "If this is the way you treat people, don't expect to stay in business, because you are going out of business." So, some six months to a year later... they were gone. There were four in all as I recall, who just turned belly-up or moved out of the area all together, and are no more, even today.

After I got off the phone, I was on my own and depressed, which is why I say, brothers and sister should be kept together to support one another, so I called Dennis. Word even got out to my dad who drove all the way down from St. Louis to visit and offer help. Naturally I said, "I got it", but as most people, I lived from pay check to pay check, and I was behind in a lot of things without a job. My dad suggested filing bankruptcy because I wasn't and couldn't continue paying for everything, especially that which was no longer ours. I explained the situation to Joyce and advised her to file jointly with me and that I had just enough severance pay to cover our expenses. Joyce said she had to think about it and I told her if she didn't, I would, and that the creditors will be coming after her, because her name was on everything.

Needless to say, we filed jointly and Joyce continued staying with her mother and dad until after the bankruptcy. Afterwards, she asked me if I would driver her and the girls, back up to her girlfriends in Savannah, GA. Well, being the sucker I am and still in love with her, I agreed in hopes to convince her to come back home; unsuccessfully, I might add.

So, I dropped her off at 12 or 1 o'clock AM in Ga. and headed back home by myself. On my way home, driving by myself and not paying attention to my speed, as I should have, having Joyce and the girls on my mind... I was speeding. It was me and three 18-wheeler trucks that were heading south toward Florida on some lonely highway out in the middle of nowhere.

They too, were speeding, but then I saw these blue lights come on in my rearview mirror and just knew they were for me. I tried to squeeze in between the trucks to let him pass by incase he was after the lead truck. He wasn't and pulled up as to swing behind me and the 18 wheeler behind me backed off, allowing the GA Patrolman to pull in behind. The trucker went around us as we pulled off to the side of the road. He asked for my license and began writing a ticket. He said that he needed $50 cash for speeding. I was shocked and never heard of such a thing, not to forget my being unemployed and broke. Being the wise guy I was, I said, "Now, let me get this straight. "You want me to give you $50 cash, right here, right now, in the middle of nowhere, in the middle of the night?" He said, "Yes sir."

Knowing I didn't have any money in my pocket, I asked him, "Well, do you take checks?" He said, "No sir!" I then asked, "Is there some place open where I might go to cash a check this late at night?" Again he said, "No Sir! That'll be $50 please, cash! I said that I didn't have it and it's a good thing too, that I didn't know where I was, or I may have tried something foolish, like making a run for the border, but I knew better. Besides He's only trying to make an honest living, so I thought it best not to do something so foolish, but this came to mind, only after I heard him say, "Follow me." I asked him, "Why" and he explained.

This is when he told me, he was going to have to lock me up for the night to see the judge first thing in the morning where he would pass judgment on me and put me on the chain-gang to work-off that money, I didn't have." I knew then, that I was in big trouble. When we got to the station house he told me to empty my pockets and then he put me in the jails holding cell. I asked, "Aren't I allowed a phone call before being locked up?"

Calls on a pay phone, only cost a dime back in my younger years, long before cell phones ever came out, and if you got the wrong number? Oh well, you were in a heap of trouble, so he reached in his pocket and put a dime on this little shelf that was a ledge on an opening in the cell door. He slowly slid it across the shelf in my direction, as he nodded to the phone in the corner. He had a serious look on his face as he smiled, as if to say, "Got you..." He said, "Make it count, or you're going be here a while." I had heard about GA, and was in somewhat of a shock!

I knew then, that I had to call someone, and not just anyone. Otherwise, I was going to be in a jail, until I worked off that $50 which I didn't have. Joyce was the only one I loved enough and could trust, although we just finished arguing and saying our... what I'm sure she thought to be, our final good-bye's, forever; and then here I am having to call someone? Right... so, I called a number she had given me. I was hoping and praying she would pick-up, and then I heard this voice which I didn't recognize say, "Hello" and I asked to speak with Joyce. She picked-up saying, "Hello." I said quickly, "Joyce, It's me! Please, don't hang-up, I'm in jail. I need your help." I explained my dilemma to her and she managed to have a friend of her girlfriend's husband, bring her to where I was because her girlfriend's husband had to work. They had to come to all the way over to Macon, Georgia and Joyce would have never found the place by herself. It was in the middle of nowhere. As she and this guy came in through the door, she saw me behind the bars and burst out laughing and said, "Can't leave you alone for a minute without you getting yourself into trouble!" All I was concerned about, was that she came... and had the money. Thank God! Afterwards, we parted.

Change in Direction

After we separated, I became very ill with a high fever and managed to pick up strep-throat from somewhere. Joyce's mom and dad offered to take me in to help me out temporarily, which I took them up on. I never felt so sick or weak in all my life. It got so bad that I couldn't even swallow my own saliva for the first day or two let alone any type of beverage or nourishment. Eventually, I was able to sip hot chicken broth in small amounts, and I lost 25 pounds in that first week before showing any signs of improvement. It took almost two full weeks to fully recover.

As I showed signs of improvement and began feeling better, my father-in-law said, "It was time for me to leave and that he wanted to make sure his home was available for his daughter and it wouldn't be as long as I was there." My mother in-law though, said that she thought I should stay a while longer, especially without having a home or place to go to, and no job. What I did have though was a weekly unemployment check which I managed to save up enough to buy a car at $250 from a neighbor across the street. Also, I still had access to the trailer we lost during bankruptcy and had been given time to pack up our belongings and get out. So, I decided, I better go pack up what I needed before the courts sent someone out to pick it up. As I did, I called Joyce to tell her if she wanted anything to come get it. So, she came and packed up everything; furniture and more that she wanted to move into storage at her girlfriend's house.

I then called my brother Dennis to come and help with the move and he took off work that day and came to help. Sometime during our packing, I received a job call with an offer to take a consulting position as a Sr. Engineering Designer for a company up in Michigan. I explained that I was in the middle of a separation and agreed on a price including travel expenses, and an asked for a $100 advancement upon my arrival. I also gave a start date to be a week from that next Monday, so I could finish packing and then be on the road. He agreed, which is normal and one's word, is usually good enough, so I continued packing.

I informed Joyce about the job and explained what was going on and that I would be sending her some money, as I finished packing up what I needed, which were personal necessities only. Then Dennis and I finished moving her stuff to where it had to go and Joyce and I said our good-byes to one another and Dennis and I left. I told him that I would like him to go with me because I didn't want to go alone and he was divorced and had no ties not to go with me. Otherwise, he would be by himself when I left. It was then Dennis agreed and was as excited about going, as much as I was, and we both really needed a change.

As we left, I decided to take my car out to interstate...I-4 for a test drive, toward Tampa. I hadn't really taken it out hardly at all or experienced how it would really perform on the road other than watching the neighbor take it for a test spin on occasion; as he was getting it ready to be painted and sell. It was a 1958 V8-Belair Chevrolet with a 348 under the hood, having a duel-power glide transmission... and I need a car to vacate the in-laws, so I bought it, as is. The interior was immaculate and I was happy.

I wanted to test it to see how it ran, so I pulled over on the I-4 shoulder and waited to make sure I was clear before opening it up to experience the power and what she would do. I wanted to see how she handled herself on the road at high speeds. It wasn't too long afterwards that I slammed the pedal to metal; pushing it all the way to the floor and holding it there... with the engine, wide open. This engine just roared unbelievably loud and the tires were smoking as they turned and squealing, as they heated up and then the car leaped forward. It had so much power, and it felt really great, as it catapulted us fast and faster with first gear being fast and second gear being faster. What really surprised me was when this automatic duel power glide transmission kicked into the upper gear when we reached 70 MPH, and that was just first, and it was with such force and a sudden jerk when it kicked into second. Wow! It felt as if we were being thrown into the back seat and then rocketed up to just under 120 MPH, in nothing flat. Man, what a set of wheels. I really like this car and it ran great, looked good and had a whole lot of get up and go.

It only needed a paint job, but other than that it was perfect and just what I wanted and needed for the trip. True, it may have looked a little strange sporting only a dingy grey primer instead of paint, but the body was perfect without any flaws and there was a lot of chrome all over it. It was beautiful and as such, I was convinced it was perfect and would make the trip. As we slowed down to the speed limit we discussed our plans and what had to take place before leaving that next morning. I explained I wanted to leave early which was on a Monday.

I planned on driving straight through in twenty four hours or less, switching drivers every 100 miles or so, until we arrived in St. Louis as a layover point for a few days before going to Michigan.

This would allow us time to visit with some old friends because this was our old stomping grounds which I had hopes of visiting. We had grown up in this area as children and hadn't seen a lot of these guys in years. I was also hoping or planning anyway, on stopping in and getting lucky enough for us to spend a night with each of these guys, while we were in town before moving on to the next person. I guess one might say that I was taking advantage of my friends and their good hearted hospitality. I was a terrible friend back then, but that was the plan to see us through until Friday, when we'd hit the road again.

Dennis really liked my car too, and suggested doing a quick sale on his car, because we didn't need two cars to haul up there and it would cost, too much. What he had was an All-American Rambler and said that we could use the money for the trip, which I agreed. He also needed to go by where he worked and see if he could pick up last week's check early and then quit his job before we hit the road. It sounded like everything was working out perfect but then we watched this Camaro pull up next to us and we were feeling good. We looked at each other and nodded, and we were off! It was a race and we both wound it out all the way, neck to neck doing about 116-

118 MPH and I was slowly pulling away, as we inched forward to gain the upper -hand.

We were having a great time, and as far as I was concerned. We were definitely the winners and we gave the thumbs up as we all laughed together, as they rocked back and forth trying to gain the edge to win, and then... it happened! BAM!!! Wouldn't you know it? I blew a head gasket and looked like a 747 coming in for a landing with a cloud of smoke blowing out from the back-end of my car like you wouldn't believe. It was so thick that a corvette, that was behind us had to turn-on his fog lamps, only to step on it and blow us and the Camaro off the road, as if we were standing still. I rapidly lost power and momentum... The Camaro kept on going and Dennis and I pulled over onto the shoulder of the road to check it out. Fortunately enough, we had just enough oil in the trunk, to add to the engine. It fired up and we nursed it back into Lakeland and parked it at the trailer.

The plans immediately changed and we didn't have the time to fool-a-round any more than we already had, nor the time or money to fix the problem. We got up that next morning and Dennis did as he said, and picked up his last week's check and cashed it. Then he quit his job. On our way out of town, we stopped at this junk yard and I explained my problem to them and wanted to know if they were interested in buying my car. I told them where the car was sitting and had the keys and papers in my hand, but that they would have to go get it. They agreed sight unseen and paid us. I know it looked funny to them, but we were already running late, and just wanted to get on the road and get it over with. I had a job to start and need to get a move on.

So, I accepted their unbelievable offer of twenty-five dollars and handed everything over including the title, as agreed. Then we were on the road heading for St. Louis and I'm sure they were shocked to find the car exactly as I told them, only needing a head gasket and some paint. At least, she made someone happy and she probably looked like a million bucks afterwards.

CHAPTER 9

"Drawn Closer to the Lord"

Beginning of a New Horizon

What I never realized is my brother looked up to me, as a big brother. I also, didn't realize how much I loved my brother until later in life. We both had a terrible beginning in life. Again, I was abandoned at fifteen but Dennis stayed at home with my dad and his second wife; Wilma, the "Step-Mother" along with her daughters. Dennis just became 12, so he had no choice but to remain at home. Wilma kicked out her own sons; one my age and one slightly older and getting married. With her being so strict and demanding; more so than our own mother; Dennis never had a chance. He followed my footstep and joined the Navy. He was 6'-8" tall and weighed about 250 pounds, but because of his up-bringing, he had a whole lot of attitude, especially when growing up with me as his big brother and I wasn't much of a brother. I hurt him a lot, long before Wilma. I didn't understand family, except that of survival and rejection from everyone. But, Dennis? He was the opposite. He was there for me and I can honestly say, I wasn't always there for him, even when he needed me. So, you can understand, I was totally taken by surprise when he decided to buddy up and be not only as a brother, but as a friend. We had a lot past memories to share on our way to St. Louis, which made separation from the family I come to love, more tolerable while I left Joyce and the girls.

The heater Dennis had in his car could really throw off some heat, so we were unaware of just how cold it really was, until we had to stop somewhere in Kentucky for gas. It began snowing and was coming down pretty heavy and began sticking. Neither one of us had anything on but a white t-shirt, jeans and tennis shoes; the typical Florida attire. We had coats but they we're bought in Florida and Florida doesn't offer heavy weight garments for winter. Rarely, the temp drops into the 20's or 30's, but for a day or two in Florida, a light jacket is all you ever need.

Wow, it was extremely cold but we got our gas and got back on the road again. It snowed most of the way to just outside of St. Louis where we spent that night in the car at a large Truck Stop. It was -10 degrees and we used our coats as covers, clinging to each other for warmth, turning on and off the engine, throughout the night, trying to keep warm and save money.

1ˢᵀ Night with Friends

We had planned on holding-over in St. Louis for three days to visit with friends before heading north to report, to this new job where I would receive an advancement of $100. Other than that, I was hoping to visit and to spend a single night with each one of three childhood friends. What I didn't think about in advance though, was who they were; poor planning on my part. Almost, everyone we knew was grown up and no longer available. Man, what a way to begin a new adventure, but this was the plan and we were sticking to it. We almost froze to death before arriving, so when morning came we needed to find a place to stay.

My dad's place was definitely out of the question. I hadn't seen anyone in St. Louis since I was a kid, but then I remembered an old buddy of mine; Ron, which I grew up with until leaving the neighborhood. He was married to this cute little thing called Debbie, who I once had a crush on. Surely, they'd have room to spare... for one night. So, we called them and were invited over where we reminisced and stayed for our first night.

2ND Night with Joyce's Friend

Come morning, we left Ron and Deb's place knowing we needed a place to stay for our second night and I remembered this girl named Kathy, through Joyce whom we all hung around together before Joyce and I moved to Florida, so I called her, knowing she was actually, a very close girl-friend, to Joyce.

They grew-up only, blocks away from each other. I explained to her what had happened between Joyce and me and about the job that I was to start, so I could have money to send home for Joyce and the girls. I also, explained how we slept in the car at a truck stop and that we didn't want to do that again, unless we absolutely had to. The temp outside was still extremely cold and was to our favor, so I asked if she and her mother would mind if we stayed the night. Kathy immediately agreed and asked her mother who said okay; thank God. I thanked her and said we didn't mean to impose, so we wouldn't be over until later that evening when it gets closer to dusk, if that was acceptable and she agreed. We showed up after dinner hour and sat around and talked a while and called it a night. Dennis and I would have been happy on the floor, but Kathy insisted; giving us her double size bed and she slept on the sofa. She didn't know it but, we were more grateful than she could ever have imagined and there was snow, everywhere. We got up that next morning and had breakfast with them before moving on and thanked them, and parted. We were like a couple lost puppies stranded, looking for another victim to impose on for one last night before moving on.

3RD Night with Friends of the Lord

Well, not really impose, but we were desperate and then it hit me; the Grammars'! Bobby came to mind; my old Sunday school teacher. It was worth a try, so I called and his wonderful wife, Sue answered the phone. I said hi and explained our dilemma and without hesitation, Sue said, "Sure, come on over, I've been expecting you." I said, "You have? Right now" and Sue said, "Yes, come-on." I was surprised at her response; so quick and decisive without asking Bob. I knew we'd be more comfortable staying with them and Dennis agreed, but before we headed over there I remembered my buddy; Benny and called him. I told him about passing through town and asked we could come by and visit before heading out. I said, "You know; to shoot the breeze, play some cards or whatever." Benny said, "Sure man! Come on over." So, we got into the car and drove to Sue's to check in.

Now, Sue and Bobby are about 16 years older than me and when we pulled up, Sue met us at the door. She had big ole' smile on her face from ear to ear and she was absolutely beautiful, both inside and out, and still is. She's an extra specially and loving person and invited both of us in, giving us a hug. Wow, it was almost like being welcomed home... and I mean in a real home with a real family. In fact, I explain to her; come morning, I would be moving on toward a new job. It was then that I could swear; recalling Sue saying, "I know", but I was too busy... explaining too, that we had to leave for a while because we we're supposed to meet-up with Benny, an old friend of mine, to visit and play some cards. This was because I use to be a pretty good at cards, mostly poker and winning. I was somewhat lucky, so I was willing to gamble on the fact I could win us a few extra dollars to help ease our trip. Besides, Benny was married and had a job and a family, whose wife was working and they both obviously had money, which I didn't have, but I was hoping to win a few extra dollars anyway. As we tried to leave; the only thing standing in our way, preventing us from doing so, was Sue. She was blocking the doorway. We tried to say good-bye and slip out to the car, but couldn't and Sue just smiled, stopping us; she apparently had something to say.

The Story of Gideon - Explained
....

Sue Said, "I knew you were coming to St. Louis" and then she proceeds to tell me that God had told her we were coming and that

I was there for a reason and this caught my attention out curiosity. I asked, "Really... why?" This now obligated me into listening and she began to speak. As she did, I pulled out a deck of cards because I was anxious and fidgety and wanted to leave. So, I started shuffling a deck of cards over and over again, as she continued to speak. Once again, Sue said, "God brought you to St. Louis for a reason" and again, I asked, why? Sue then said, "Because God wants you to get closer to him." I said in disbelief, "Right!" What I didn't expect though was an eye-opening experience that could have only come from the Lord.

Now, Sue was very close to the Lord and He must have put the story of Gideon in her spirit to share with me, because she asked me if I had ever heard the story about Gideon. My response to her I'm sure, would have been no, because I don't really recall ever hearing about Gideon before, so she proceeded to tell me. As Sue goes on, she said Gideon was told by God to go to war against another nation to set Israel free and Gideon wasn't sure he was the right person for the job. He was so full of doubt that he even questioned God by asking him to give him a sign. Sue went on to explain that later in that evening, in prayer; Gideon had explained to God what he had in mind. Gideon said he would lay a fleece outside the door and asked God to let the ground be dry in the morning and the fleece wet. Gideon was expecting a miracle that would prove this to be God's will.

When Gideon woke up that next morning, he went out to check the fleece and it was just as he asked. In fact, it was so wet that Gideon rung it out; filling a bowl full of water. Sue went on to explain that Gideon must have thought it wasn't much of a miracle; that someone may have been passing by and heard him praying and just poured water on it. Gideon may have also thought too, that the ground was dry because there was any rain.

So, Sue went on to explain the reasoning behind Gideon's doubt. Gideon had so much doubt that he approached God a second time; asking God not to be angry with him but that he would like God do one more test with the fleece, only this time, Gideon reversed his request. He asked God to let the ground be sopping wet in the morning and to let the fleece be bone dry. Gideon knew, only God could do this, and it too, was done just as Gideon had asked and Gideon Honored God's request and the Lord was with Gideon; a Mighty Man of Valor.

Luke 4:12 *And Jesus answering said unto him, (Satan)*

It is said, Thou shalt not tempt the Lord thy God.

However, Gideon did, so to speak and then afterwards, I too, was asked by the Lord or possibly, the Spirit of God, to put him to the test, due to my lack of disbelief, of what Sue had told me.

Reference: *Gideon's Fleece Tests: Not once, but twice.*

(Judges 6:35 -40)

35. *And he sent messengers throughout all Manasseh; who also was gathered after him: and he sent messengers unto Asher, and unto Zebulun, and unto Naphtali; and they came up to meet them.*

36. *And Gideon said unto God, If thou wilt save Israel by mine hand, as thou hast said,*

[If] *Gen 15:8, 1st Sam 14:9, 2nd Kings 20:8, Luke 1:18*

37. *Behold, I will put a fleece of wool in the floor; and if the dew be on the fleece only, and it be dry upon all the earth beside, then shall I know that thou wilt save Israel by mine hand, as thou hast said.*

38. *And it was so: for he rose up early on the morrow, and thrust the fleece together, and wringed the dew out of the fleece, a bowl full of water.*

39. *And Gideon said unto God, Let not thine anger be hot against me, and I will speak but this once: let me prove, I pray thee, but this once with the fleece; let it now be dry only upon the fleece, and upon all the ground let there be dew.* [anger] *Gen 18:32*

40. *And God did so that night: for it was dry upon the fleece only, and there was dew on all the ground.*

Put me to the Test

After Sue shared the story of Gideon with me, she continued speaking about whatever; I'll never know, because from somewhere... someone with an audio voice spoke to me. It was during my shuffling the deck of cards. This voice said to me, "Put me to the test." Now, this voice was as clear, as if someone had spoken to me, from directly behind me... in the same room.

In fact, I was so sure of it that I even looked over both my shoulders to see who was with us. I then turned back around to face Sue and asked her, "Is someone else here?" Sue said, "No, we're alone; that there was just her, me and Dennis and I thought that to be strange, because I had just heard this voice behind me and was being told that there was just the three of us? So, I questioned myself; "Where'd that come from?" It was then I felt led from within as if, it was God who was speaking to me. Naturally, in my disbelief... I said, "Yeah, right." But I knew someone had spoken to me, but who? (I'm Sorry that I ever doubted you Lord.)

It was then I began talking to the Lord from within saying, "Okay; if it's your will for me to stay in St. Louis, prove it to me. I'm going to cut this deck of cards in half and when I do, if it's an Ace, I'll know it's your will... for me to stay in St. Louis." This was all taking place in right in front of Sue, as she continued talking away about; God only knows what. Just as I finished saying that from within; I stopped shuffling the cards and held them in my left hand and began sliding the fingers on my right hand... up and down on the deck while my thumb followed on the other side; searching for just the right place to part the cards. As I did, I stopped at what I thought to be the perfect place where I would find an ace and I grasped the cards, to divide the deck into two piles, as I had always done. This was my way of my being Mr. Cool. This is because, as I grabbed the cards, I would snatch them up with a sudden jerk and a quick snap of the wrist, as I would be saying... "Tah-Dah, as if the card I was looking for, would magically reveal itself.

But, not this time! Just as I was preparing to flip these cards over, I hear this familiar voice speaking to me again which stopped everything as I heard it say, "uh'uh, top card." Out of total amazement of hearing what I thought I heard, and out of curiosity; I gave in and placed the top half of the deck I just cut... back onto the bottom half of the deck making it complete; setting in my left hand. Then, using my right hand, I slowly slid the top card from the top of the deck, lifting the edge upward, ever so slowly to peek at it before flipping it over, and surprise: An Ace Shocker! What I saw was none other than the face of the card I ask to draw, but told to use top card; the Ace of Diamonds! A smile came across my face, as I showed it to Sue, and explained.

I told her exactly, what had just happened and she only laughed at my disbelief and then again, said to me, "See, I told you that God brought you to St. Louis for a reason; to get closer to Him." As she was saying this, I had already put the ace back into the deck and was in the process of shuffling it again and Dennis was just standing there taking it all in, as an innocent by-stander and a witness.

As I Shuffled the cards, I spoke to God once again in disbelief saying within, to myself... that what had just occurred, had to have been a fluke. Like Gideon, I explained to God, "Right, you're going to have to do that again." Because I needed to have confirmation... due to my disbeliefs, and as I did this; I stopped shuffling. It was then that I began to separate the cards as I had tried earlier in hopes to reveal yet, another ace... to see if it was actually God's will for me to stay in St. Louis. As I began to do so; once again, I heard the same voice that had spoken to me earlier, before I turned the cards up to face me. It was as perfectly clear that time as it was the first time, stating exactly the same phrase, as before. I believe He did this to enable me to relate to the answer in a more positive manner, at my level of understanding and as to allow me to believe in his will and I knew then; it was the Lord. Only, his voice this time had a slightly higher pitch in tone saying, "UH'UH... TOP-CARD!"

So, once again, I slowly set the half-deck of cards on top of the others and slid off the top card to expose yet, another ace. Only, this time it was the Ace of Spades. I leaped with the joy, knowing... what Sue had said to be true, as I displayed the second ace and explained again, what had just happened. She laughed even louder recognizing the miracle that had just taken place, even though it was through the use of a deck of cards. Unbelievable one might think, but no it wasn't. It is pure truth and could only be that of God; as you will come to understand and I knew then, what Sue had said... to be true and I excepted it.

This actually happened and I did accept the fact that God wanted me to stay in St. Louis, which included Dennis to get closer to the Lord. We could find work and our own place later, but for now, Sue had to explain to Bobby that we would be staying with them. Their decision would be shared with us later that evening, but until then we headed over to Benny's house.

Honoring Commitment

On our way over to Benny's to play cards, about a half a mile or more from the Grammer's, Dennis confronted me with a question. First keep in mind that its 10 degrees outside in the dead of winter and in the middle of the day. There's snow everywhere and it had been pushed up off to the side of the road, as to allow vehicles passage and it was still snowing.

Note: Not once did my brother's car have any kind of over-heating problem in or out of Florida, where even the winters are hot by nature. So, you can understand why this is such an unusual event to occur. It happened precisely, at the right time, just as I spoke the inappropriate answer. Let me say too, that this car never had another encounter with this problem while Dennis owned it. It only happened after my response to Dennis's question. My response was completely negative to that, which was not in the agreement with that I had committed to, earlier.

Dennis was like the Devil's Advocate saying, "Doug, you're not really going to stay here in St. Louis are you? You need that job because Joyce and the Girls are counting on you to send them some money to survive on." I hesitated to digest what Dennis had just said. Then I answered Dennis by saying, "No, you're right... the girls need the money, so I guess I'm going to take the job. "BOOM," no sooner than the words left my mouth... the engine light came on indicating the engine had over-heated and steam began bellowing out from underneath the hood of the car, blinding our visibility. Let me remind you too, that this only occurred precisely as stated during that event, when I responded negatively about staying in St. Louis, after my commitment to God.

We pulled the car off to the side of the road and we both jumped out to check the car in hopes to see what was wrong. We couldn't see anything but steam coming out from beneath the hood and it wasn't clear where it was coming from or why! All we did is open the hood to assess the situation, and the steam bellowed out even more; almost blinding us from seeing underneath the hood. I unscrew the radiator cap to see if the radiator was empty, but it was full. It was then I said to Dennis, "Well we're going to have to stay in St. Louis now, because we can't trust this car to get us to Michigan. Also, with the kind of luck we had been having, we'd probably break down somewhere in the middle of nowhere and freeze to death." Unknowingly, as I made this claim, I was honoring my commitment of stay in St. Louis and the steam appeared to be diminishing. So, I put the cap back on the radiator and closed the hood. We got back into the car and as we did, I told Dennis, "So we're staying, okay?" Dennis agreed and cranked up the car and we were off to Benny's. As we left, I said, "We may as well go and play some cards; we might get lucky and win some money." So, we drove to Benny's without ever having another over-heating problem with his car and I agreed to honor my commitment to God.

Obviously, God had other plans for me, but I'm a hard headed person by nature and somewhat forgetful, as to recent events or agreements. This being said because when it came to the Lord?

Well, I wasn't walking or honoring the Lord as I should have been. In fact, I really hadn't walked with the Lord much at all since He visited me in my room other than reading the Word on occasion. I know now, that I seemed so ungrateful, as I look back at myself, but people do change and I had a long way to go.

All I can say is; like many, I slacked off and I'm sure I hurt the Lord and I'm truly sorry Lord, but thank God for being, such a Merciful God. He wasn't through with me then, as He isn't now, nor will be, for the Lord does Love me, and change is an on-going process that never seems to end. Praise God and Thank You Jesus! For the Lord hath said, *I WILL NEVER DESERT YOU, NOR WILL I EVER FORSAKE YOU. (Ref. Hebrews 13:5.)*

Remembering Our Commitments

As I said, God had a plan for me, but I was not aware of it at the time. Therefore, I did not realize the value of commitment. In the mean time I was going out foolishly to play poker and take advantage of an old friend, just to line my pockets with his money. Before we got there, I stopped somewhere to break a ten dollar bill to split with Dennis. This was all the money we had between us. After we arrived at Benny's we sat down and visited for a while, reminiscing over things that we had shared in the past and then headed down stairs into his family room to play cards; better yet, poker! I believe too, this was the last time I ever played the game. At first we started out slow, playing for pennies, nickels and dimes, and graduated to quarters, halves and then dollar bills. I was winning from what was a few dollars to five and then ten dollars. When I hit twenty dollars in winnings, as I recall; Benny wanted to play some more to maybe win back some of the money he lost. So, with it getting late, we agreed to start playing with ten dollars bets, set as the limit. Before I knew it, I was holding $40 in winnings. Dennis folded and Benny seemed a little disturbed and asked if we could bump it up to twenty to give him a chance of winning back his money. Now, I may have been suckered in and again, possibly not, but before Benny and I continued playing, I said something to Dennis that more than likely changed everything.

I said, "Well Dennis, we have enough money now to get us up to the job." I really can't explain it any other way, except that God obviously had other plans for me and it only took a matter of minutes and I lost it all, everything; even the ten dollars we came with. Maybe we were snookered, but I doubt it was Benny.

Benny asked, if I wanted to keep playing and I said, "No man; I lost everything, between the two of us." Now Benny; being the nicest of friends that a friend could be, said "Really?" I said, "Yeah man! I'm supposed to start a new job this Monday up in Michigan and I stopped by to visit while passing through St. Louis. I didn't expect to lose everything, but hey that's life." Benny confirms, "We're friends, right?" I said, "Yeah, man."

He said, "Alright then, we were just playing for the fun of it, right?" I smiled and said, "Right." Then Benny held out his hand and gave me back my ten dollars and we said our good-byes, shaking hands and Dennis and I headed back to the Grammer's. On our way back to the Grammer's, I told Dennis at least we have ten dollars to get to Michigan, forgetting my commitment. I said, "Things will work out okay, when I get the advancement."

We arrived at Bobby's and Sue's late and they were waiting up to let us in and then we talked for I while. I explained my marriage issues and Bobby told me, my marriage was through. We spoke some more and called it a night. That next morning was Friday and after we had breakfast, with me being the hard headed person I am, I didn't think twice about my commitment and began preparing to leave. I was so self-centered. I started saying my good-byes and Sue was surprised that I had decided to go. She reminded me I was to stay and I explained I needed the job for Joyce and the girls to survive. Sue said, "Okay." I really think she suggested my calling first or just maybe, I was led to make the call to confirm the job and the advancement. I'm not really sure, but I do remember making the call to speak with the person who was hiring me. I expected a confirmation and ignored staying in St. Louis with the Grammer's; to attend church and get closer to the Lord. I thought only, about the job.

So, before I went any further with packing the car I agreed with Sue and made the decision to make the call before leaving, to double check and re-confirm my new job. Basically though, I was more interested in confirming the fact of having the $100 agreed upon, waiting on me, which I was in desperate need, because the job was already agreed upon. I knew it was there and I knew too, that I would be completely broke upon arrival.

So, I called the guy I had been dealing with and when he came to the phone he said, "Doug, I'm glad you called!" I asked, "Why?" He said, "I've been trying to get a hold of you all week. You haven't left Florida yet, have you?" I said, "Yeah, my brother and I are in St. Louis at a half-way point, so we could visit some old friends for a few days before reporting up there. We were just getting ready to get back on the road and I wanted to call, just to reconfirm things and that I would still be able to get that advancement from you, as soon as possible."

What this guy said to me next, really set me back at first; giving me a reality check! He said, "The job fell through, so don't bother coming up." It was then that I realized I would be staying in St. Louis, just as Sue had said. Everything is in God's hands, thank you Lord. I not only come to realize that the commitment this guy made to me... wasn't going to happen but that when we make a commitment to God, we had better be committed, because first and foremost, God is committed to you and me and we better honor our commitments, especially to God.

God loves you, He loves me and He loves all of us. We're all created in His Image and His Likeness. He is the Creator and He does Loves each and every one of us... unconditionally. The fact is that He loves me so much that he made provisions for both, Dennis and me while Joyce and I were separated. He provided us, not just any place to stay, but a place that would have a family; the kind of family that was committed to each-other; more importantly though; committed to God. This family attended church regularly and out of respect, we did too.

This is a family life in which we hadn't known and as we stayed, we come to know and love the Lord or at least I did. I had hoped or expected my brother to do the same. We come to learn more about the Lord and about family. The kind of family with a whole lot of love, which we came to know at the Grammer's; something we missed out on earlier in life.

The agreement to stay meant sharing a two bedroom home with their boys. The boys shared a room up-stair that appeared to be more like a dormitory. It was huge with five beds side by side, each having a dresser in front of each bed, adjacent each of the boys and a large closet. What an arrangement. The master bed-room was next door and they only had the one bathroom.

It was for all to share. Bob was not making the kind of money he could have been but it met the family needs and now? Well, he had two extra mouths to feed. I don't know how they did it but God too, had a hand in that, because there was not only a place for everyone but there was always enough food for everybody; blessed and prayed over. The only stipulation was that we attend church regularly, which we did; not just Sunday School & Church but Sunday & Wednesday evenings, as well, as family.

God Honors Commitment

We stayed with the Grammer's for what appeared to be approximately six months. I'm not really certain of the exact amount of time. It may have been more or less, but Joyce and I were separated during that time frame, which is why I say this.

Neither Dennis nor I had a job at the time. We tried to find work but the economy was really bad. I literally had close to 500 or more resumes sent out all across the country in hopes of land something, anything; be it a high-end or a low wage job, but nothing materialized. I did however; qualify for unemployment but Dennis didn't. What I did receive though was eighty dollars each week, which I believe I split with the family for groceries and to have gas money for us to search for work, but to no avail.

We both ate well, but didn't gorge ourselves like we had come to know, before staying with Sue. I'm approximately 6'6" and my brother and I looked very much like twins to most but he was a couple inches taller and three and one-half years younger than me. Originally, when we came to St. Louis, we weighed in at approximately 250 to 255 pounds each and lost enough weight where we were weighing 218-220 pounds. We were mean and lean. Well, I wasn't mean but I was lean and as for my brother? Well, he was lean too, but he also had a bit-of-a-mean streak in him that he just couldn't shake.

I remember in our teenage years I bullied him so much into thinking I was so bad that he never confronted me, but once. In his attempt to do so, we were home alone and where I upset him over something and he lost his temper. He charged me putting me into a corner with both arms swing at me like a set of wind mills. He was coming at me hard and strong and I come to realize he was going to get the upper hand, unless I did something quick. I looked for the one and only shot that might stop him, otherwise it was curtains for me and there it was an unprotected nose as his arms were swing behind him, so I only had time for one good shot, on the nose… and POW! It worked! I nailed him and he backed off saying I was always bullying him and beating him up and he said, it's just not fair. I backed off after that because I knew next time I might not be so lucky.

Also, I don't believe Dennis knew how close he really was in defeating me. Had he known it would have been pay-back time, but again he never knew! I remember too, hearing how he took on guys throughout high school that I knew I wouldn't want to tackle, but then again, because of such, he developed a real mean streak, which is why he was in the Navy for such a short stretch. He had anger management issues and I'm sure I was the cause of some of them, but I'm sure our family childhood wasn't any help to either one of us with all the abusiveness we encountered. I only mention this for a reason, because I recommended Dennis to go down to the shipyard in St. Louis for a job. I knew too, that this place was full of rough necks, but that he'd fit right in.

One week before I received a call from Joyce is when Dennis went down to the ship yards; down-town St. Louis and he had just cashed his tax return check for $460. While there, he went to get something to drink. As he did, he was bumped into and when he reached for his wallet to pay, it was gone. He turned around real fast to see where the guy was that bumped into him and he saw him standing just adjacent to where he was standing in this cafeteria. Dennis caught him looking up at him with two other guys who had quickly turned their backs to him, as not to be obvious, but it was too late. Dennis realized what happened and by their actions... they were guilty, so he confronted them.

I was at Sue's when Dennis came home. He was beaten up, bruised, black and blue with a black eye and a cut on his face. He proceeds to tell me the story about what had happened and that he was beating the tar out of these three guys when they yelled for help and five other guys came out and jumped in on him and beat him up. So, Dennis came back home just to get me for reinforcement. He was serious and looked into my eye's; his big brother, so wise and tough and said, "Come on Doug, between you and me, let's go kick their tail." I told him I stopped that kind of stuff and that we were staying at the Grammer's. I didn't think it was a good idea to be bailed out of jail, so I bowed out and said, "No." I did however offer him a solution. I told him to tell them a story, which we shared earlier. Dennis was married but separated too; actually divorced and still wore his wedding ring. I guess he did so in remembrance, as I did. I shouldn't have said what I did, but he needed help, and this came to mind.

I told him to confront them and tell them that you just received that tax refund and it's something you needed for your wife and daughters who are counting on it, because you're separated and they'll give you your money back. Dennis looked at me and said, "Are you crazy?!" I said, "Believe me, it'll work! They'll feel sorry for you and give your money back." He said that I was nuts, but he went anyway. I stayed and I don't remember, if I prayed for him or not, but God was watching out for him, because he came back wearing a smile from ear to ear.

These thug's may have lifted his wallet, but when he went back and shared the story I told him to; out of pity or fear one, they gave him back his wallet and his money or at least, most of it. They apologized too, for spending $30 to buy a few drinks but they offered him a job beginning at the end of the month.

Personally, I think they figured anybody who was crazy enough to approach them after what he had gone through and with him being as big as he was... they knew he would be back for more. So, rather than having an enemy looking for them... one at a time, when they were alone, they made friends with him and gave him a job, and as for Dennis? Well, he fit right in and accepted their offer. It was shortly after that, we put Dennis's car into the shop to have the clutch replaced. The cost was expensive and I knew we didn't have the money. I don't know what happened for sure, but Dennis must have sent his money home. Either that or used it elsewhere, because he was broke. At least I was receiving an unemployment check every week like clockwork, so I figured we could get the car out in a couple weeks unless we could borrow some money from Bobby and Sue, which I'm sure they didn't have either, so we didn't ask.

Through those months I had grown in Christ and was attending Revival this particular week, when Joyce called me out of the blue and ask for me to come back home. I wanted to make sure I heard her correctly and asked, "So, you want me to come back home?" She said, "Yes." I was extremely excited and had been praying for this day, but I remembered what had happened the last time I said I love you where she wouldn't respond, so I put together a little test right there. I said "I love you", and instead of waiting for her response, I followed it with the question; "Do you love me?" Joyce responded by saying "Yes" and my response to her, was quick and simple. I said, "Well then... you had better say it, because the last time I ask you; you wouldn't say anything!" It was then that Joyce opened up and said

"I love you." I said, "I love you too, and always have; I'll be home, as soon as possible." I was so excited that when I got off the phone, I was bursting with joy.

So, I went into tell the good news to Bobby and Sue. Bobby made the statement, as to try and let me know, so I wouldn't be caught off guard or disappointed, by saying; things don't always work out like you would like them to. I on the other hand said, no! Things are going to work out just fine. His final remarks to me, were a little offensive as he said, "Your marriage is not going to work." Sue however, wished me well and I know God had a hand in this; and here's why; we were once again, complete as the perfect, "Love Triangle"... consisting of three.

> **1-John 5:7** *For there are three that bear record in heaven, the Father, the Word, and the Holy Ghost: and these three are one.*

It is said that marriage is like a circle; never ending which is true, but Love is like a triangle. The perfect example is the Trinity within the Word of God, for God is Love! There's God the Father, the Son (the Word) and the Holy Spirit. God the Father is mentioned first, because God the Father is above all things. Therefore, the only way marriage can exist is to include God above all things. Distance apart, has no meaning, but what does have meaning, is to seek God's will. In doing so, Joyce and I were once again, on the same plain; the base of what is called: "The Love Triangle" where God is above us; where we seek his will and honor our commitment to God. The closer we draw to God, the more we come realized our Love and Commitment to God... and each other, but more importantly, to God.

God Honors Prayer
············

After Joyce's call, I told her I'd be home, as soon as possible, which must have lead Joyce to believe I was leaving for Florida immediately, which wasn't the case. When I didn't show up that week-end, she realized I wasn't coming as she had thought. So, out of being worried and angry; she called to speak to me but got Sue and asked for me to call her. So, I did and she was furious.

She wanted to know what happened and why I didn't show-up. This opened the door for discussion about things, needing to still be addressed and she agreed, so we spoke.

I mentioned I was in the process of attending a revival at a Non-Denominational, Full-Gospel Church that practiced the Gifts of the Spirit, which is why I didn't come. I went on to say too, that when we get back together we're going to church and not, to just any religious church or organization, as we had done previously, but that we would be going to a Non-Denominational Church. One that would draw us closer to God and she agreed. This is because we needed it for ourselves and our Love Triangle with God, and for our children's sake, who needed to know God.

I also, mention Dennis's car, as our only means of transportation; needing a new clutch and that I was waiting on my unemployment check to come in that next Friday in order to have the money to get Dennis' car out of the shop. We also, discussed a few other things, but all in all, we were in agreement and that we would put God first in our marriage and would start attending church regularly, as a family. Afterwards, I agreed to come home that next week-end.

It was later that week when I found out the cost of repairs for Dennis's car would be $82, which we didn't have. Also, I had not prayed to God and ask if it was His will for Joyce and me to get back together, but God knew my heart and my intentions, which I believe; is why God worked, so closely with me. So, what I needed to do was to go to God in Prayer, which I did explaining the cost of getting out Dennis's car, so he could drive me down to Florida, just to turn around and drive all the way back to St. Louis, because he had a new job to start that next Monday. Also, with Dennis not working at the time and having no money and as for me, I had little money, if any myself. My unemployment check was due at the end of the week but it was only going to be for $80, which would not even be enough to cover the cost. What I really needed... was another miracle.

The money I needed was twice that of my unemployment check. So, what I needed was unrealistic; a double check in an amount to help things come together. I knew too, Bobby or Sue couldn't help, so I turned to God in prayer with yet another fleece. I explained my situation to God, as if He didn't already know, but He knew long before I asked. I didn't know anything about the complexity of my request until long after the fact when I would come to realize how God was actually working with me to answer my prayer that could only, be answered through a miracle; an intervention of God! So, you must understand; The Lord knew I was going to lay this fleece down and had already made provisions; months, if not years before to honor my request, which I didn't know at the time. God had already taken care of everything and He honored my request, which was my third and my last time, to lay a fleece before the Lord.

In my prayer, I explained that the only way I could see all of my needs being met; was if I were to get a double unemployment check in the mail that was due Friday and that if I were to do so; I would then know it is God's will for me to go home to my family. Otherwise, I was going to stay in St. Louis. Now, that's a pretty steep request; stepping out on a lot of faith… expecting an answer. I also, didn't realize, just what I was asking, but come Friday when the mail was delivered, I went straight to the mail box, expecting to see my prayer answered. I weeded through what appeared to be 7 or 8 pieces of mail, if not more, looking for my unemployment checks. At first, I found one, which I put between my lips to free up my hands to take another look, for a second check that wasn't there! I was so disappointed because I was expecting to get that money. Afterwards, I put the mail under my arm and pulled the unemployment check from between my lips and opened it. As I did so, I noticed something had accompanied the check that hadn't seen before. It was a small slip of paper which read, "Due to the high cost of postage, the State of Florida would be sending out double checks every other week, effective this week." Glory to God and Praise unto the highest! God is so good and merciful.

Wow! Now, this was a real miracle! I was looking for two checks when what I had really asked for... was a double check, and I was totally shocked! I reached in and pulled out the check, leaping with joy. It was exactly, and I do mean EXACTLY, what I had asked for; thank you Lord. There was a check made out to me for $160! Praise God! God is so good! Thank you Jesus! Even now, as I'm telling this story, my heart is filled with so much gladness that my eye's fill with tears, knowing just how much the Lord loves me. Thank You Jesus! His love is real!

I hadn't lay down a fleece in months since I sought God's will about staying in St. Louis, but now; I must have been lead to seek God's will a third time, out of desperation, I would think, but He said to me before; put me to the test, so I did... one last time. I can't help but wonder if it was God's will for me to do this, because of what He had in store for me, but as I was waiting; waiting on the Lord, expecting an answer... I did receive again, exactly what I had requested!

I ran up to the house yelling and hollering out loud, "Dennis, let's go get the car, and pack up; we're going home!" I opened up and shared with both him and Sue about the fleece and how the Lord had answered my prayer. It was then, Sue said something to me that made me realize I would have to cease turning to God with what I had come to know, as the fleece. I share this with you too, because he told me to put Him to the test and I did, but there's something I didn't know.

Sue said, "God honored my fleece, but what I was doing... was wrong." She went on to say, I was telling God what I wanted in life and not allowing Him for other options, and that I narrowed my options to only two, when the Lord may have other plans; better plans... for my life. She went on to say that what I had been doing was not turning to God to show me the way, when in fact; what I should be doing, is ask for His guidance and but dictating to Him what I want. She was obviously led to tell me this as I'm telling you. Don't do this unless, God instructs you to do so. He says, ask and you shall receive, just have faith and as in Salvation; just ask, believe and receive... in Jesus name.

My only advice to anyone, even thinking about laying a fleece, is to search the Word of God and find out first, what I come to learn, which is to seek the will of God, above all else.

> **Matt 6:33***But seek ye first the kingdom of God, and his righteousness; and all these things shall be added unto you.*

To do otherwise, would be to do something we shouldn't be doing, which is to test the Lord. Remember too, that Jesus told Satan; thou shall not tempt the Lord thy God. I didn't know this at the time and felt strongly led to do what I did and yes, it did prove to be as Sue had stated. True, it was God's will for me to stay in St. Louis and to get closer to Him, but my advice to you, is not to think about testing the Lord, but read the Word and see what Jesus says after being tempted by Satan.

> **Matt 4:7** *Jesus said unto him, It is written again, Thou shalt not tempt the Lord thy God.*

This is why I can honestly say, "Do not... do this." I only did what I did, because I was so strongly led to do so; especially, when I heard the Lord say to me, "Put me to the test". There is no doubt in my mind; it was the Lord and His will. This is confirmed to me by Sues explanation, as to why I was back in St. Louis and by being told what to do while cutting the cards; not once, but twice with the constant reminder that I was to stay in St. Louis while I tried to convince myself otherwise, as well as the way things unfolded, as they did. This included the loss of the job after coming into St. Louis, only to return home to honor our commitment in marriage to one another and to God. Our commitment to each other is to honor the sanctification to one another in marriage and family, as well as our commitment to our Lord and God; God the Father, the Son and the Holy Spirit.

I was exactly, where God wanted me to be; in the right place, at the right time, and He proved it through His gentle persuasions and

I'm so, stubborn; stubborn as a mule sometimes. It's my nature and I suppose as most; I was living for myself.

What I should have been doing was remembering to put God first! All I can say is thank God for His Love, Mercy and Grace and for being... so Patient.

It was by my arriving and staying where God wanted me to be, so that I would develop a closer relationship with the Lord where I come to know and feel the presence of Lord's Spirit upon me. As I look back now, even to when I was just a child setting on the edge of my bed... looking at the dresser with the three stacks of coins; I come to realize through the years, especially, in my adult years; that the Lord has been with me all my life, even before for then. He knows all of us; each and every one of us and yes, even before we were born, including you.

God also, has a plan for you, as He does for me, and it feels great... to feel His presence, knowing that the Lord is here working in our lives and actually to the point, if you allow Him. By doing so, you may even see His mighty works, as they unfold right before your eyes. Give credit where credit is due.

It's not by luck or coincidence, or karma, fate, destiny or whatever name you want to call it, but there is someone in your life that loves you. He is the one watching out for you... and He is trying to protect you, but we don't always recognize His presence or His hands in our life. Unbelievable, so some may think, but trust me; God is with us, and if God is for us, then who can be against us? For we are his; Alive-N-God, which is a saying that I have come to know from my oldest daughter, Valerie; a true blessing! But you too, are a blessing, and God wants to bless you. All you need to do is to listen to that small still inner voice within... calling you; it's the voice of God's Holy Spirit.

Broken Bottle

Another event that occurred just before leaving St. Louis was when I was returning from visiting my Aunt. Instead of waiting on a bus transfer, I decided to enjoy, the beauty of a peaceful Sunday afternoon, by walking the last mile to Sues.

Everything was closed and the streets were empty; no traffic and surprisingly spotless; clean of any debris accept for an empty upright soda bottle that I just happened to notice in front of some store. I walked past it as I continued and three guys sped by me from behind, shouting obscenities as they passed and I in turn, yelled back. They turned right at that next corner, squealing their tire and racing to the next right turn, and so on, and so on.

As I listened, I could hear the squealing tires at each corner, echoing through the alleys between the empty buildings, as I looked for a place to escape or hide, but there wasn't any. I feared the worst and as I did, they come up from behind me; screeching to a halt, as they slightly passed me by, bailing out of the car, to do me bodily harm. I believe I said within; Oh God, help me. What am I going to do and as I did, this bottle came to mind. So, I swung around, stepping over to pick it up and approached them; rapping it on a concrete lamp post next to me which I never did before, bursting it, revealing shards of glass. As I approached them, I ask one question; "Who wants to wear this thing first?" Needless to say, they climbed back into the car and disappeared. I swear that bottle was the only debris I seen for defense and truly believe it was obviously there, for a reason. I didn't know where to go and had no place to turn, but to God. Only then, the bottle came to mind; to pick it up and rap it on the pole, with a quick sudden jerk, causing me to appear as the aggressor, and they left. Thank God for that bottle. Sadly, but gratefully, I believe it was there, for a reason; to rescue me in my time of need. Thank you, Lord!

He really does take care of his own. I also learned not to be so aggressive, because Jesus says that we are to love one another including our enemies, and to even pray for them. We should always help them and share where we can, for we never know whom it is that we are entertaining. It may very well be an Angel or a person, and to do unto the least of one of these, is to do it unto the Lord, which is why we should love one another. For we are all created in God s image and have His Spirit dwelling within us; calling us to repent from our sinful nature, and to guide us into all truths and righteousness. Amen? Amen.

CHAPTER 10

"Restoration - by God"

Journey Home

Dennis and I packed-up, said our good-byes and headed on down the highway. We decided to exchange drivers every 100 miles, as to drive straight through, non-stop, as we did before. Only now, returning to Florida. We were headed East through Illinois, swinging into Kentucky and heading to Nashville, then Chattanooga and due south through Georgia, on into Florida. The trip was faster returning than leaving and Dennis still had to turn around to return to St. Louis to start his new job, by himself.

We only had one problem that caused us to slow down, costing us a couple hours on our trip to Florida. I was fast asleep with the radio blaring in the back-ground. We were just outside of Paducah, Kentucky on a long straight section of inclining highway which was actually a toll-road at the time, but now: I-24 that would take us into Chattanooga. The traffic on this stretch of highway was scarce because of it was new and actually, a toll-road back then, and by driving it? We could drive on it wide open, making great time at 70 MPH, give or take.

As I slept, Dennis was driving with the radio on and the vent window open as he enjoyed his coffee and cigarette, when all of a sudden, all heck, broke out! I couldn't complain about his smoking because I too, smoked once, but as I slept I was awakened by his burst of anger. He was just ranting and raving over something, and I was half-asleep and didn't know, but he just kept griping, and fussing and then it happened; I was awake.

I looked over at him and said, "Hey man... what your problem? I'm trying to sleep here, what's your problem?" Why are you cursing and carrying on like this. I'm supposed to be sleeping and I can't! You woke me up! So, what's going on? What wrong man?"

Dennis explained that he just finished his cigarette and flipped it out the vent window and because we were staying at Bobby's and Sue's, we had lost a lot of weight." In fact, both of us lost so much weight that we dropped from about 260+ pounds to about 215. He said his wedding ring was too big and loose, and flipped off his finger when he flipped out his cigarette butt.

I asked him what's the big deal, because he had been divorced for a year or longer and he said that it had sentimental value, because he still loved her and had hopes of getting back together with her someday, too. Well, what could I say or do?

I said, "Well, pull the car over... let's go find it." Dennis said, "We'll never find it!" And I said, "Yes, we will... now pull the car over, and we'll go find it." Dennis asked, "Are you nuts? We've been driving too fast and too far, to find it." And I said, "Just pull the car over, to the side of the road and stop; we'll find it, believe me... we will find it."

So, Dennis pulled over and we got out, stretched our legs and began walking down the middle of the empty highway. There wasn't any traffic to worry about, though we kept our eyes open for traffic just in case, and the ring of course. I figured we'd be able to find it on the road, if it was lying there. Dennis began fussing again saying, "I told you, we'd never find it. We're wasting our time." I said "Yes we will, we'll find it! Now, just keep looking and we'll find It." and I really did expect to find it.

After walking for what I believed to have been far enough to cover the distance from where we got out of the car to where we were standing, I turned around and looked up toward the car. It was a spec in the horizon and I said to Dennis, "Well, I guess this is far enough." which was about two miles or more and Dennis then said, "I told you we'd never find it." I said, "Yes we will... now, when we walk back to the car; you walk on the shoulder of the road and look in the grass, as I walk back in the median." "Dennis said, okay, but we'll never find it." I said, "Just Look! I'll be in the median and we'll look together."

As I stepped into the median, I closed my eyes and began to say a prayer: "Lord, I'm coming to you today to ask you to let me find my brothers ring, because it means, so much to him. It says in your Word to ask and you shall receive. It also says, whatever I ask for in your name Jesus, it shall be done to glorify the Father, who art in Heaven. So, I'm coming to you right now and asking in the name of Jesus to find my brother's ring, and that when I open my eye's; I expect it to be the very first thing my eyes focus on. It's in Jesus name I pray and give thanks, and all the glory to God the Father, Amen."

As, I opened my eyes looking directly toward the ground in front of me; it was almost like a miniature person standing in the grass... waving a super bright flash-light into my eyes to get my attention. Well it worked, because what I was looking at was my brother's ring which happened to be, in just the right angle and position, to allow the sun's rays to bounce off the rings... directly into my eyes. It was just what I asked for and done in such a way that I couldn't miss it, even if I tried; causing me to focus my eyes, as I had asked; on the first thing I saw. It twinkled and shined, so brightly, all I could say was; "Thank You Lord and Praise God the Father who art in Heaven!" Thank you!

I yelled to Dennis, "Hey Dennis, I found it!" He said, "Really?" I told him that I prayed to find it as I walked out onto the median and there it was. Now, I'm not certain how or what I told him exactly, but I would think that I gave God all the glory then, and if not... I'm doing so, now because without His intervention and the answering of my prayer; finding it was like finding a needle in a hay stack; impossible, but we found it! So again, "Thank you Jesus, all Praise, Honor, and Glory, to God."

Family Re-United

We arrived in Lakeland sometime later and I went straight to my in-laws house, as a place for me to unpack and stay. They were completely surprised and caught off guard, as I walked in.

They had no idea that Joyce and I were getting back together and in fact, they hadn't heard from her. Well, needless to say, Joyce wasn't there and I felt a little awkward, but finally, she showed up and they wanted to know what was going on. Joyce explained her decision and asked if it was okay to stay with them until we got our own place, as soon as possible. Since I wasn't working, I had plenty of time to look for a place, but what we needed to live in proved to be, too expensive for the money we had coming in. All we could do is hope and pray for something that was less than the going rental prices that were averaging close to $350, give or take for a two bedrooms/single bath apartment. The prices seemed outrageous but then one day our prayers were answered. There was a house being renovated and near completion. We rushed over and offered $90; agreeing to finish renovations to make it livable. Afterwards, we moved in and as we did the owner came over to see the changes. He said, "Wow, I'll be glad when you move out, so I can get a $140 or more for this place." Again, I reminded him of our rental agreement for $90 a month even after we finished the renovation which I did finish, and as agreed; he honored our agreement.

Joyce was working at a convenient store and with what she was making; we just did make ends meet due to the low house rental, and what few needs we had. Thank God her car was paid for, but I needed to get a job, and fast. It wasn't more than a week or two, upon completing the renovation and moving in, that I received a call to report to a job in Mobile, Alabama. So, I packed up and the plan was, to leave Joyce and the girls behind at her mother's for a week and bring them on up that following week-end, but it wasn't meant to be. I was misrepresented as something that I wasn't and needed the job, but had to decline.

Upon reporting to work that morning I was given a stick full of drawings for a new plant that were piping and instrumentation drawings, referred to as P&ID's, which is the primary road map to any successful job that consisted of 50 to 60 D-Size Drawings. I was asked to review them and that we would get together after lunch and discuss my ideas on how to approach the task at hand.

So, I laid them across the drafting table and went through all these drawings rather quickly, and the more I seen what the task involved... the more I began chuckling to myself in a quiet, but worrisome tone, shaking my head in disbelief. I may have even asked the Lord, "What did I get myself into?"

Well, it soon became time for lunch and I took a break for a quick lunch, only to return almost immediately, knowing what I was about to face. What was required of me was to provide them some answers, but I was totally, at a loss of what to say.

Finally, they returned and asked me how it was going, and I said with a little bit of a hesitation; saying, "Hmmm, not so good." The only thing that came to mind is that honesty is the best thing to do. So, I went on to ask, "What exactly did you think you were hiring to do this job?" This caught them off guard I'm sure, but they stated, "A Design Engineer, why?

I went on to apologize for any misunderstanding and informed him that I had explained to the placement agency that I was a Design Draftsman and not once had I claimed to be an Engineer and that they had the wrong man to do the job. I also stated, not to worry; I wouldn't be charging them a fee for being there because of the misunderstanding or mistake and said that I would be leaving, as I apologized again. He asked me to explain this situation to his boss and he in turn called the plant manager to come down to hear this, which I explained to them, as well. I was thinking to myself, that one of these guy's heads are going to be rolling; pardon the terminology, but in other words, someone was going to be fired over this, but not me; I quit.

They stepped back for a moment and then returned, and much to my surprise; these gentleman thanked me for my honesty. The manager then asked me, after reviewing the drawings, if I felt that I understood what was expected and would I be able to proceed, even though I wasn't an engineer. I agreed, but surely not within the time frame allocated to be completed and that I may run into some areas where I may be lacking in experience.

It was then that he said, not to worry, that he had other engineers that would be more than willing to help me accomplish any question I may have, and as for time? He said that I could have whatever manpower and resources I needed, but I had to respectfully decline and I was treated with great respect, as well.

He said that he would call the temporary services company that brought me in and would personally give me a recommendation anytime I needed one... for my honesty. With that I bowed out and headed home. I believe this was when I learned to turn to the Lord in prayer when sending out resumes or applying for a job by asking Him to close any doors He would have me, not enter and to open the door to where he would have me be." I've done this for many years and have always managed to feel and know that I was, right where I was supposed to be.

Well, everyone at home was surprised what had happened but honesty, truth is the best policy! It wasn't more than a day or two later and I was hired again, by a different company.

I had to report back to Mobile, this time and felt led to take the whole family with me, so we packed and headed for Mobile. Thank goodness our girls were only $2\frac{1}{2}$ and $5\frac{1}{2}$ years old which made packing and moving, much easier. We began in a motel room for 1-week and thank God for the swimming pool. It was perfect, considering it was summer and that we were in a motel. We eventually, moved into an apartment complex which had a two pools; a standard size for everyone and one for kid's.

We found a local church that wasn't exactly what we wanted but we wanted to make sure we were there as a family... and for the Lord. We were doing fairly well, but Joyce was soon expecting again, and started dropping hints of moving back into Florida. So, I began sending out résumé's again, but nothing was taking place at the time. All I could do was to check back periodically, to see if there were any changes or needs in the Central Florida area, especially in Lakeland or the surrounding area's and still, there wasn't anything available, anywhere.

There is one story I really enjoyed hearing about while in Alabama when I came home one evening, as usual and Joyce called me aside into the kitchen. She said "Let me tell you what kind of day, I've had." She went on to say, she was doing something else in the back of the apartment and heard the girls laughing and saying, "Wee!" So, she snuck in to see what they were doing and in shock, she screamed, "No!" What she saw was Veronica, who is our youngest daughter, who had climbed up onto the kitchen table and was hanging from the chandelier. If that wasn't bad enough, she also added that Valerie grabbed her by her legs and used them to swinging her around the table in a circular motion. She told them what they had done was wrong and that someone could have been hurt and not, to do it again. They agreed and went back into their rooms to play.

Joyce began preparing dinner, and heard Veronica singing "Praise you Jesus... Praise you Lord! Praise you Jesus... Praise you Lord" over and over again, and as she did; she was dancing. Dancing around the perimeter of that kitchen table with her hands stretched upward to the chandelier, holding her head back. She was having fun, just dancing in circles, praising the Lord. Joyce saw her and called out to her to get her attention and asked her what she was doing. Veronica said that she was praising the Lord. Well, Joyce for the most part, can be a bit of a smart aleck at times and just couldn't refuse. So, Joyce asked, "Oh yeah? Well, where is He?" Joyce said that Veronica looked up toward the chandelier, pointing her finger and said, "Right There!" Joyce said she felt a little eerie and said, "Okay..." and turned back around and continued with dinner, leaving Veronica alone and let her continue with what she was doing. That story really helped us as parents, realizing we must be doing something right.

Joyce was getting bigger and bigger and the due date was fast approaching and was only weeks away. She asked her doctor about traveling and he of course said that it was against his recommendations. So, we packed her and the kids up to move to Florida anyway, which is where she wanted to deliver the baby; in Florida, and not... in Alabama, which put her closer to home.

So, we unloaded the things she needed into her mom and dad's place and got her and the girls settled in, where I visited, for the rest of the weekend before heading back to Alabama. It was one of those sad times where a decision has to be made for what was consider to be the best for everyone, even though it felt as if, we had just gotten back together, only months earlier.

It was late Sunday afternoon when I headed out to Alabama to return to work. I began hoping and praying that week to find a job in Lakeland and it wasn't until that Wednesday when I received a call. I was asked if I would be interested in working for a company outside of Lakeland that I had never worked with before, and I said yes. I was so anxious; I called on Thursday to see if they had made a decision, as of yet, and he said, "No, it'll probably be tomorrow." which was Friday, because the person to be hired, was to report to work that next Monday.

Well, I prayed all the harder, so I could be home for the delivery of our new addition, but come Friday morning, I was disappointed with the news that they decided to go with another.

I explained why I needed this job, to get back home with my wife who was expecting to deliver anytime, but that didn't help. I asked too, to be kept in mind should something else come along. He agreed and we ended the call, where I went right back into prayer and claimed that job, which I just missed, to be mine... in the name of Jesus. I claimed that they had made a mistake and the individual they really wanted, was me. I trusted in my prayer by claiming it in the name of Jesus and I, expected a call... confirming that the job was mine.

In the meantime; my present boss came in and explained a job task that came in for another individual, requiring him to go inside a Cyanide Tank of all things, to get internal piping measurements. He went on to explain that there were no other means of entry into this vessel except for that at the top of the tank. He explained that Cyanide is so deadly; that it only takes thirteen particles out of a million to kill you and because of this; he would be required to wear a rain suit and use an oxygen tank.

I was so relieved to hear that this was his job, and not mine, but then he informed me that I would be going in the tank with him, because it is mandatory to be on a buddy system upon entry. I naturally, declined and this boss said, "No, You're going with him and you're going to have to wear a rain suit, too. That's what you were hired to do" and I said, "No, I was hired to draw and not to jeopardize my life, especially when my wife is expecting to deliver a baby, so get someone else to do it or do it yourself." He said, "You're going! So, be ready come Monday morning and the two of you are going to have to share the oxygen mask, because we only have one." It was then I come to realize that companies have no concern about their employees' well-being, as long as the job gets done. Thank God for OSHA.

This gave me all the more incentive, to get out of there. I then asked why I was expected to go and he claimed that if, the other fellow was to pass out that I was strong enough to carry him up the 25 foot tall tank wall and back down again, to safety. I then asked, "What if I was to pass out?" I only asked, because I was much larger than this other individual. He said, he would have to drag you over to the bulk-head of the tank and set me up against the wall to go and get me some help? I said, "No, I don't think so, today's my last day." So, I prayed all the more, claiming victory on the Lakeland job, claiming they made a mistake and want me.

Well, surprise! It was about 3:00PM when I received a call from this person again; who told me that they had made an error and that it was me that they wanted. He went on to say that they somehow managed to mix-up the résumé's and asked, if I was able to report on Monday. They didn't have to ask me twice; I accepted. Praise God! God is so loving and caring, and will help us, if we only trust, believe, and have faith in Him. Yes, He's so good, and always with me, and always there, for you too.

As I've said before, the Word says the tongue is a powerful instrument. So, be careful of what you ask for or what you say. You may just get what you ask for, as I did. Other examples are where my wife and I have been taken advantage-of by others.

I could mention names, but choose not to. It's usually the people and not necessarily the company. We were either charged too much for a service provided or given something in-lieu of what we thought to be buying, and in some case charged money for a something we didn't receive. Because of events like this, I would ask to speak with the manager and discuss the issues and they either worked it out with me or they didn't, and if they chose not to... then I would tell them that the way they ran business, was wrong. I also, remember saying, that if they were to continue treating people like this that they would soon be out of business. There were four or more places, and each and everyone one of them that have since, closed. The Word also says not to curse people with the same tongue that we praise and worship God with, for the one we curse, is also made in God's Image, and the Holy Spirit may be dealing within them. So, I'm trying not to be negative, toward anyone, anymore. Remember too, there is power in name of Jesus and the unbridled tongue, so be careful what you ask and in what you say; it may come about.

Iranian Hostages

This is but another example about a big event that took place in Iran, where 52-American Citizens and Diplomats were taken hostage, blindfolded and held as prisoners from: November 4, 1979 through January 20, 1981 which days numbered: 444 days.

This event took place while I was working with a couple different companies; alongside others who too, were temps', as I was, also referred to as Job Shoppers; Professionals. There is this one person I come to enjoy spending time with, named Dennis Evens. We shared the Word of God together and became close friends and associates. He also, did other work elsewhere, that I envied, where he worked for the Lord, as a preachers' preacher, having meetings with other pastors that came together in a group where he spoke to them as a teacher; a person of authority, sharing the Word of God. It was after learning about this, that I opened up and shared with him, my stories, dreams and visions.

I don't really know, if he truly believed what I shared, but he was definitely impressed over what I shared with him, where we sat together, side by side in the office. I remember him telling me that he had never known anyone, to have so close of a relationship with the Lord, where the Lord was working with me, so closely and to having so many visions and dreams. He used to leave me notes on my desk telling me how blessed I am or how much the Lord loves me, and that the Lord has plans for me. I really didn't understand what or how, but he tried to encourage me to get a degree in theology through the Berean Bible Course by mail, which I began, but eventually quit, for personal reasons.

It was after this that the Iranian Hostage crisis took place and where we attempted to rescue them, but failed. Dennis and I talked about it, where I told Dennis that these hostages would be held for 444 days, and only then would they be released. Dennis asked, "Where did you get that number from?" I told him that I didn't know and that it just came to me. I don't believe he believed me, but we were worked together and discussed the events as they aired on the news, numerous times. My answers to his questions were always the same: they're freed on day 444.

Then one day it happened. It was the 443rd Day and Dennis came in the office all excited calling my name saying, "Doug, you were right! We just made a deal with Iran to release all the hostages... tomorrow! He went on to say that they were being flown to W. Germany and then to the United States. I said, "You're Right! Tomorrow is the 444th day, the day when they're supposed to be, released." Afterwards, we returned to our desk.

Come next morning, we reported to work and Dennis came in saying, good morning to me and then said, "Well, today's the day! The 444th day and the hostages are going to be on their way home, any time now." I agreed, but still Dennis wanted to know how I knew that they would be released, and I could only say, I don't know other than something inside me told me, 444 days. I'd like to say it came from the Lord and maybe it did, but as always, I really don't know for sure, and that's a fact.

I believe it was just before lunch, if I remember correctly, when Dennis came over to me and said, "Well, it sounds like you were wrong! They just said it was too late, and it would be tomorrow before they would be released to come home." What could I say, but what I had been saying all along, since the beginning. "Nope! Todays the day; the 444th Day and Dennis, interrupted me to remind me. Saying, we're talking about Iran here and that they just announced it wouldn't happen until tomorrow and again I said, "No, today's the day; the 444th Day!" Dennis had accepted what they were saying on the radio, but I refused to believe otherwise, and it was close to quitting time when Dennis came back to my desk and said, "Doug, How did you know?" I said, "How did I know what?" Dennis said, "How did you know today would be the day?" He then said the radio just announced confirmation that the hostages were own their way to West Germany and would be coming home from there, and he asked again, "How did you know? Who told you?" All I could say was, "I'm not sure." I remember Dennis asking, "Did God tell you?" and I would say, I didn't know because I wasn't sure. I just knew something inside me said the 444th Day and I stood on it, claiming it as such, accepting nothing less, nothing more. Only God knows for sure and what my tongue confessed, but I'll say this. The Spirit of God does dwells within me.

Family Addition

So, this is why I believe I was hired instead of the other guy. I confessed it... with my tongue; claiming it to be mine, in the name of Jesus; trusting and believing, having faith that I would receive that job, and I did! So, I packed up all of our remaining belongings and furniture and hit the road to surprise Joyce and the rest of the family with the good news. Joyce was so excited and happy when I came in. We were together again, as a family, and that we would soon be moving into our own place. It wasn't much longer after that, that we were blessed with the birth of our son, Joshua Earl; our latest families addition. We were so excited about our new blessing, from the Lord; our son!

We all have dreams and visions and I can only say this because of what it says in the Bible; that the young men will have visions and old men will have dreams. Well, I've been blessed with both, especially with dreams. This being said, because of my son, who was only four days shy of being three.

My Sons Blessings

It was early, one Saturday morning when my son came into our room to disturb our sleep. He said, "Dad, hey dad! Wake-up! I got something to tell you." As we woke I said, "What is it son?" Joshua said, "I saw God." and I said, "What?" He said, "I saw God." It was then I corrected him and said, "No! No one has ever seen God. You may have seen Jesus, but not God."

Well, Josh just stood there for a couple moments and I could almost see those little gears spinning round and round in his head. Then he looks right at me and said, "Then I saw Jesus!" So, I asked Joshua, "Were you sleeping?" Josh said, "Yeah." Then I said, "Oh, so you were dreaming" and Joshua said, "No!" I said, "Well, you said you were sleeping, yes?" Joshua said, "Yes, but He woke me up." I then asked, "He woke you up?" followed by; "What happened next?" It was then that Joshua in his innocence of being only three years of age, he looked into my eyes, having my attention and said, "He picked me up in his arms." With remembering my experiences I had in years past, I had no reason to doubt him, but I just had to ask; "He picked you up... in His arms? He said, "Yes." It was then that I asked, "Well, what did He say? Did He, say anything to you?" Josh said, "Yes, He told me He that loved me." I thought I'd push the issue and asked a few more questions. So, I asked, "Well, what happen next? Did he just disappear?" He said, "No, he put me back into bed and walked out the door, with two angels." I thought to myself, Angels? Then I thought to myself, ah-ha, got you now; trying to see if he made this up or what. So, I went on to ask him, yet one last question, where I asked him, "What were they wearing?"

We attended church regularly and we always spoke of the Lord, reading the Word to him and his sisters every night followed with prayers. I'm sure we mentioned angels in passing, but I really don't recall discussing what angles wore. So, his next response was enough proof for us to accept what was saying to be true, when he said, "Long white dresses!" Well, I had him repeat this event to us daily, weekly and then monthly... for years to come and then on occasion, as he became a teenager. He was, too young to make-up this story and I don't really know, if he actually remembers the event, or just telling us the story through the years, but the event actually occur and I knew it may serve him well one day and it did, much later in his teens years.

Like other kids, he had begun experimenting with drugs, including the hard stuff. As such, we were forced into making an unwanted decision. We thought he may be doing drugs but didn't know the first thing about them for we hadn't done so. We also, came to realize that he was stealing from us and when I noticed things missing, I confronted him. He claimed not to know anything about it and I chose to believe him and let it ride until it continued. Then I was at the end of the rope. I didn't ask him the next time something came up missing, I accused him as the only one that could have access which would take a key, unless someone literally broke in, which was not the case. So, I back-handed him when he denied it and told him next time I'd beat him and if he ever stole anything from his mother again, I would have him arrested. He agreed, but did so anyway and then I did the unthinkable. I had him arrested to teach him a lesson. I explained the events to the arresting detective who assured me I could drop the charge, if I did so, within a given time frame.

That was a big mistake! We were assured that we could drop the charges and get him released, but that I would have to do so before 30 days were to pass. So after the end of week one, Joyce and I went to see him, and Joyce and I were excited about seeing him. She brought him under garments and some flip flops. What I didn't know though, was just how much this whole event was up-setting Joyce until later which is why it's called, "Tuff Love."

When Josh stepped into visiting area, Joyce's face lit up. Josh was glad to see his mother, but he didn't want anything to do with me. I expected as much, but spoke to him anyway. I made an offer to get him out of jail, but with certain conditions, which his mother was well aware of, but he wasn't interested. I thought after spending a week in jail that he may have a better attitude, but he said he had friends that were going to come down to bail him out. So, Joyce and I agreed to leave him in there. We knew his friends wouldn't come, but he had false hopes, which we in turn, had hoped to teach him a lesson. What it did though was to teach Joyce and me about the meaning of, "Tuff Love." It hurt, as we turned to get up, Joyce asked him why he looked like he was losing weight and he said that the food was really nasty, and that he wouldn't eat it. I said that he had better get used to it, because we have only x-amount of days to drop the charges and get you out or he was going to be there a long time and that no one would be able to get him out after that. He said he wasn't worried about it; his friends would get him out.

Well, our visit time was ending and we were getting ready to leave and as we did, Josh asked his mother if he could get some money from her. He said the only thing available to eat there was sweets and they cost money, which were just candy bars. So, Joyce gave him a $20 bill and we said our good-byes, and that we would see him next week. We then got into the car and cried.

During our second week visit, I asked where his friends were and he said they're coming. I said, sure they are, and then I explained to him the facts of life; the real difference between friends and family. I told him family is blood and will always be there for you. Whereas, friends cannot always be counted on, especially when you really need them, but again, family really cares and will be there, if you want them, which is why you don't steal from family, but he insisted on waiting on his friends.

It was then that I decided to share a story with my son, as to why his friends would not come. I also, explained to him that he was smart enough to figure this out and to think about it.

I asked him why on earth, would his so called friends spend their hard earned drug money to bail you out? I said if they did, then they may not have enough money left to buy their drugs, and even if they did, now they have to share them, which means fewer drugs for them. So, I asked, "Do you really think they're coming down to bail you out and still his answer was; yes, they will. So, we left and went back to the car and held each other.

We visited on the third week and my son approached his mother. He asked her to ask me, to get him out of there. He was out of money and someone had stolen his flip-flops and other items. He said, he couldn't take it anymore and swore if he gets out, that he would never do anything to go back to jail again. He apparently had enough and has since done an about face, but I believe the event he had as a child, which he repeated over and over to us through the years is what had helped him break free. There is more to the story than this but the fact is that he settled down, got married and has blessed us... with three grandchildren.

I could go farther, but will only say this: I had to hire the most expensive attorney money could buy to help us to prevent Joshua from serving 15 years in prison, and we beat the case but, only because of money, and it's true what they say; money does talk... most of the time. Thank God for my career and the money I had or we would have lost big time. It could've crushed our hearts and come between us, but God is gracious and loves us!

The experience of raising him during and after those moments cost us more than tens of thousands of dollars, but more like a hundred thousand plus. Fortunately though, the Lord has been with us and he now has a family. He's become a good worker and does well, having a great home with a dock on a canal that leads into the Gulf of Mexico. He's always taking his family out swimming or fishing and enjoys watching the Manatees swim up and down the canals, including huge fish. That's what it's all about; freedom, love, family and above everything else; God Almighty, Lord of Lords and King of Kings, who dwells within. I believe too, that his blessing of having been visited, which he remembers, also helped him to overcome issues, and settle down.

As I said before; he's married now, in church, and life goes on, but this was truly, a case of unconditional love, as well as tough love. I would never wish anything like this on anyone and would only hope and pray that those of you who face a similar situation? That you would think twice before you relinquish control of your children into the hands of government. Always turn to God, friends and loved ones first. The cost and heart-aches are over-whelming, but we're never alone.

Yes, the Lord is with you and all you have to do; is but to ask in faith, trusting and believing in the Lord. He will guide you into truths and knowledge in ways that men cannot. Another thing too, is to take the time to read and share the Word with one another, each and every day. Say prayers together, as a whole. Allow your children the opportunity to speak with an open heart and an open mind for the needs of friends and family, as well as themselves. It may surprise you and even open your eyes toward the tenderness of the ones you love and open your heart toward things you may have otherwise, not known, be it good or bad. It will also bring in closeness into the relationship most parents may never know and a bonding toward love and trust that we can all learn from, and count on, especially in the child's time of need. They learn how to open-up and trust you in a positive way.

Also, to read the Word of God will fill your heart, soul and spirit with God's Holy Word, and in this you will come to know the Lord in ways that only God's Holy Spirit can lead you, as He dwells within, opening your awareness to the presence of God.

It is here that you can truly love and worship your creator in ways you otherwise, may not as the spirit speaks on your behave in ways that are unknown to men. Also, as you grow in the Lord and abide in His Word, he will abide in you and he says to ask what you will and it shall be done. So, trust in the Lord for God is faithful and He loves you.

John 15-7 *If ye abide in me, and my words abide in you, ye shall* ***ask*** *what ye will, and it shall be done unto you.*

CHAPTER 11

"Blessings of the Lord"

Trust in the Lord

So, as I was saying before, I had taken my wife back to Florida, only to return to Alabama. It's there where I didn't want to be, and came to remember and realize the need to trust and believe in the Words of the Lord, which I hadn't been doing as I learned staying at the Grammers, while Joyce and I were apart.

I needed, but to return back toward the Lord for guidance and approval; focusing on what I come to know, as truth. I had only, but to ask, believe and receive; asking and expecting to receive in the name of the Lord, as I had done before, expecting to receive that which I had asked for, as if what I was asking, had already taken place. It's because of this, and through my faith and believing in the Lord, that I knew I would receive what I had asked and I landed the job outside of Lakeland. Thank you, Lord.

So, as it says in the Word of God, that whatever we ask in the name of Jesus; it shall be done to Glorify God. So, this is all any of us have to do, is to turn to the Lord, accept Him in Love and Faith as our personal Lord and Savior whom we can trust and believe in

Him, for His Word is Truth! Know too, that we only need but to ask in His name; trusting and believing, that it has already taken place. It's called stepping out in faith; trusting and believing, in the Lord and this is how I come to learn to rely on the Lord. Especially, with me becoming a temp where I grew into becoming a Sr. Design Engineering Consultant, and shortly afterwards, I incorporating myself as; DDT Services Inc.

As such, I was making two to three times or more than before as a direct employee. I reached out as such, when I realized that a room full of direct employees working as a team, beneath a boss, consisting of 10 or more; all of whom have high hopes of moving into the boss's position when he retires, but just not very likely due to conflicts of interest for everyone involved.

There's only one problem with this idea, which is, that they all looking in hopes to fill that one position and some may be vindictive to another, due to their high hopes, of filling that job themselves. They may feel more qualified due to their seniority, knowledge, experience; hard work and company dedication, but can only lead to major problems, for everyone and the company.

This can cause morale issues and discontentment among the team, due to one of the team members being favored over another and for what; a few extra dollars? Most corporate leaders however, through previous experiences I'm sure, would be better off bringing in an outsider. Someone more experienced and qualified to replace the boss; leaving the team intact to continuing to do the job they're trained to, without hostilities.

Those who are smart enough to see the writing on the wall may however move on, realizing their inability to move up the corporate ladder, if ever. Those who do not see it as such are usually, the young people; the innocent and naïve, lacking the experience to move forward. They will be content for a time or until they realize, as others have; what has taken place and providing whether or not, they have acquired enough experience, only then may they move forward to greener pastures, elsewhere.

I know this, because this happened to me when I come to realize how business works, but only after my stepfather shared a story with me. He said while he himself was a young man, just getting started in life, that he had an eye opening experience early in life. This is where he came to realized how business really works, and manipulates people... to their advantage.

He went on to say that he along with others went to be interviewed for a job that was advertised in the local newspaper by a man that would be his boss. This boss showed interest and then asked what sort of wage he was looking for. Afterwards, his boss apologized, saying that he was a little younger and less experienced than what he was looking for and counter-offered him considerably less, which Gil had accepted, needing a job.

Gil began working just outside the boss's office and this older gentleman dressed in a suit and tie, carrying a briefcase entered into his office. They spoke awhile and then the boss asked what he was expecting for a salary. After he had stated what he would like to receive, he said the boss responded by saying; "I'm sorry, but that's much more than we are willing to pay. What we're really looking for is a fresh young man right out of school that has no experience that can be trained in our ways. We could however consider you for the job, but only if you were willing to accept the wage that we are willing to offer for your services."

Gil said he stormed into the boss's office upon hearing what the boss had just said, without even knocking; asking, "Hey, what the heck's going on here? You told me you wanted an older, more experienced person and offered me less, only for this guy to come in; the guy you told me you wanted to hire, and then you tell him... you want someone younger, less experienced to train and learn company ways, only to offer him less money? He looked at the guy and said, I'm out here!" and they left, together.

It's because of that story and my being laid-off from numerous jobs which I thought to be safe and secure, offering benefits: sick days, holidays and vacations, but more importantly a secure job? Not so! I came to realize it was just talk where I made less money, and because of it, my family and I suffered.

I come to realize that temps are usually, the first to be hired to test the waters, so to speak... prior to hiring on direct employees and temps are usually, the first to be let go, which is why they do so well financially. They are hired knowing the inevitable will occur, upon completion of the assignment and because of this... they ask for more and get it. Where-as, the direct employees have that false sense of security, expecting temps to be laid-off first, thinking themselves to be safe and secure, but surprise! Direct Employees are let go after the first wave of lay-offs and some are surprised to see some temps staying. This happens because the temps that began the project are key people who understand it best, and can finish the task up to, and through plant start-up; the end of the job, should any issues arise.

Otherwise, directs employee's, as well as temps, are eligible to receive unemployment, but usually the temps are able to find work first, being released first... before the direct employees are even let go. This makes finding a job a bit more difficult for those who are direct, and when there aren't many jobs to be found locally, both directs as well as temps are forced to reach out, into other areas beyond. This is the reason I was headed to Michigan and passed through St. Louis, only to stay with the Grammers and then return to Joyce and the girls' 6-monthes later, where we moved to Alabama, only to return to Lakeland as a family, where Joyce would bring our son, into the world.

Professional Experience's

Like most, I preferred being a loner and was referred to, as I had said earlier: A Senior Design Engineering Consultant, which is a glorified name for Job Shopper, as a Senior Designer that began, as nothing more than a draftsman. I have worked in most all areas, from mechanical, structural, civil, concrete, electrical, architectural, machine, tooling and more; for defense, aircraft such as F15 and F16 decoys, aerospace including the Space Shuttle and the Skylab Orbital

Space Station (America's first Space Station) as well as, jet engine test stands, Poison Sniffer test stands, Reverse Osmosis System and Marine for an unman Submersible & US Mini-Submarine for the US Navy. I worked for numerous mining and chemical facilities across America. A lot of these places had asked for me to return as many as 4, 5 & 6 different times. All of which I loved, enjoyed, and miss dearly, as they were all challenging; mentally and physically, where I would be present during turn around and start-ups, on some jobs.

The thrill to negotiate wages, travel expenses, room and board including job duration was a real challenge in itself and none of this would have been possible, if it had not been made available to me. It all began with me meeting the young man that was in the Job Corps, who just happened to be passing through the St. Louis Grey Hound Bus Station; all predestined I believe by God.

That's where I was, when abandoned just after becoming 15 years of age. There's absolutely, no doubt in my mind that it was the Lord who was watching over me from that point on and has seen me through the years, making it more abundantly clear as time went on from childhood, to meeting Joyce, and I being married throughout my entire life. In fact, we've been married now, 50+ years and all is well, thanks be unto the Lord our God; God the Father, the Son and the Holy Spirit. Thank you, Lord.

As time came to pass, I come to realizing by learning from past experiences, to ask the Lord to close the doors where He would not want me to be, and to open the door where He would have me be. It got to the point where I would do this, almost always; each time I sent out hundreds to thousands of Résumés, all across these United States. My responses were as much as 10% or more and I received many offers for numerous positions that I found hard to choose from or where to go, except for where I felt led; turning the other jobs down and passing them on to others, sometimes for a finding fee from various head hunters.

Failing the Lord

There had been times in life, that I chose to be in a particular place without asking for guidance, thinking to myself; I got this or I wanted to be here or there; forgetting or just failing, to ask the Lord for guidance. Such was the case, in accepting an assignment at this one particular company that was first-class and where there were Air-Force Generals working on the premises to assist and provide an over-view of things to come, which we were all striving toward. There were a lot of young men and women; of all ages, whom were well dressed. This one particular day, there was this really beautiful looking young lady who had passed by me, which I chose to ignore, as I continued working. My associates chose to gawk and to make obscene sexiest jesters about her and what they would like to do, as they laughed in agreement with one another. I chose to ignore the conversation and to keep my head down, and continued working.

My choosing to do so left the door wide open for ridicule and accusations, especially from a small, Napoleon type individual that I will refer to, as Jim. Jim noticed that I hadn't joined in and asked me questions that I've heard before, and as before, I tried to skirt around them, but to no avail. He asked something basically like, "What you think Doug? Isn't that nice, and wouldn't you like to spend some time alone with her?" I responded by saying, "No man, I'm not interested." It was then, that Jim asked me, "Why not? Are you better than us?" I said something to the effect, stating: "No, but I am a happily married man and have three beautiful children. So, thanks, but no thanks." He acted confounded and surprised.

I obviously, insulted him; not intentionally, but never the less... I insulted him, and he wasn't going to let it lie. So, he exclaimed aloud, "Look what we have here, Mr. Goodie Two-Shoes that is too good to look at another woman? I said, "No, man, it's just that I'm a Christian and happily married to the woman I love." He laughed and continued with his remarks saying something similar to, "Hey, fella's, Doug's a Christian and thinks he's better than us, what you think of Mr. Perfect?"

This went on for a few days including one individual named Al who had invited me and my wife over to his home on several different occasions in Alabama where we worked together before at another company, as associates. I considered him to be a good friend and when he joined in... I reminded him of such. Now, he didn't deny it, but he did not come to my defense either and even joined in on the harassment or at least, just stood by, as it occurred, laughing with the others. I really don't remember exactly what happened, but what I do remember, is reminding him of how he had told me that he too, was a Christian, but no one seemed to care, because he had joined in with their: Ew-la-la remarks over the woman who had passed-by. I even went a step further, reminding him how he had told me that he use to teach Sunday School to the children, and still... he only smiled as the insults came, which I try to ignore for days but again, to no avail.

Jim came to my desk regularly until finally, I had my fill. Instead of praying about it, I let the ugly... inside me, come out; failing the test, as Jim reminded me of being a Christian who was better than him. Then, I said that I was no better than he is and if he wanted me to prove it, I could stop being a Christian, just long enough to kick his butt! Well, needless to say, silence returned, and all appeared well and over with, except for one little thing; I failed God and Jim, whom I was probably there for.

I believe this may have been one of the last times, if not the last time, that I would decide to go on a job without asking for all the doors to be shut, except for that one place, where God would have me be. I really blew this opportunity. I wonder as I look back, even now! How many other opportunities have I blown? All I can do is ask is... Please, forgive me Lord.

I did however, manage to stay on the job for 16 weeks and created 16 separate conceptual drawings, all which were feasible. Jim was bad enough, but as for my boss? I questioned him about what he wanted, because he never appeared happy with my work and always said, "Well, put that one away and let's try another."

Only this time, I had reached my limits with him too, when I showed my boss my latest concept. He said, "Good! Now, let's put this one away and try another." I opened my drawer and strummed my thumb across the edges of 16 drawings and asked, "What's going on?" I went on to say, that what I was doing was a waste of time and tax-payers money, and that anyone of those 16 drawings was feasible and would work just fine. He wasn't very receptive to my complaints and didn't want to hear it, and had only one thing to say to me, as I complained. He pointed to a phrase beneath the title block, stating..."Quality, Not Quantity!" He said, "This is what we are striving for, and if it means that we needed to do 99 drawings, then that's what we'll do. I reminded him of my position and told him, that he might do this, but I didn't want to stand before a Congressional Investigation and with that being said, I informed him that I quit.

Afterwards, I went to the highest ranking General I could find on the upper floor and knocked on his door. As he looked up, I asked if he had a moment where I could speak with him, and he invited me into his office. I introduced myself and explained that I had just quit my job, as not to be involved in a Congressional Investigation. He asked me what I meant, so I explained in detail, including the Engineers name. I also believe the phrase; Quality not Quantity" meant just that; Quality, instead of quantity. Afterwards, I apologized for interrupting him, but felt led to tell someone, which is why, I come to him.

He thanked me and as I left, I knew that I had burned a bridge and that I would never be able to return, but I recognized a pattern, which I did not want any part of. Most companies, from past experience would never have asked or told me at any time to make a career... on one drawing. I may have taken it personally and shouldn't have, but I've never repeated a drawing anywhere before or felt insulted, or as if I were being bullied or picked on in addition to what had taken place earlier with Jim. It was either that or to be fired, for generating 99 drawings which was absurd and would have taken, nearly two years at one per week.

I loved working in my profession, but that love soon turned into hatred and despair, where I began taking all this personally. That was the main reasons I quit and shared this event with someone at top to stop such nonsense. Otherwise, this guy would have brought someone else on board to replace me; into the same environment where they would have only continued in his ways, which needed to be stopped, since he couldn't be reasoned with.

So, after the fact, I took the time to re-evaluate the way everything turned out which seemed to be stacked up against me. I realized too, that if I was there for a specific reason... I'm sorry Lord, but I failed you, again. I didn't see it and took things too personally and blinded myself with what was being done and willing to fight back one way or another, which is not that of Love, but that of hatred and again, I was unhappy with myself. I also knew that I took this job, without asking, the Lord guidance.

Second Opportunity

It was too many months later or longer, following that incident when I was watching the news following diner where I heard that this particular company, whom I had been working for, was actually under a Congressional Investigation. I'd be lying if I were to say I wasn't surprised, because I expected this with the accepted practices and quite possibly that, of only one man. I don't really know what the out-come was nor did I ask, but then one day out of nowhere, surprise! I received a call and was asked, if I would like to come back to work at this same company. What a shocker! I accepted the position and returned to the company and noticed the engineer I had been working for was no longer to be seen. I then asked, "What had happened to Bob?" I was informed that he had been relocated into another position, elsewhere. Then, I noticed too, that Jim was missing and questioned his whereabouts. I was informed that he too, was relocated and a changed man. I said, really? What happened? He went on to remind me how most of the guys would stop after hours for a few drinks directly across the street from the office. He went on to say, one night Jim drank a little, too much and crossed-over a double line driving home, killing a Florida Highway Patrolman. I was floored and much to my surprise, I felt lead to see him. As I did, I noticed that he truly appeared to have had a complete change; a different outlook in life, and he viewed life in a whole different prospective. He spoke softly and I don't remember what took place between us at that point. I was in a bit of hurry being on company time, but did want to visit, for a few minutes to let him know that I cared and that I was thinking about him, which was well received. He thanked me and we said our good-byes and that was the last time, I saw Jim. I only wish that I would have made more time to see him and shared the Lord, as I should have. But by his actions, I would like to think he already met Him or at least, I would like to believe so. Otherwise, I blew it but again, and I wonder sometimes in life, how much of a disappointment we are, as we try and hope to serve the Lord, but fail. We should only, strive for perfection and look to the Lord for forgiveness and guidance.

Smiling Fish Dream

I want to share a dream with you where I out fishing on a flat john boat and the best I can recall is, that I was all by myself and fishing, with only a ten pound test line. I had hopes of catching a fish or two, but I never dreamed that I would catch a fish, anything like the one I caught. I had just thrown in the line, and somehow, managed to catch a fish immediately, and what a fish he was! He appeared to be about 36 to 40 inches long. I really didn't have any idea as to how big he was or how much he weighed, because I've never caught a fish, quite like this before in my entire life and I never had the chance to weigh him. Judging by the size of the fish, I would've thought that he'd give me quite a fight, but he didn't. He just drifted slowly, up along the side the boat, which I thought rather strange. I realized as he did just how big he was, and that my 10 pound line would never pull him on board. So, I reach down to grab him by the gill.

I refer to this fish as a "He", only because, as I lifted him out of the water, I was in total shock and disbelief of what I was seeing. Instead of looking into the face of a fish, I was looking into the face of a man. He had no hair to speak of, and his face was a smooth, flesh tone as one would imagine and it blended in with scales of a fish, where a man's hairline would begin.

As I lifted him out of the water, I was in awe of the fact, that he was indeed, a fish... with a man's face. He didn't speak, but looked up at me, making eye contact and his eyes blinked several times, as if to get the water from his eyes to see me, as one would normally do coming up from out of the water. Only, he had a big smile on his face. I was so taken back and surprised of what I was witnessing that out of fear and not understanding; I dropped the fish back into the sea and woke up from my dream. I really didn't have any understanding of what this dream was about at the time and thought it to be rather strange and shrugged it off as another one of those crazy or unusual dreams I have from time to time, but this one, was so real, I couldn't let it go.

I did however, share this dream with a few people I know, and they reminded me of the Lord telling Peter that He would make him a Fisher of men. However, I didn't think about it much because, after all who am I, to think of such a thing? Who, me; a Preacher? So, I too, let that idea go, as I shrugged it off, forgetting the impact of dreams that I've had, throughout my life.

Too Many Dreams
....

As a reminder, I live in Florida; Mid-Florida, and as such, we have hurricane threats, just about every year. Sometimes we may only see one or two or none, and then there are some years where we have had a slew of them, all lining up, one after another. As shown, below in the images provided by NOAH, these storms in this satellite view were literally unbelievable, as a "Parade of Hurricanes" that happened in 1995, when all my dreams of hurricanes first began and have done so, every year for over 20+ years now. Why, I don't know. A lot of these came across the state from every direction, so it would appear. In fact, three of which crisscrossed right over us in 2004; Charley, Frances, and Jeanne were separate by approx. 2

weeks apart. These dreams were surreal that I would seek immediate refuge, whatever I could find. It was almost as if, they had a mind of their own and would follow me wherever I went; tearing off the roof tops of houses or buildings, just to get to me. But, they couldn't do it, due to my surroundings, where I would always be barricade within a reinforced concrete shelter. I would wake my wife, saying that's one, then the next dream would come, and I'd say, that's two, then there were three, four and so-on and so-on.

I remember in 2006 being the year that my wife and I, along with her three brothers, and one of her two sisters, were getting together for a family reunion, on a seven-day cruise. The cruise-ship was destined for the Carmen Islands and Cozumel, Mexico. There were ten of us all together, most of whom came from other parts of the country. At first, there wasn't much, if any concern about hurricanes, until the week of departure came into light.

Everything was planned nearly a year before with everyone paying in advance to receive discounts given to us for booking early, so hurricanes were out of question at that time. It was only as the departure date come into light, that hurricanes were talked about, one forming in the Atlantic. It was just days before we would depart when hurricane "Ernesto" came into the picture looking, as if it would go into the Gulf of Mexico and ruin our trip. I told them not to worry. True it was going west but I told them it would swing north and miss the gulf all together, which it did. It calmed their concerns, as I told them the weather would be just fine for the trip, and it was perfect. Ernesto hit Cuba and turned north, entering Florida through the everglades; passing over N. Lake Okeechobee, and back out into the Atlantic; re-entering into, and through N Carolina and on up into N America.

These storms still come every year, 2005 being the worst year for hurricanes, having so many and the year, 2015... I believe to have been the least amount of hurricanes. I still continuously have these strong dreams, pointing them out as to whether or not were going to hit right here in Florida or not, and they've been fading with each passing year, so it would seem. As of this year though, I've not had a single dream I can remember except for one that was a near miss in December last year, which was probably Hurricane, Otherwise, I haven't seen as many coming toward us, as before except a few that turning northward, up the Coast or east of the states, out into the Atlantic ocean, but they have slowed down considerably, including two for this year still coming. So, I suspect I'll continue having these dreams. The Bible says young men will have visions and old men will have dreams and as much as I hate to admit it, I'm not as young, as I once was, but I'm blessed with dreams... every night. Some which are pleasant and some that are not so pleasant. I also, have some that are scary where I tell myself, It's only a dream and others that happen occasionally, where they are nightmares that will jerk one right out of sleep and again, I remind myself that it was just a bad dream and to think about something else. I don't know for sure how many I have dreamed about the returning of Jesus but I do know this... He is coming someday... soon, which I share more, later.

1995 - Parade of Hurricanes
(Compliments of NOAA)

FISHER OF MEN

True, some may have thought that my dream may have been a way of the Lord speaking to me; for me to step up to the task in becoming, a fisher of men. That thought though, I shrugged off. That is, until I was on my way home, finishing yet another job, only this time I began to wonder; what next, as I packed to leave.

I then went out to the car and put all my belongings in the trunk, only to turn around and go back inside to say my good-bye's, as I always have and then hopped into the car to head on home. As I headed homeward, I realized that I hadn't sent out any résumé's, as of yet nor made any contacts to line-up my next job, as I would normally do. It was because of this that I was a little concerned about it, wondering... where I'd be going next.

I usually send out résumés even before leaving a company, but things, just happen so quickly with this job, where I had been working, that I apparently, put it on hold. So, I hadn't taken the time to do so, as of yet. I thought about it as I drove down the highway, wondering to myself, where I'd be going next and asked the Lord, "What's next? Where am I going" wondering to myself, "Why am I here?" I also asked, "What purpose do I have in Life?" It surely wasn't to, just work. I couldn't see any real purpose, or direction in my life, which is why I began speaking to the Lord, knowing my life was near, half-way over.

All of this took place as I was driving in the fast lane, minding my own business with no one around me. There wasn't anyone in front of me or behind me, and as I did; I entered into a vision. I visualized myself driving across, what is best described as a "Bridge of Life," Straight and narrow, from the beginning of one's life, spanning across time to the end of life. Only, this bridge was a representation my life, as it was, and yet to come.

As I continued to watch, with these questions in my head, I could see myself where I appeared to be about halfway across the bridge; when actually, I was on a main highway that was a toll road. However, in my vision, I appeared to be traveling on a bridge where there was nothing but a great body of water on both sides, as far as I could see. All of a sudden, amongst all this began appearing fish, lots of fish; swimming on the surface of the water, similar to the fish that I had dreamed about, where I was fishing on a johnboat. As in the dream, these fish too, had the face of a man on every one of them. It was then that I come to realize that I had received an answer, in regard to my dream, and my question. As to what purpose I had in life, where I felt lacking direction; not knowing where I was going and therefore, I was seeking guidance; asking the Lord and found my answer. I knew right then and there, what I needed to do in my life and the answer was simple. I needed to prepare myself to move forward, to serve the Lord for it is God, in whom we should trust. As I came to this conclusion, I also realized my surroundings and that I was fast approaching my exit to continue on my trip home.

As I did this, I began thinking of the possibilities of getting back into school; a University where I could learn more about the Lord and the possibilities of obtaining a degree; in theology. It's only because of this, that my desire grew to educate myself and to prepare myself to serve the Lord, and to share Jesus with others. I wanted to help lead others toward the one and only true way of having Eternal Life... Life with the Lord of all creation: the Father, the Son (Jesus) and the Holy Spirit. For the three are, one; one God! There is none other. He is the Creator of the Universe; the Heavens and the Earth, and of all things that ever existed, or presently exist, and yet... to come, for He alone is God! There is no other God, except for the One and Only, True Living God; God Almighty, the Great I AM and the God of our Salvation, who was and is, and forever will be, GOD! His name is above all names and there is no greater name... than Jesus.

As I've said before, I usually put together my résumé and send them out in great quantities, sometimes hundreds to thousands at a time. This is what I referred to as, a shot-gun blast; all across America. There have always been more jobs than needed, right here in the United States without me having to leave the country. Eventually, I incorporated myself to gain a tax advantage that worked well for me, as DDT Services, Inc. This opened doors to travel. I now had a tax deductible corporate expense account, so I could travel across the country, using less money at a lower taxes, none of which I knew much about, except for having, a CPA. He was a registered IRS

Agent and kept me out of trouble and away from audits, so I could concentrate on the job and making money because, I was somewhat of a workaholic making 6 figures.

So, when in search of any Design Engineering, Consulting positions, I always tried to stay close to home, in Florida. Only, as a last resort when there were no other jobs available, locally or in the state, I'd go out to other places. Again, I only did this because of the lack of these types of jobs that forced me to reach out to Tampa and the St. Petersburg areas, or Orlando and beyond; sometimes out of state. As such, I would have to fly home for the weekend every other, 2 or 3 weeks, when possible.

I truly, dreaded this point in my career, but the money was always top dollar, which allowed me the means to provide what was needed to meet my family's needs, as a provider. I was not necessarily the best father that I would have preferred to have been, but I always tried to stay in town, close to home, as to be with Joyce; my wife; who is my best ole' pal, ole' buddy, ole' friend of mine, and my lifelong lover and companion. A real blessing from God, who has blessed me with her and I would like to believe after our years of marriage; she is blessed with me. In turn, God has blessed both of us with three beautiful children, whom are now grown and married, providing us with seven grandchildren that are all fast approaching adulthood, if not already there. All these are a blessing to us as a product of the Love which we have for one another. This is the only reason why I dread being away from home, which separates us from one another; as a family, and puts a lot of responsibility and burden on Joyce, especially when I go out for weeks, months, or longer.

Being on the road away from home and family can be lonely, but I made it a point to call home nightly and to send my wife flowers at her office, as often as possible, to make her feel special and to let her know that I love and missed her. The jobs were pretty good considering my background, but I had the desire to be a successful business man and hopefully, a better father than my dad. There are those times too, where I loved it, but then again, dreaded it, but had to keep working. Sometimes, if it were summer; I would take my family with me on a summer vacation, but before any job or this would ever happen, I always made it a point to ask for the Lords protection when looking for a job. I would ask Him to close any doors where He'd not have me be and to open the one door, where He'd have me be, and by doing this... I knew, I'd be exactly, where I was supposed to be.

So, I began tossing the idea around of going to school, only to set it on the back burner, but once again. I knew that I would need to find a job near home where going to college was possible on a long-term job, for at least a few years or more. So, until then, I had no real choice, but to send out my résumé, yet again.

I did this several different times, where I would go to work for various companies after my vision. One of which was located up in Huntsville, Alabama where I'd be on contract with a company doing a job for Redstone Arsenal, which is a military base that deals with ordinance and storage bunkers.

Before I left to go to Huntsville though, I went in to speak to a gentleman; Bob who had a business being relocated in the little town where Joyce and I called home. Bob was impressed with my credentials and said he wanted to hire me but didn't have the space to bring me on board, until his new office building was complete. He said that he'd be in touch in a month or two and to keep in touch. This is why I accepted the short term position in Huntsville, but Wow! The possibility of a job at home meant that I had a real possibility to stay local for years and obtain a Theology Degree and prepare myself, as a fisher of men.

Born and raised in St. Louis, Missouri, Glasgow Village. Attended... Glasgow Elementary, Riverview Jr. High and Sr. High Schools. Abandoned at fifteen: at Grey Hound Bus Station, Joined Job Corps for GED and 2-year Drafting Certificate: San Marcos, Texas.

Graduated at eighteen and began 40+ year Professional Career in Engineering, as Draftsman, to Senior Design Engineering Consultant; generating 2D and 3D Computer Generated Drawings. Founded privately owned company: DDTServices, Incorporated Contracting 40+ Companies within America for Various Facilities: Mining and Chemical to Military: US Navy, Air-Force, Aerospace, including NASA. Attended FL Christian Life University: Associates Degree in Theology, and Retired.

TEN COMMANDMENTS

I was really so excited, but I had to wait a little longer. It was the week of Thanksgiving that I reported to work in Huntsville, and I wasn't sure or very happy about it. I already missed being home and this wasn't the best time of year to be away from family or for finding a job, considering the Holiday Season, but I needed the job. I arrived in Huntsville a day early to locate the company where I'd be reporting to and to find a place that would be safe and secure, as my home, away from home. This also, allowed me the convenience of being able to report to work, in a timely manner with little or no traffic. In doing so, I paid for my room, a week in advance and then prepared myself to report to work, by calling it a day. I prepared to go to bed early and get a good night's sleep, but only after checking in at home with Joyce, where all was well, except for me not being there.

When morning came, I reported to the job-site bright and early as I had planned. The entrance of the building consisted of two double glass doors in which were open and I went on in.

Immediately in front of me was the receptionist and I was somewhat taken back with what she had on her desk. It was a huge L-shaped desk and was almost completely covered with a manger scene from one end to the other with little room for her typewriter, having enormous figurines that were standing at least 14" to 16" tall. This naturally caught me by surprise and then I noticed behind this display, was the receptionist. She greeted me with a great big smile on her face as she peered over the scene and welcomed me, asking if she could help me. I smiled at her, giving her my name and of the person in whom I was to report.

She mentioned that he hadn't come in yet and offered me some coffee since I would have wait on him. I accepted the offer and sat down across from her. As I did, I complimented her Manger Scene, stating it to be the biggest desk display that I'd ever seen.

I looked in awe and mentioned to her, that I had heard on the radio, on my way into town that It was sad to hear, but that Alabama would be removing the Ten Commandments from the State Capital Building and that there would no longer be any Manger Scenes on display any longer at any of the government facilities, as I nodded toward the Manger Scene on her desk. Then I asked, "Isn't this a government job, I'll be working on?"

She was a very attractive, middle aged woman, well dressed with high-lighted short blond hair and very well-mannered, and wore the biggest smile that only brightened the day. She didn't have to say a single word to me, and her smile only grew, even bigger as she leaned back in her chair. As she did so, she then pointed directly over her head, and behind her, hanging on the wall which I hadn't noticed do to the size of the manger scene, was a tremendous display that was awesome. As she did so, I too, grew the biggest of smile on my face, as she said, "Yes, but we're a Christian Company." All I could say in response to that was, Thank you Lord! I knew right then, without a doubt, that I was definitely where I was supposed to be, looking upon, two tablets... displaying the, "Ten Commandments." Glory, to God!

Worked Myself... Out of a Job

∙∙∙∙∙∙∙∙∙∙∙

Well, it was only moments after our discussion that my boss had come in the front door and took me back to where I would be working. He said he wanted to take me out in to the field to view the task at hand and that I would need my hard hat and to bring a pencil, clip board and tape measure, should I need one.

Well, I brought everything requested, as I've done this so many times before, on other jobs. I listened to what he had to say as he explained what was expected of me. I was told that this piece of equipment that I would be measuring, was designed in inches and feet back in the mid 1950's and made to last for decade and longer except things have changed. The bomb casings, needed to be upgraded in meters now, instead of feet and inches. He said the weight of this machine alone, is equal to three machines made by Japan that are similar in design but not of the same weight or quality of material which is why they would not last as these were engineered to do, which is why I was there. He went on to explain the difference to me and the dilemma they were in. He said that the company that had engineered these units, was sold to another, which they were unable to find any records on and therefore, left in a position where field measurements was the only way to address the situation. This was because they had no real documentation or means of authenticating arcuate measurements other than that of field measurements, which is why I was brought onto the job.

We arrived at the facility where the machine was already in position and ready to run, except it needed to be up-graded. He left me there for an hour while he went in to speak to those inside the inner office building. When he came back he asked if I had started yet or gotten what I needed to get started. I said yes and that I even recorded all the pertinent information I could find on various tags and labels with the equipment name, model and serial numbers including manufacturers and more. I went on to show him the two pages, where I had drawn the equipment in two separate, 3-Dimensional, prospective, hand sketches.

I had produced views showing all the field dimensions I had taken, in their respective places, which I would normally do. I don't think he expected that from me, but took a look and said, Wow! Man, your good and I thanked him, saying it's part of the job. As we drove back, I explained that if he didn't mind, I would like to take an hour or two to see, if I could run down the manufacturer of this equipment to determine who presently has ownership of the original company, knowing they don't usually just close up, never to be heard of again, but sold to another.

My boss agreed to allow me this time to do it and in doing so, I searched and located all the owners, up to the manufacturer who currently owned and had all the equipment's engineering drawings and specifications. My boss was shocked and asked how I was able to do this, while he was unable to so. I explained that I had taken the model & serial numbers, and by using them and the internet; I followed the paper trail from company A to B, to C, to D and then Company E. Five in all, if I remember correctly, all of which I documented. Each contact sent me to the next company, all of whom, I collected: names, addresses, phone numbers and the person in whom I spoke with, including dates and times, all the way up to the current owner.

I stated too, that they could provide him with just what he needed, and that they could even do the engineering to expand on what requirements were necessary with precise measurements all based on machine design: geometric dimensional tolerancing. I explained that they had not only had all the existing drawing as such, but replacement parts, if needed, including the existing equipment drawings on all existing equipment, as it is had been originally sold and installed. I also informed him that they could easily up-grade and transform this machinery to meet his needs.

My boss then thanked me as he accepted all this information I run down for him and in the process of doing so, he semi-smiled and informed me that my services were no longer necessary, but not to pack-up just yet. This all took place around 11 o'clock, just before lunch hour on my first day, on the assignment. Now, this is what you call: "Working yourself, right out of a job!

Reprieved from Reassigned

Knowing I had another job waiting, I began packing to head home, but before I could? My boss came back in and introduced to another gentleman, named Zane. He said that he heard what I had done and could use someone like me. I was willing to bow out of the picture with good reason, which I explained to Zane. I said that I was there basically, to buy myself some time while waiting on a job back home in Florida, where my family was waiting on my return. He asked when I was to start and I said it would probably be after the first of the year, which I would have to take, if I wanted the job that would only give him a month or more of service. He then asked, if I'd stay until then to help him, which I agreed.

So, I began working with Zane on a different facility where we would implement design to address issues to recover the highly energized materials, extracted from the old existing bombs. Those would be the bombs passing through the first facility that I had originally been hired to provide a service. This is where the upgrading of existing equipment, would take place, extracting these materials being removed from older, out of date bombs, that were worn out and showing signs of aging with material break-down to eventually, create new up-to-date bombs.

Only, after the process of extraction would our facility receive those materials to run through another process, where these materials were liquefied, up-graded and made ready to be placed into static-free containers for shipment into yet, another facility. These facilities were located, totally separate from one another, even miles apart, for obvious reasons. Such as, to prevent the total devastation and destruction of any series of a complete process, but only that of one unit, or facility, that may consist of four or more; should a devastating incident ever occur, like that of an explosion. This is why there are various steps at different facility before shipping to the next phase, as was the end product, where I had been transferred, that would be shipped to another facility, where they were introduced into new bomb casings and again, sent to another storage facility, for future use.

I never cared much for these types of jobs, but somebody has to do it. These types of jobs have proven their usefulness in being effective through the years, in the event of war or to ensure not only Freedom in America, but to those around the world who are seeking Freedom and Peace within their region. This jobs main benefit's then, are as Americans, being able to help others.

I had only worked in this facility, less than 2-months, when I received my call to report to my new job in Florida, I'd been waiting on. So, I accepted and asked to provide my current place of employment, at-least some sort of notice, preferably 2-weeks, which is customary and the least I could do, and Bob agreed.

I then went in to see Zane and explained that I had received my call and would be staying on to finish what I could, but was giving him a 2-week notice. This was done as to allow him to find someone else and bring on board, if necessary. It would also, enable me help someone to pick up, where I was leaving.

The one thing about jobs like this, and many others that I've reported to through the years, as a consultant, is that we're not sure what we're getting into. Well, at least, not until after the fact. In most case, we have a general idea of what the client's expectations are, but then there are those we just don't know. This is why I come to learn... to reach out to the Lord and ask for his guidance and this one was a prime example, to my question.

I happened to like this particular job, though it was somewhat dangerous, but mostly because of the people and friendships developed. It's those in whom I met, like Zane and so many others, through some 40 plus years and thanks to Facebook, I've been able to keep-up with a lot of these people. There is one other particular thing that I really miss most though, which Zane had introduced me to. It was getting together for lunch on Thursdays, where Carrabbas would open not only, just for the blessings of Great Food, but the Word of God and to enjoy the fellowship with one another. It was a real blessing, thanks to the owners and management of the local Carrabbas Restaurant.

CHARTER 12

"Last Days to Retirement"

Finally, Home Again
....

Well, I finally began the job that I had been waiting on, to get me back home and reported to work immediately and assigned a task to create a new facility and all seemed to be going just well, but before we started, I had to lay down some ground rules. I mentioned I had a large family reunion that we hadn't had in decades. That it was a prepaid, 7-day Caribbean Cruise that I would not be able to cancel nor could we change the dates, as it was purchased with a discounted and paid in full a year in advance. To do so meant that we would forfeit any refund or ability to change the dates. He agreed and the I also mentioned that I had been working 60 to 70 hours a week on a lot of my previous contractual assignment and would like to hold it down to a 40 hour work week if at all possible, for a couple months, if not longer. He said he would try but two weeks later... I was at it again, and continued doing so the whole time I worked for this company, but right in the middle of the job, much to my surprise. He allowed time off time off for our family reunion cruise.

I also, took advantage of being at home and registered to attend classes at "Life Christian University" being held at the Word of

Life Christian School Campus in conjunction with the Word of Life Church. This school is where children would begin with first grade and work their way through up twelfth grade graduation, including where students could register as I had, to continue their education by attending, Life Christian University. I had hopes of obtaining an Associate's Degree, followed by a Master's Degree and then pushing on to a Doctrine in Theology; something I've wanted to do for years but always on the go from here or there. I just never seriously considered it or gave it much thought, until now, because I never seemed able to sit still long enough to consider do so, but as for now? It appeared doable, so I went up to the University to inquire about attending.

The economy appeared to be satisfactory and the job was promising. So, I began attending classes being taught by Pastor David White where he and His lovely wife, Miss Debbie had dedicated their lives to the Lord and founded, The Word of Life Christian School and Word of Life Church, which was so much more than just a church and school. They reached out with open arms to other ministries from feeding the poor to spreading the Word of God, not just locally, but in South America and other countries around the world. I was so proud to become part of the family with my wife and children, and our children's children.

My oldest Grandson attended their school from first grade up to the day of graduation as a senior, Graduating as Valedictorian with a 4.0 grade average throughout all his years of schooling. This opened the doors where he received a four year scholarship at the newest university in all America called, "Florida Polytechnic University" where he began in 2015. His goal is to become an Industrial Engineer, much like that, which I had been doing, before retiring. His graduation from college is yet to happen but forth-coming.

Stepping back for a moment; he was only in the Sixth grade, when I first began this new job that I had longed for, making it possible for me to attend college at the Life Christian University. All of which fell into place that year when returning home to work for FEDINC, Florida Engineering and Design, Inc.

All was well and I had begun working there as a direct employee having benefits, but had the desire to switch over into a Contractual Agreements through my own company; DDT SERVICES, INC. All seemed to be working out well afterward, which was to my benefit, with more money and less the benefits. However, I was able to financially manipulate my salary and have tax advantages, not available as an employee; compared to being contractually hired through my own company. This also helped open doors for me to register in college and begin classes where I was so excited to finally settle down and attend college.

Living the Dream

I began classes which was leaning toward Theology and finished up the first year. I was pleased with my ability to do as well as I had and was anxious to get started into the second year, which came quickly, especially attending school 2 nights a week.

I had always tried to keep work separate from my private life, including school as well, but only able to attend, do to my ability to be flexible, if necessary. However, after I had begun the second year, I was asked to go to a job-site, which was located in Nebraska? Yes, Nebraska of all places, and right in the heart of winter. Burrrr... I feared, not being able to continue in my education but much to my surprise, I was allowed to continue via computer and offered classes via DVD, which was a blessing.

I eventually, got to a point where I had to return to the home office in Bartow, Florida to continue there. I also, continued my education in my second year working toward an associate's Degree and was so excited and proud to be graduating soon. I worked, so hard to get there and personally speaking, I was the first in my family to have obtained a degree of any kind, wanting to go for my Masters, and a Doctrine. I really had big dreams.

Dreams... Do Come to an End
············

Unfortunately, something occurred that one would think to be a stumbling block, in front of me. The economy was on a downward spiral after the elections in 2008; industry in general, was slowing down to almost, a complete halt. Finding work was becoming scarce and I'm the kind of person who doesn't like taking advantage of others; not even an employer. So, I spoke to Les, a friend and associate of mine through the years; explaining my thoughts and intentions, and he asked if he could join me. So together, we went in to speak to the Owner/CEO of FEDINC, to make an offer... to save face; for both of us and money, for him.

There is nothing like leaching off anyone, especially a business when they have little next to anything coming in, as profit. The only real task, I personally had, been to continue with my education and graduate after that Semester, in the following year; 2009 with an Associate's Degree and be the first to do so in my family. Afterward, the Monday prior to Thanksgiving; 2008, we asked to speak with Bob and were invited in to have a seat. Then he asked us, what was on our minds. So, we explained our concerns about work, and that it appeared to be in a downward spiral; slowing down and becoming scarce, as was the economy.

He agreed, and we asked if he had anything pending or prospects we weren't unaware-of, which he didn't. We then explained that being responsible in having enough work for others, as well as ourselves had become more difficult and to receive unearned, non-productive wages, was unjust. So, we suggested we would be happy to temporarily step aside until after the first of the year in hopes things may pick up by then, because things are often slowest around the Holidays. He agreed and we shook hands as he thanked us and asked, if would you like to leave our things in our offices, which we agreed and left. After leaving and going into the New Year beginning 2009, I continued classwork to keep me busy, until I graduated with my Associated Degree. It was during this times, upon graduating... I began feeling considerably bored, having caught up each week's normal task and chore list around the house; inside and out, waiting on a call that hadn't come. I'd check in on occasion at FEDINC, but nothing was available. So, I was basically, unemployed, fit as a fiddle with all my body parts being young, strong and healthy, without any health concerns or issues except for the C-Pap I wore to obtain a good night sleep and therefore, feeling energetic and want to do something, to do anything. So, I began visiting Word of Life Church and Word of Life School while waiting for my third year to begin at the Christian University. In doing so, I asked, if there was anything that I could do for them in between classes where I could donate time in repairs and/or provide proposed changes with additions that I may be able to assist in or create drawings that I would generate, having 40 years' experience in doing so, professionally.

Ministry of Helps

They agreed and this began taking place before I graduated, as a Ministry of Helps Project for college credit and continued, up to and past, graduation in 2009. I enjoyed this and it was productive. So, I continued from early spring up to and through, classes that were to begin in August, but something came up, where I couldn't continue and filed for Social Security disability.

Until then, I did the finishing touches by adding base boards along the walls inside the ladies restrooms and provided drawings for a new industrial stove and hood arrangement to be installed in the kitchen. I also, rebuilt their pantry and storage areas for food and other items. I then converted several other rooms, by adding much needed, miscellaneous storage shelving to meet various needs. I then created drawings for a new library with computer stations and 19 or 20 separate book shelves fabricated from pressure treated 2x12 lumber. They were 48" Wide x 84" Tall x 12" Deep, having a top and bottom, plus 6 intermediate shelves. After these bookcases were assembled, they were stained with a dark cherry wood, by others, which was a big help. They were extremely heavy, weighing approximately 225 to 250 pounds each, due to their being fabricated from wet pressure treated lumber. It took 2 to 4 people to move them around for staining as they laid the cases on the floor, facing upward with protection clothes beneath them. When dry the Pastor and I had moved one or two together before he had strained his back and forced to quit. So, I realized that by standing them up, in an upright position, that I could lift them by myself, using my right hand in the middle of one of the upper center shelves, just below my shoulder level. I just needed to position my right hand while in somewhat of a squatted position, and then stand up-right. By doing this, I could lift the whole book case by balancing it with my one hand, while using my left to stabilize it. I could only do this because I'm such a big guy. By doing this, I was able to carry each shelf and place them where I needed to bringing them together, forming little 4'x4' cubby holes between them, all along the right wall of the library.

The remaining book cases were spread out along the opposite wall where computer work stations were set up. These bookcase shelves combined provided a little more than 525 L/F of shelving for all the books, leaving space for additional future books that would be coming in. There were three large round reading tables placed down the center of the room with 6-chairs each, finishing the Library with a checkout desk, next to the libraries entrance.

I was also asked, if I could provide layout drawings developing a new children's church that could serve as a church and lunch room and convert into an auditorium; having a stage with background drop, to allow for plays and baptisms to take place, with his and her changing rooms on either side. All of which was to take place in an area that is encompassed within three existing buildings. One of which ties two separate adjacent building together through the use of a long, glassed faced wall, full of large windows looking out into the exterior area where the new Expansion is to take place. This is hallway linking the existing Sanctuary to the adjacent, toddlers Sunday school classroom building, which will encase the new proposed facility.

The only confirmation required was to ensure that the existing sanctuary's, tall sloped roof-line could be continuously extended with a perfectly matched sloping roof; extending over to and tying into... the adjacent building with ample vertical clearances. This would completely cover the area where the new facility building, is to be built. As such, this would leave a rather large exterior opening covered, linking the 3-exist. Building's together with only having, to add the exterior wall and stage to finish and complete the enclosed area. Everything appears feasible and should work, and was given to the church for future expansion.

Upon completion, I was asked to layout some plans to create a concept for a new, larger sanctuary that would be capable of seating 1200+ people. While in the middle of developing this, there were a couple guys who began constructing in the area that was taken from the arrangements, I provided for the new library.

However, no sooner than they began, they were unable to continue the task due to other issues needing their attention, elsewhere. This is when I stepped in and said I would build the shelves and do what was necessary to finish the library before school would start. Especially, since I was available and hadn't heard anything form my previous client where I had worked last.

As, I had said previously, I was a big man, weighing 300 pounds at 6'6" and capable of lifting and carrying my own weight if necessary, which each of those book cases being made from pressure treated wood, came close to. I really didn't have anyone to help lift and move these, accept by doing it by myself. So, as far as I can tell; it was though my lifting, moving and positioned them, as required, to tie them together and anchor them to one another, including the walls that I began swelling. It became predominate throughout my body: from my legs looking like tree trunks up to my arms and hands, down to my fingers.

My wife stated that my hands looked like Mickey Mouse hands because they had swollen so much, that they appeared to be double in size, having both, fat hands and sausages for fingers. I didn't feel any pain and my forearms, where they had swollen, as well. Enough so, that I told her in response to her saying that I had cartoon hands looking like Mickey Mouse that I also had the arms of Popeye the

Sailor man. I remember coming home and letting out that famous call of laughter from Popeye, saying Olive... Oh, Olive Oil... I'm Home! Yack, ack, ack, ack, ack, ack, ack, ack, as I would hold my arm up and be waving with those Mickey Mouse hands.

Life Changing Event
....

Well, my wife began her career as a nurse upon graduating Traviss Vo-tech... Now: Polk College, in 1983 in an Intensive Care Unit (ICU) at a local hospital. She left there a few years later to work with a Cardiologist for a quite a few years, only to leave there and settling in at a medical clinic where she worked for another Cardiologist, before transferring into Rheumatology.

She's been in Rheumatology over ten years and what a blessing she's been. She loves me and was so concerned about my well-being that she made me an appointment to see the Doctor whom she had worked for and now this doctor is my Rheumatologist. I met with her and she too, had concerns and sent me to the lab to run a blood test: Seropositive Rheumatoid Arthritis Prognosis. This test determines whether or not I have anything to be concerned about and if so, what? Well, Needless to say, it came back positive and she told me that this test is based on a scale factor, that if the count indicated, is 55 or above, it was positive proof that I indeed have RA; Rheumatoid Arthritis. I ask, what my number was, and if my memory serves me correctly, she said 278. I was really surprised and then she told me that I also have Osteoarthritis. She went on to say, that I was fortunate enough to have caught it early. Otherwise, it may not have shown up for years, but do to my aggressiveness while working at the church? I caused it to show itself and she wanted to hit it aggressively.

So, she put me on a regime of medication that consisted of two weekly injections, consisting of Methotrexate and Enbrel. All of which were to provide me a self-induced, suppressed immune system, along with approximately 200 pills, weekly. I didn't really understand fully what this entailed, but went along with the diagnosis to stop the swelling, and for the most part, it worked. Only, this is a disease that has no cure and for the most part, a disease that causes my immune system to be fooled into thinking that I am the enemy. Because of such, it attacks my joints where my bone join together, such as hips, Knees, feet and toes, shoulders, arms, fingers and up and down my whole spine; back and neck. Some days are worse than others when it comes to flare up issues, and usually, somewhat noticeable to very noticeable depending on the weather, with incoming cold fronts and/or humidity. It can be extremely painful at times. So much so, that it feels similar to a pair of adjustable vice grip pliers having a wheel to tighten or loosen the grip. If you were to snap this tool onto a fingers knuckle joint and slowly tighten it until it is as snug as you can stand it? Then remove it by snapping the jaws open and turn that wheel an additional 360 degrees tighter.

Now, try to snap that back onto that same joint, if you can. The pain only grows and there is no letting up until you release the swelling, which is like releasing the jaws of those pliers from your finger joint. Wow, what a relief! This is the best way I can think of to explain such pain and it occurs when left untreated or when a weather front comes in. Now, just imagine several areas on your body's joints, anywhere and everywhere... at the same time. Thank God it hasn't been that bad for me, but there are those times, when they are multiple areas, and Ouch. Just when one area is letting up a little, then another area flares even worse and is so painful, you no longer feel the other pain any longer; not that it stopped or is no longer there. It's just that the body seems to block the pain in one area to allow you to deal with the next area, if that makes any sense... Thank God. I explained this pain to the doctor, as being similar to a horsefly biting you, but how quickly you forget about that horsefly when the horse steps on your foot. Suddenly, the horsefly's bite is so insignificant; the pain is basically, meaningless... in comparison.

However, I come to find out what the meaning of having a self-induced immune system, actually means. It's due to these medications that I take, that provides me a self-induced suppressed immune system, similar to that of a person having aides. The only difference between the two is this. I actually, have an immune system, only mine, is self-induced and suppressed, as to protect my body's joints from self-destruction. However, there are those occasions though, where I may need to stop taking these drugs to allow my immune system to build back-up temporarily, to fight off an infection, unlike that of Aides, which is a disease that completely destroys the immune system, permanently! So, I too, like them, must avoid people who are sick and contagious, as it could literally prove to be fatal for either of us. It's because of this, and by my not understanding, or not knowing better, that I didn't heed the warnings, as I should have. I managed to pick up a virus from one of my granddaughters that had a 24 hour cold/virus and wouldn't you know it? A simple common cold, which she threw off in just a matter of a day, took me twelve weeks to shake off.

I had to go see my primary doctor who put me on two or three different oral antibiotics in an attempt to get control over this virus, all of which failed through the months. It's hard to build up something I didn't have; an immune system. I had to wait for mine to strengthen to even attempt to work but, nothing! It had gotten so bad that I was having difficulties breathing. So, I was put on a nebulizer that induced a medicated mist, as to basically kick start my immune system and suppose to help me breathe, but to no avail. After a week or more, I found it more and more difficult to breathe and I felt as if, I had emphysema. I know about this disease, only because it is a very bad disease which I wouldn't swear off anyone. My stepfather died from it and like him, I found myself sitting on the edge of my bed. It got so bad that I pondered the idea, since nothing seemed to be working, gasping for breath; on whether to go or not... to the hospital.

I realized, that if I went to the hospital, that I would only be routed to the Emergency Room and NOT admitted without my doctor's authorization. So, I call my doctor's office and asked to speak with him. The doctor came on the line, asking, "Yes Doug, what can I do for you?" I then explained, almost in tears and with a hoarse, raspy throat, that I was having great difficulty in breathing and was only able to sit up, gasping for breath. I explained that the nebulizer wasn't working and felt that I was about to pass out, and was preparing to head-up to the Hospital.

It was then, I asked him if he could admit me, and meet me up there. He explained that he would rather have me come by his office first, and try what he referred to as a, "Hail Mary" of all things. He said, if that didn't work by the next morning, that yes... he would gladly meet me there. So, out of desperation, I went to his office and explained that twelve weeks has passed and still no improvement and that I had been off the medications that suppressed my immune system since I first began, showing signs of having an infection; reminding him of the other attempts he had taken, that hadn't done anything. He explained that it was due to my disease; but that my immune system must have strengthened its self-enough by now and then proceeded to give me two large injections where the sun doesn't shine... Ouch!

As he did, he explained that I should see results come morning and that he would be calling me early. He said if this doesn't work... then he would meet with me and admit me into the hospital. The only thing I didn't think about is that I was driving, and it was rather painful to use peddles, but I made it home and come six o'clock in the morning, the doctor called and said, "Good morning". Then he asked, if I was feeling any better or whether or not there were any signs of improvement. I thanked him for calling and said on a scale of one to ten; ten being yesterday when I first called... that I felt much better, possibly a five or better, but definitely better, as I thanked him again. My immune system had finally kicked in and beat this thing that day and just in time. Thank God! I hate this disease. It was a couple weeks later when I began my medications once again, as my Rheumatoid was already beginning to attack me, yet again. It's because of this one incident that I come to realize the importance of me being seclude from others, as to prevent any possible contacts through physical contacts such as shaking hands or just breathing an air-borne virus. So, basically speaking, I'm an indoor hermit like that of a prisoner in my own home by choice, which is when I quit working, and filed for Disability Social Security. This is when I stopped thinking of returning to work again or going out and about, as I once did. It's in my best interest, including attending church. Everyone wants to shake hands, hug you or pray for me and I just can't, do it. In all honesty... it breaks my heart, as I would like to continue school too, and to see people and go places, but never will. I miss the fellowship and communion and it's also, quite depressing, but Thank God! He's with me and still loves me, praise the Lord and thank you, Jesus.

Well, 2016 came and still, nay a call had been received and I didn't expect one, because I have decided to remain retired. I made this decision after the virus episode and went back into my office and cleared out everything. I gave my library collection of engineering books to others that would have better use for them than I, and explained my unwillingness of being retired, against my wishes, but decided it to be best. I thanked my boss for the opportunity of working with him and said my good-byes.

So, after 40+ years in engineering and now having an Associate Degree in Theology, I'm retired. I love the Lord and have throughout my life and people have prayed over me for a healing from the Lord. I either receive it or I won't, but I have adapted to my circumstances. I know full well too, that I should never come in contact with people in general, in or out of an office, or wherever. So, like I had said, I gave up on returning to my old job, where employees were allowed to bring their sick children into the office to stay in a room that was directly across the hallway from where my office was. I had asked about relocating but that was not possible. So, considering that and the air ventilation system being capable of transferring a virus, I decided otherwise. That's when I accepted the fact that I will remain retired and be content with my Social Security Disability. I qualified and received it without any difficulty: completely applying for it without any assistance due to having the proper medical documentation from my Rheumatologist. It can only worsen where I could be bed-ridden or even die, before it's over. She has been exceptional caring toward me and all patience in reality with a pleasant personality and the ability to really help easing pain. Know too, there is no cure for this disease. I'm so blessed in having such a lovely blessing, as my wife, who just happened to be working for my doctor. Both have a heart of gold, having the ability and desire to make a difference in helping others.

So, it's be since 2009; I consider myself, completely retired at 59, being disabled and living like a prisoner within the confines of my own home, where I remain most of the time, except for contacts via the phone or computer. On occasion, I do manage to go out of the house to doctor appointments or the store and sometimes, I may eat out or go to a movie, but usually, on special occasions. Otherwise... again, I avoid public as much as possible, but when I am out... I keep a mask in my wallet. If, I hear someone sneezing accessibly, sniffling, or coughing, I avoid them and go in another direction and when surround? I'll hold my breath and get out of there immediately. If the exit door is too far, I bring out the mask since I have no immune system.

Should someone stop me and ask, "What's with the mask?" To say I'm sick is better than telling them I'm avoiding people, and it works well. Even with those at the front door soliciting. I've even had one person cover their face and apologize as they backed off their steps. I'm not mean and it's a pretty terrible thing to do to others, but sometimes, it's the only thing others seem to understand, instead of answering questions, as they try to carry on an unwanted conversation. I just don't want to, nor can I afford getting to get sick. I'm not paranoid, but I do ask people if anyone in the doctor's office is sick, when preparing to go in for a visit. Especially, when it comes to the dentist office where they get, right in my face. If there is anyone having a cold or virus, or whatever? I reschedule, just to play it safe. Getting sick, like I had from my granddaughter, was a wakeup call... to try and stay healthy, if not for myself; for my wife and family. Others have prayed for a healing, while laying hands on me, but to no avail, but that's okay... for the Lord is with me, always.

So, needless to say I stopped going to church or providing services any longer, releasing all the concepts I have done for them, should they decide to continue. It wasn't a wasted effort and gives those in whom they approach a general ideal. I even stopped providing services at the church, rendering all the concept drawings I had done for them. I also, ceased continuing college classes or attending services at the church in fear of making contact with people in general who always come up in my face to smile and greet me and my wife, which is nice to be thought of, but followed with a handshake or a big hug. I would politely stop them in their tracks as I would take a step backwards to protect myself and explain the situation, and then sometimes they would want to lay hands on me and pray for me that would lead into a conversation, reminding me that Jesus can heal any disease. This I know and have been prayed over and have prayed for myself many times, but I'm still waiting and trusting in the Lord to heal me. As much as I would love to go to church, to sing and worship, I stopped attending, but I had asked the pastor on occasion, if he would like to come over to the house and possibly have some fellowship and communion. However, I suppose, out of their respect, is why he has not come.

So, I had become like that of a house wife and having to learn how to cook, to keep peace in the family with Joyce who was still working. I began treating her like a goddess: serving her burnt offerings until she caught on and told me to learn how to read a cook book. So, I began to cook and do the dishes, wash, dry, fold and hang-up the clothing, include putting them in their proper places. I vacuum, sweep and mop the floors, clean the tub, shower and toilets, take out the trash, feed the dogs, and so much more, and still found time to read the Word and give thanks. Things could be worse but I'm so grateful for all we have. God is good and he takes care of us, meeting all our needs.

I also, enjoy listening to; The Joy FM Radio" station out of Central Florida, watch TV or just spending time, communicating with people on the Computer. I also, go out and sit on our front yard park bench to enjoy the warm sunny days staring across the lake; watching the ducks that come across the lake to be fed, which I try to do daily, and life... is good. Especially, since my wife retired 8 years later and by having my body breaking down on me, I have backed off slightly, due to my limitations, but again we feed the ducks together and she does most of the picking up now, where I can't. I just wish I had the energy and ability to do more for her and especially, the Lord, which is why I decided to finish my book, because I really want people to know, God is what life is all about and that he is with us, always.

CHAPTER 13

"Jesus Never Fails"

Wake-Up America
....

America best wake up, as we are told to Love and Pray, not just for one another, but family and friends, as well as our enemies, for we're all made in the same Likeness and Image of God, and should not curse anyone with the same mouth we praise the Lord. This should not be & America best start praying.

AMERICA IN NEED OF PRAYER
....

Dreams are Powerful and I'm a believer in dreams for the Lord does speak to me through dreams and the following dream has been revealed to me on Sept. 14, 2001; "The Day of Prayer" that came to me a few days after the day of attack on WTC's, which took place on Sept. 11, 2001; commonly known as... 911!

Post 911 - DREAM
....
(Sept. 14, 2001)

I was entering into a path of darkness and was in search of a way out. I was afraid to enter into the darkness because I feared that I might not be able to find my way back. Darkness was inevitable and it had to be confronted. As darkness fell upon me, I prepared to enter. An officer of sorts, possibly even an Angel came to me and said to lay down some stones as I entered into the darkness, so that I would be able to find my way back out.

I questioned him about the possibility of not being able to find the rocks and he said not to worry. As I looked down onto the path leading into darkness he spoke, telling me to place my rocks between the other stones that were already placed before me. The stones appeared to be small and were spaced just far enough as to allow me to insert my rocks, one at a time, between them. These rocks when laid between the other stones, created a straight and narrow path, which would lead back from the darkness, into the light.

Note: I began to awaken, but before I did, I turned around to continue this dream, because I didn't understand the importance or significance of this particular dream. He smiled at me, as to already, knowing what it was I wanted to ask, and this is what I understood the interpretation to be.

Interpretation

The darkness; is the war that America is entering, as it engulfs us. The rocks being laid represent the foundation and path leading to the war. It is through the Americans prayers, which were once few as the small stones but are now many, as all Americans unite in prayer and faith in God. It is through the Americans prayers and trust in the Rock, which is our very foundation. He will guide us and bring us out of the darkness into the light.

Note: Personally, I'd like to see <u>America</u> to have an <u>Ultimate Victory</u>, but only if, America turns to God in prayer and seeks Gods will. Until then, America is definitely, In Need of Prayer and we are still in a war that was declared immediately following the attacks on America and it will take a peace treaty to end, but with whom? We war not, against a nation or country, but with terrorist... without a home base, so the war continues.

We must find Love, Peace & God.

Some people, or should I say... most people have faith in some sort of God. Even if, they don't believe in one, other than themselves, as if they themselves are the only one they care about. In their eyes, they are the only god they believe & trust in.

However, in my 70+ years in this world I come to know, that there is, but One God, The One and Only True, Living God. There is none other, especially one that offers a Resurrection into an Eternal Life that is, "Never Ending." Only One! Praise God!

It is, He alone, who is the God of all Creation and offers Salvation as a Gift to all, who is the Only God, that offers all people, through His Precious Blood; the sacrifice that only He and of His Life alone, has provided, all of us who trust, believe and receive Him, as Lord of Lords and King of Kings. As such, He makes Life Anew, including a Resurrection into an Eternal Life. To do otherwise is a complete failure and of that which is not meant to be, which comes through denial of Jesus and to deny Jesus and His Salvation? Is to be denied by God! This is because if you deny God you have already judged yourself and will suffer the second death not intended for men but Satan and his fallen Angels who are facing an Eternity of Fire and Brimstone, which is that of an eternal damnation that is intended; Again, not for Man; created in the image and likeness of God, but intended for Satan and his evil ones, for Satan is a Liar and Deceiver, but God is: God the Father, the Son, and Holy Sprint and the three alone are One: One God, and They alone are the One and Only, True Living God and Creator of all things that ever were, are, or are to come; from the Heavens to Earth, including all Creatures; Big and Small. This includes man and women, who gave names to all creatures whom were created; not only as caretakers, but given dominion over all things created, including to Love God with all your Heart, Mind, Soul & Spirit.

I sometimes tell people the story, where God put Adam into a deep sleep, and took out one of his ribs to form Eve; and He created both; Adam and Eve, and as Adam woke? He looked over at Eve, to take look at God's Creation, and as Adam beheld Eve's purest form of beauty, laying there naked and asleep? Well, this next phrase is something I made up where Adam saw Eve and said, "Woe...Man!" So, Woman, it was, is, and has been, passed down through the ages... as, "Woman."

Sorry about that! I'm bad, but you'll not find; Woe-Man in the bible anywhere but, as good as it may sound. It is not in the Word of God, but thank God for His Love, Mercy and Grace, and especially, the Creation of Man and Woman who were made in the image and likeness of God and why we should love and pray for one another, including our enemies, for we are God's.

Prayer of Salvation

I cannot really explain why I loved my mother so much, even though she has since passed on. With all the abuse I came to know, I still continue to love her. I love her so much, and it really hurts; even to this day when I think about it, but nothing compared to the loss following the call I received one day; when I was asked, if I wanted to come see her one last time. I was told that she had been admitted into the hospital with diabetic complications and if I wanted to see her before she passed on, I better come soon. They give her 72 hours to live at best. So, I drove up to N Carolina with my son, Joshua. It gave me the opportunity to reminisce and share the good times and bad times during my earlier years, as a youth. I knew sharing the bad times would not set well with her and she asked me; why on her deathbed, that I would bring up such terrible events to remind her of these things?

It was then that I told her; I did so to let her know that I loved her and that I forgive her, and then I opened up and shared Jesus with her. I prayed for her forgiveness and salvation before she passed. I even find myself on occasion still praying for my mom, as well as my dad, whom I had the chance to share testimony with too, before his passing. I prayed for the Lord to have mercy on them and to forgive them... and to accept them into Heaven. It wasn't their devious doings that brought them their ill fate.

We all know who's to blame for that, and we all know why Jesus shed his blood; for all sinners, including our brothers and sisters, mothers and fathers, including friends and loved ones, and even our enemies. So, share the Gift of Salvation with someone you love; a family member, a friend or even a stranger. This is because it is through Jesus Christ alone that we are saved, but only through our acceptance of Him as Lord and Savior, and yes, we can... you and me: can make a difference in helping others, by praying and leading them into salvation.

Jesus is Coming... Soon

There is this one dream, where I had been shopping inside a big man's store known as Nathans Big Man's Store on the south side of the town square, which is referred to as Munn's Park in down town Lakeland, Florida. As I exited Nathans, I was looking toward the Park before me, coming out of the door. As I did, I saw what appeared to be storm clouds, pushing in where the wind began to be picking up, with some pretty brisk and gusty winds beginning to sway the trees back and forth. They began shedding their leaves, which I took a fast glance at, to see which direction, the storm would be going. As I glanced from the Northeast to the west, all I could see is that we had one heck of a storm coming in, fast... from the East.

As I was making an observation trying to size up the situation, is when I noticed a woman carrying a bag full of items she had just bought from one of the merchants stores located on the west side of the Park. She had a little girl with her leading the way to head toward her car.

She was carrying her bags in her right arm and switched them immediately, from her right arm into her left arm, and as she did, she screamed out a shrilling scream that could put fear into anyone's heart. She did this while she was looking toward the Eastern Sky, reaching as quickly as possible for her daughter and then swept her up into her right arm and ran back into the store, seeking cover and shelter. After seeing her reactions and hearing her scream, I began to investigate what was happening by looking above her and sweeping my eyes toward the skies above the park, as I also focused on the swaying trees where the wind had really picked up in strength as the storm cloud moved, so quickly out of the East. As I did, I gazed into the skies looking for a tornado.

I continued sweeping my eyes to the Eastern Skies and as I did, there was to huge Angel Dressed in white, standing there, floating in the air, having a huge long Golden Horn, which he was preparing to blow into the Air, and when he did? This sound was so mighty, that it filled all the Earth. I recognized this angel to be Gabriel, whom I've read about several time before in the Word of God and the sounds coming out of this horn were Extremely loud, a sound that blew out two very distinctive long winded notes that sounded, as if blurting; TAAAaaa - DAAAaaa...

As I looked closer, I could see the darker clouds were being pushed out of the way, making a clearing for what appeared to be... the coming of the Lord of Lord and King of Kings coming within huge bright white flashing clouds that came rolling in as the cloud appeared to be expanding in size. As this occurred, I woke up and never did see Jesus.

I only got to see the clouds and what I believe... will be an event that will take place someday, soon! I have shared this dream with others in the past who have told me of similar dreams and obviously, we have seen something forth-coming, but no man knows the day or hour: not even the Angels, nor the Son of Man; meaning Jesus, but only the Father, who is in Heaven. It looks to be a great day but in truth, it will be a sad day, as there are so many who will weep, having not heard of, or accepted Jesus's... Salvation.

CHAPTER 14

"God Bless America"

In God We Trust

America, best pay attention and become aware of the things happening within our Beloved and Blessed Country of Freedom!

I would hope that this may be of interest to you, which is something I felt led to write about and wanted to share. The reason being is that it's interesting and utterly amazing... how much proof there is, in referencing the origin of The Unites States of America, based from the Word of God and yet, we have those who wish to fool themselves by accepting anything else, but truth. I am a Christian and can only hope that others are as well; breaking away from the tyranny of others to have God Given Rights, as a Government of the People, by the People and for the People; We The People, in whom it is... "IN GOD WE TRUST" as a Sovereign Government within these "United States of America" as One Nation... "One Nation Under God" and "Blessed is the Nation whose God is the Lord."

I hope this will give you some food for thought and may come in handy by shedding some light on the U.S. Constitutional Rights.

Especially, Freedom of Religion, and not... Separation of Church and Government, as some people claim or miss-quote.

Why some people... cannot Conceive or believe this country was established through the use of the Word of God, is truly hard to understand when there is so much evidence to prove the opposite. The following only indicates a small number of the many, many items which reinforce the case; that America is truly Blessed and that God has been with us, since our creation of these United States and why The United States of America; humbly pays tribute and honor to the Word of God, and people.

The following are basically: **Recognized** Holidays without Pay, and Honored Paid **Celebrated** Holidays, to help Quality of Life.

> *We* **Celebrate** **New Years Day**, *like that of a Blessing from God, Entering into a New Year; shrug off the old... for the New.*
>
> *We* **Celebrate** **Civil Rights Day**... *Honoring the Man... helping bring* **Martin Luther King's Day**,.. *Civil Rights... into Reality!*
>
> *We Recognize Valentine's Day as a Day of Love and not that of a religious holiday but a day to express one's love, to another.*
>
> *We Recognize April Fool's Day as a day for those who choose not to believe or accept truth, and tell lies, jokes, and pull pranks.*
>
> *We* **Celebrate** **Good Friday**: *the Day Jesus Defeated Death for our Sins against God, purchased by His Life and Precious Blood.*
>
> *We* **Celebrate** **Easter**; *Jesus Resurrection Day; defeating death by raising from the dead on the 3rd day unto Eternal Life for all!*
>
> *We* **Celebrate** **Memorial Day**; *a day of remembrance of*

those who are, or have served, and given their all, to serve our country.

We **Celebrate** **the 4th of July***, as America's Birth Date; where we won our Independence, and God Given Rights, for Freedom.*

We **Celerate** **Labor Day** *as a Day to honor and remember the hard working individuals who help industrialize this great nation.*

We **Recognize Veteran's Day** *to give Honor & Praise to those who are, have, or sacrificed all, to serve and protect our country.*

We **Recognize Halloween** *to give Honor & Praise to those who are, have, or sacrificed all, to serve and protect our country.*

We **Celebrate** **Thanksgiving Day** *to honor the Lord for all His Many Abundant Blessings he has bestowed upon us, as a People.*

We **Celebrate** **Christmas;** *the recognized date of Jesus Christ birth; the Son of God; our one & only true living Lord & Savior.*

We **Celebrate** **Hanukkah,** *during the Christmas Season, but through the use of a Jewish Menorah.*

We **Recognize Kwanza** *– African America Family Celebration.*

It's our Right to believe or not to believe and if they choose not to believe, it's their right! We have no more right to force others, as they have none, to deny us. of our own 1st Amendment Rights.

That's why we have "Freedom of Religion" to do as we wish, or not at all. This is our choice. This means... Freedom of Religion and NOT... Freedom FROM Religion, as some would believe. So those who chose not to believe should not try to destroy that which also, provides them the very rights... they stand on. It's these God given rights that were established within America's foundation; the U.S. Constitution that gives them the ability to stand up and be heard including the right to criticize these same rights without fear of reprisal. They instead, have a total lack of respect for both God and Country; the same country they claim as their home; the Home of the Brave and the Land of the Free, including God Fearing people. These people also have the nerve, and truly are... unbelievable; thinking they're rights, outweigh our rights within the Constitution, which are equal!

America... The Blessed
....

America has truly been blessed in so many ways since its creation. Again, this country was built upon freedom, such as is evident in The United States Constitution, especially that, which is referred to as; "Freedom of Religion."

The United States Constitution; is to the United States... (We the People), as the Bible is to the Church (We the Believers.) This country was without a doubt, created through a Christian point of view, established by the very Word of God, as the perfect example. It's very foundation was not laid by just ordinary men, but by inspired men. Inspired by whom... one may ask?

Well, read our currency and our coins; "In God We Trust" and "The United States of America." We also, have the song "God Bless America" and Our Pledge of Allegiance to Our Flag, "One Nation Under God."

There is the song too, America the Beautiful; "God shed His Grace on Thee and Crowed Thy Good." Even the Declaration of Independence says, "We Hold these Truths to be self-evident; that all men are created equal; that they are endowed by their CREATOR with certain unalienable rights; that among these are Life, Liberty and the Pursuit of Happiness." (This interpretation, which I believe to mean; to seek and reach for that which your heart desires, but only if you do-not encroach on another individual's, "Constitutional Rights.")

Yes, there is a God; God the Father, The Son and The Holy Spirit! The Three are One; One God, the One and Only, True Living God; the Head of the Church, (We the Believers.) In the same manner is this country established: Washington D.C., the District of Columbia, "Not a State", but the "Head of States", The United States, (We The People.) Washington, the Head... being One, consisting of three Branches: "The Executive Branch, The Legislative Branch and the Judicial Branch."

Our Judicial System... is the finest in the world; again, established after the perfect example in the Word of God. We have twelve jurors like that of the twelve disciples and the Judge standing for Justice, as Christ... the Son of God standing in Righteousness. We have a Prosecuting Attorney too, much like that of Satan, standing before the Righteousness Judge; Jesus. As he convicts and condemns us for our wrong doings, but then... standing there in our behalf is our Defense Attorney, who much like that of the Holy Spirit of God, is pleading on our behalf, for our Mercy. Praise God! How Blessed... We truly have been.

Our country has monuments erected all around this country leading to the Word of God and is embedded in artifacts throughout America, especially in Washington D.C. within, and on the top of and inside the Washington Monument and even the Supreme Court Building, just to name two.

Above the entrance leading into the Supreme Court is the likeness of Moses carrying the TEN Commandments which houses our highest court in the land, consisting of nine Supreme Court Justices; One Chief Justice and eight Associate Justices. The way the Justices are set-up, reminds me of the Jewish Menorah, consisting of one main candle in the Center like that of the Chief Justice with four additional candles on either side, equaling eight associate candle lights like those of the Associate Justices that total nine Supreme Court Justices in all. I say this because Washington D.C. is the Head and Capital of The United States of America which is referred to as the light house... to light-up the way for Truth and Justice, both here and around the world. The Supreme Court sets on top of the Hill... in Washington, for all the world to see. It also, say in the Word too, that you don't light a candle stick and hide it beneath a basket but set in on top of the basket to let your light shine Brightly.

America... it also say in the word of God that we as Christians are the Salt of the World and if the Salt loses its savor, what good is the salt, so stand up and Unite America, as it was intended and become as one; The United State of America; the Blessed, and In God We Trust, for it is because of Him that we have been so richly blessed! Ignore Him and we will become divided and shall not survive, so unite! For to deny is to be denied.

To separate state from Church is to separate government from God; our countries very foundation! The two were meant to stand together, hand in hand, similar to two people standing before the Altar... to be United, as One. To separate would be to divorce or to divide! Jesus says in Matthew 12:25, "Every Kingdom divided against itself is brought to desolation; And every city or house divided against itself shall not stand." This is not intended for a Unite Country The United States of America.

It's for this reason we must go back to the basics, "In God We Trust", as it was in the beginning of this great country. We too, need God; the very fabric woven into this great country called The United States of America. It's the only way America will remain as an inspiration, a hope and a light like that of a light-house; standing for Truth and Justice, as does Jesus Christ... our Lord & Savior, for Blessed is the Nation whose God is the Lord.

In closing Let me add something else too, that most people may not be aware of. If you were to look at Washington, as if you were flying overhead, coming into Washington from the East... to the West, approaching the Washington Mall as if it were a runway at an airport; you would notice that there are monuments strategically set up in the fashion of a Cross. The U.S. Capital represents the base which you would pass over first. As you travel up this cross, following the Washington Mall, toward the Lincoln Memorial, which is at the top of the Cross, you'll first come upon the Washington Monument representing the Heart of the Cross. To the right of the Washington Monument is the right arm of the cross that reaches out to the White House and at the opposite side of this cross is the left arm, that reaches out to the Jefferson Memorial... and if this cross were to be lift into an up-right position, this cross would be facing toward the East! The question is this: "Was this accidental or intentional, as it were in the creation of this great country: America?"

Again, this country WAS established using the Word of God as a Foundation and this Foundation is the Rock: Jesus! This was done to ensure the existence of America and DC in general to be like that of as a beacon of light and hope, for all the world to see, in hopes that the World too, would seek Freedom; the same Freedom we have in the United States of America; in whom it is; In God We Trust, almost 250 years now and still the most powerful nation on Earth. Thank God and God Bless America, We the People, and those who Represent, We the People. Amen.

SCRIPTURE

Ecc. 12:13-14

13. Let us hear the conclusion of the whole matter: Fear God and keep his commandments: for this is the whole duty of man.

14. For God shall bring every work into judgment, with every Secret thing, whether it be good, or whether it be evil.

All Mankind fell into Sin; Through Adam and Eve and through them... all have fallen short of the Glory of God, but through God's Love, Mercy and Grace? There is Salvation through the perfect Sacrifice of God's only begotten Son; Jesus Christ who sacrificed His Life to pay for the remission of our sin, so that we may have Eternal Life, and live life more abundantly... through our Faith and Trust to Accept, Believe and Receive Jesus Christ, as our Lord and Savior; The Lord of Lords and King of Kings, who is the Alpha and the Omega, above all things that ever were, are, and yet to come. For Jesus is the Word and the Word is God and Jesus is our Salvation. The Good News to share with all; out of Love and Prayer for others Salvation, as says the Lord, and to Love and Pray not only for our Friend, Family and Loved ones, but our enemies, as well. For we are all made in the Image and Likeness of God, and it is God, who so loved the world that he gave His only begotten son, so that whosoever believes in Him shall not perish but have Eternal Life. Amen! I am a whosoever.

Note: God truly loves all of us and as such, we too, should Love, for the Greatest Commandment of all, is to Love God, with all our

Heart, Mind, Body and Soul, and our Spirit, for God is Spirit and with all man being made in God's Image and Likeness? We are God's and He is with each of us and yes, He loves all People, as should we, including sharing Jesus Christ, as Lord and Savior.

Mathew: 28:19- 20

19. Go ye therefore, and teach all nations, baptizing them in the name of the Father, and of the Son, and of the Holy Ghost:

20. Teaching them to observe all things whatsoever I have commanded you: and, "<u>Lo, I am with you, always</u>", eve unto the end of the world. Amen. (This is TRUE, Always!)

CLOSING THOUGHTS, SALVATION & PRAYER, WITH SCRIPTURES.

As we are introduced into life; a life of sin, which we know not there-of, we are quick to learn the meaning of right and wrong. Only then does the awareness of sin become apparent, as we age and come into the realization of our very being. It's though this awareness that we too, come to know the meaning of time that opens with a whole series of questions that only begin to beseech us, as to; why are we here, and where does it all end, as we age? It's then we begin to know fear... the Fear of Death; which God had warned us about, as punishment for man's fall from God's will. This then leads to the question: Who is God?

As we come to know God, we realize too, the fear of God and what destiny lies ahead; death, which God had not intended for man. We were actually intended to live and to walk and talk, with God forever; that is, until the fall of man came into light. God's Word is Truth and because God's Word is Truth, we were separated from God, which was Satan's demise for Satan hates God. God too, is Satan's Creator, but Satan tried to put himself above God, and there can only be one God; God the Father, the Son and the Holy Spirit, for the three are one. The father of lies fell out of God's favor and was cast down from Heaven to Earth, and is destined for hell and has tried to get back at Father God through God's children. So, Satan; being the Father of Lies, deceived man... causing Adam and Eve to fall from God's Grace, therefore surrendering our God given Earthly Authority to Satan, which he successfully did, through their fall, from God.

This fall is what God had warned man about; that they shall surely die, if man proved to be disobedient to God and partake of the forbidden fruit on the Tree of Knowledge, which man did take and eat there-of; both Adam and Eve... into sin. This then explains why man was doomed to eternal separation from God and was in need of intervention, by a Savior... or destined, to die!

We all needed someone who is the Perfect Savior that could bring us back into Righteousness with God, as it once was originally, as it were intended with the creation of man. We truly are loved by God because we are in fact, a part of God. We are created by God, as were the Angels, but we are above the angels, including Satan, for we are created in the very image and likeness of God Himself. Again, we were given authority and dominion over this world, but we gave this control over to Satan; separating us from God, and became in need of a Savior. It is then that Jesus stepped down from His Thrown in Heaven and came into this world through a virgin birth... to break the bonds of sin passed down through man; to live and die... for all mankind, through the shedding of His Precious Blood. His blood was not tainted with sin but shed to pay for all man's sins, which is payment for our sins, so we might be reunited unto God, forever and ever, into an everlasting life. It is through Jesus' and His Resurrection that occurred 3-days after His crucifixion when He arose from the dead, proving He Lives, and has defeated death; setting the captives free, including you and me, and had known us, since before we were born, offering us Eternal Life with him, forever.

To receive this Salvation; we must first recognize someone greater than us, who is God; and that we were born into sin. We need to confess in prayer, that we are sinners and destined to die, which leads to hell, but that it doesn't... have to be this way. So, we need to pray and seek God's forgiveness, confessing our many sins throughout our life, and accept Jesus Christ, as Lord and Savior: God's only begotten son, whom He gave unto the world, that whosoever believes in Him, shall not perish, but have Everlasting Life. If you accept and believe; say this prayer.

Lord, I come to you in prayer and accept Jesus as my Lord and Savior and ask that through your Love, Mercy, and Grace, that you wash away all my sins and unrighteousness, with the precious Blood of Jesus, saving me, making my life anew and filling me with thy Holy Spirit, to guide and show me the ways in which I should go. It's in Jesus name I pray, and give Thanks. Amen...

So, if you meant this prayer; you are saved, but you will need to come and know the Lord, that comes with reading the Bible, and attending a good Christian Church that loves and honors God where you will be strengthened and come to understand and know how to walk with the Lord regularly. As you do you will grow in the Lord, which is God's Holy Word, written by men; inspired by Gods Holy Spirit; about truths, and the Lord's will, who will show truths, and speak to you, and inspire you to move in the ways of life that He would have you follow, where you can and will grow, for He is with you... Always.

2-Tim 3:16-17

16. All scripture is given by inspiration of God, and is profitable for doctrine, for reproof, for correction, for instruction in righteousness:

17. That the man of God may be perfect, thoroughly furnished unto all good works

<u>**Romans 12:1-2**</u>

1. I beseech you therefore, brethren, by the mercies of God, that ye present your bodies a living sacrifice, holy, acceptable unto God, which is your reasonable service.

2. And be not conformed to this world: but be ye transformed by the renewing of your mind, that ye may prove what is that good, and acceptable, and perfect, will of God.

John 14:23-26

23. Jesus answered and said unto him, If a man love me, he

will keep my words: and my Father will love him, and we will come unto him, and make our abode with him.

24. He that loveth me not keepeth not my sayings: and the word which ye hear is not mine, but the Father's which sent me.

25. These things have I spoken unto you, being yet present with you.

26. But the Comforter, which is the Holy Ghost, whom the Father will send in my name, he shall teach you all things, and bring all things to your remembrance, whatsoever I have said unto you.

www.ingramcontent.com/pod-product-compliance
Lightning Source LLC
LaVergne TN
LVHW091534060526
838200LV00036B/601